THE SCARECROW AUTHOR BIBLIOGRAPHIES

Studies on Clarín:
An Annotated Bibliography

by
DAVID TORRES

Scarecrow Author Bibliographies, No. 79

The Scarecrow Press, Inc.
Metuchen, N.J., & London
1987

Library of Congress Cataloging-in-Publication Data

Torres, David.
   Studies on Clarín.

   (Scarecrow author bibliographies ; no. 79)
   Includes indexes.
   1. Alas, Leopoldo, 1852-1901--Bibliography.
I. Title. II. Series.
Z8020.95.T67 1987 [PQ6503.A4] 016.868'509 87-4362
ISBN 0-8108-1993-7

IN MEMORIAM:

AGUSTIN LARA

CONTENTS

INTRODUCTION

Distinguished bibliographers of Hispanic literature such as José Simón Díaz, Hensley C. Woodbridge, and Theodore A. Sackett would probably agree that a "complete" bibliography is a <u>rara avis</u> indeed. This statement is particularly true of Leopoldo Alas "Clarín" (1852-1901), whose stature as a novelist, short story writer, and literary critic continues to grow rapidly. More than 900 books, pamphlets, and articles have been published on Clarín since 1880, and dozens more will undoubtedly appear even as this volume goes to press.

Nevertheless, my goal has been to compile a descriptive bibliography of every reference I have been able to locate on Clarín, regardless of length or critical value. The user of this volume shall decide which items to consult or ignore in accordance with his own judgment or objectives. If nothing else, short reviews can serve as a barometer of literary tastes or personal prejudices, or simply as an historical perspective--for example, the three-paragraph commentaries on <u>La Regenta</u>. Therefore, the word "studies" in the title of this book should be taken lightly for many entries.

This bibliography confines itself to books and articles written in Spanish, English, Italian, French, Portuguese, and German. With few exceptions, only doctoral dissertations listed in the standard reference tools have been included: <u>Dissertation Abstracts</u>, <u>Revista de la Universidad Complutense</u> (Madrid), <u>Index to Theses Accepted for Higher Degrees by the Universities of Great Britain and Ireland</u>, and <u>Dissertations in Hispanic Languages and Literatures</u>: <u>An Index of Dissertations Completed in the United States and Canada</u>, up to the summer of 1986.

Each article is counted only once, regardless of the number of times it has been reprinted, or the number of journals in which it has appeared. In this regard, Spanish editors are largely to blame, by not acknowledging receipt of manuscripts or by not notifying writers of the approximate date of publication. Under the "publish or perish" pressures of the academic community, a scholar cannot afford to wait four or five years to find out if his research efforts have been accepted or rejected.

The length of an entry does not necessarily reflect the value or length of the item itself. Some titles are self-explanatory, while others call for longer descriptions. In some cases I have added one or two sentences to make the entry more meaningful or useful. Entries without a description are those which I did not examine personally, or which upon examination did not require comment.

vii

Benjamin Disraeli reportedly once observed that there are three types of lies: plain lies, damn lies, and statistics. Even so, the following facts and figures may provide some food for thought. If my statistics are correct, at least 150 items on Clarín appeared prior to his death in 1901. The earliest would seem to be Ricardo de la Vega's in the February and March, 1880, issues of Madrid Cómico. In 1881 Alas' friends, González Llana and Sánchez Calvo, published reviews of Solos de Clarín. That same year, San Juan wrote an article for La Ilustración Gallega y Asturiana, and the Navarros protested against Clarín's opinion of their play.

Of greater interest are the polemics with Bonafoux (1887-88) and Bobadilla (1892), as well as the scathing pamphlets against Clarín: Palacio's Clarín entre dos platos (1889), Fray Mortero's Cascotes y machaqueos (1892), Gener's El caso Clarín (1894), Cuéllar's Dioses caídos (1895), De las Heras' El besugo Clarín (1895), Martinete's La autopsia de Clarín (1895), and Siboni's Pan de compadres (1898).

Approximately 120 books and articles on Clarín appeared between 1901, the year of his death, and 1939, the year that marked the end of the Spanish Civil War. While many took the form of recuerdos or obituaries of limited critical value, special mention must be made of Sáinz Rodríguez's address, La obra de Clarín (1921), Valentí Camp's Ideólogos, teorizantes, y videntes (1922), Suárez's biographical sketch in Escritores y artistas asturianos (1936), and Cabeza's biography, Clarín, el provinciano universal (1936).

Between the end of the Civil War and the year 1950, only about 88 studies can be counted. Notable during this period are the Epistolarios (1941, 1943) compiled by Leopoldo Alas' son, Adolfo, and another biography (1946), this time by Posada, a long-time friend. In Obras selectas (1947) Cabezas made available many forgotten pieces by Clarín.

The avalanche of studies--more than 450--began in 1951, the 50th anniversary of Clarín's death, and 1952, the centennial of his birth. During 1952-53, José María Martínez Cachero published the first annotated bibliographies ever compiled on Clarín. These magnificent contributions in the 1952-53 volumes of Archivum undoubtedly inspired many new studies; unfortunately, his bibliographies are now over 30 years old, and even at that time the bibliographical entries were not as complete or informative as one might hope.

Clarín has had the good fortune to be studied by scholars of the caliber of Martínez Cachero and Sergio Beser. During the past ten years, other specialists-- notably Ibarra, Ramos-Gascón, Richmond, Sobejano, Thompson--have contributed excellent studies to an ever- growing bibliography. French interest in Clarín has also become an important factor, as clearly demonstrated in the well-documented studies by Blanquat, Botrel, and Lissorgues.

While editions of Clarín's works lie well beyond the scope of this bibliography, it is interesting to note that relatively few of his books were reprinted between 1901 and 1951. One of his young admirers, Azorín, observed in Clásicos y modernos (1913): "Clarín fue violentamente combatido en vida; después de muerto se ha ido haciendo en su torno el olvido." In Les Maîtres du roman espagnol contemporain (1907), Vézinet omits Clarín but devotes a chapter to Echegaray, who was not a novelist. Mario Méndez Bejarano, in his book La literatura española en el siglo XIX (1921), does not even mention Clarín as a novelist; his only reference to Clarín is to his introduction to José Quevedo's poem. The oblivion of the first two or three decades of this century was so great that in 1923 the famous bookseller Antonio Palau y Dulcet felt compelled to write: "Como la mayoría de críticos literarios que en vida son leídos, Clarín después de muerto resta casi olvidado. Sus obras se venden poco." Clarín's Obras completas (1913-1929) were discontinued after only four volumes, all of which are extremely difficult to find today. As late as 1946, Baquero Goyanes penned an article entitled "Clarín, novelista olvidado." Fortunately this neglect has been corrected in recent years, but Clarín still awaits the compilation of his complete works.

Many aspects of Clarín's life and works remain to be examined. For instance, a perusal of this bibliography will reveal how little of Clarín's correspondence has been published to date. Not one letter to or from Pereda, Alarcón, Ortega Munilla, Balart, González Serrano, or Bobadilla has come to light as yet, unless one counts Pereda's letter about Juan Ochoa, which Clarín himself published in the April 9, 1898 issue of Madrid Cómico. His known correspondence with Menéndez Pelayo, Galdós, and Picón is probably quite incomplete.

There exists a crying need for a new biography, one that will consolidate in a scholarly fashion the best data in those by Cabezas, Posada, and Gómez-Santos with the research of the past forty years. Stylistic studies are also needed, considering the fact that Clarín was such a staunch defender of the Spanish language and an advocate of correct usage.

Until Clarín's complete works are published, we need more bibliographical studies on his writings in specific periodicals, such as those undertaken by Narciso Alonso Cortés on Madrid Cómico, Sergio Beser and Laureano Bonet on the Barcelona press, and Dionisio Gamallo Fierros on El Solfeo. Hopefully, future studies will appear in Revista de Literatura, Cuadernos Hispanoamericanos, or similar journals with a worldwide circulation, so that all scholars can have easy access to them.

Compiling a bibliography entails much more effort than some people suspect. Boswell's assertion that one has to read an entire library in order to write a book seems less of an exaggeration when one considers the vast number of works and journals that must be examined in order to compile a bibliography. The task becomes very difficult in the case of local or short-lived 19th-century Spanish periodicals, many of which were destroyed during the Civil War of 1936-39. Even when complete or partial runs exist, certain libraries' hours and regulations tend to discourage and frustrate scholars.

This bibliography was compiled intermittently during the past six years at the following libraries: The University of Illinois at Urbana-Champaign, The University of Texas at Austin, the University of California at Berkeley, and the Biblioteca Nacional of Madrid. A note of thanks is hereby extended to Mr. José Luigi Bartoli of New York for his assistance at Columbia University and the New York Public Library, and to all the professional librarians and clerks who assisted me, particularly to Ms. Pam Lindell and Dr. Sara de Mundo Lo at Illinois, and Ms. Pauline F. Crawford at Angelo State University. Of all _clarinistas_ and _clarinófilos_, Professors Gonzalo Sobejano, Clifford R. Thompson, Pierre L. Ullman, and Frances Wyer Weber have been the most helpful by supplying copies of their studies.

As Moratín's Don Hermógenes might have expressed it (in Latin, of course, for greater clarity): _Finis non coronat opus_. This bibliography is far from complete; it merely represents the beginning of what may soon require a second volume. To this end, reviewers are invited to notify me of any pre-1986 entries omitted here. Undoubtedly many more articles on Clarín still lie buried in the periodicals of the United States, Latin America, and France, not to mention the numerous _almanaques_ and _ilustraciones_ of 19th-century Spain which may have escaped my attention.

DAVID TORRES
Angelo State University
San Angelo, TX 76909

October, 1986.

ABBREVIATIONS OF PERIODICAL TITLES

AIA   Archivo Ibero-Americano (Madrid)

ALE   Anales de Literatura Española (Alicante)

ASNS   Annali della Scuola Normale Superiore (Pisa)

BBMP   Boletín de la Biblioteca de Menéndez Pelayo (Santander)

BH   Bulletin Hispanique (Bordeaux)

BHS   Bulletin of Hispanic Studies (Liverpool)

BIEA   Boletín del Instituto de Estudios Asturianos (Oviedo)

BRAE   Boletín de la Real Academia Española (Madrid)

BSCC   Boletín de la Sociedad Castellonense de Cultura

CA   Cuadernos Americanos (México)

CCU   Cuadernos de la Cátedra de Unamuno (Salamanca)

CE   La Correspondencia de España (Madrid)

CH   Crítica Hispánica (Johnson City, TN)

CHA   Cuadernos Hispanoamericanos (Madrid)

CLC   Cuadernos de Literatura Contemporánea (Madrid)

CN   Los Cuadernos del Norte (Oviedo)

DAI   Dissertation Abstracts International (Ann Arbor, MI)

DHA   Diálogos Hispánicos de Amsterdam

DHR   Duquesne Hispanic Review (Pittsburg, PA)

EM   La España Moderna (Madrid)

Estlit   Estafeta Literaria (Madrid)

ExTL   Explicación de Textos Literarios (Sacramento, CA)

Hispano   Hispanófila (Chapel Hill, NC)

HM   El Heraldo de Madrid

HR   Hispanic Review (Philadelphia, PA)

IAL   Indice de Artes y Letras (Madrid)

Il EA   La Ilustración Española y Americana (Madrid)

Il Ib   La Ilustración Ibérica (Barcelona)

KRQ   Kentucky Review Quarterly (Lexington, KY)

LBR   Luso-Brazilian Review

LdD   Letras de Deusto (Bilbao)

LL   La Lectura (Madrid)

LLNL   Les Langues Néo-Latines (Paris)

LN   La Nación (Buenos Aires)

LOS   Literary Onomastics Studies (Brockport, NY)

LT   La Torre (Puerto Rico)

MC   Madrid Cómico

MLF   Modern Language Forum (Los Angeles, CA)

MLJ   Modern Language Journal (Madison, WI)

MLN   Modern Language Notes (Baltimore, MD)

MLR   Modern Language Review (London)

MLS   Modern Language Studies (Kingston, RI)

NRFH   Nueva Revista de Filología Hispánica (México)

NT   Nuestro Tiempo (Madrid)

PMLA   Publications of the Modern Language
            Association of America (New York, NY)

PSA   Papeles de Son Armadans (Madrid)

RABM   Revista de Archivos, Bibliotecas y Museos
            (Madrid)

RC   Revista Contemporánea (Madrid)

RCEH   Revista Canadiense de Estudios Hispánicos
            (Toronto)

RCHL	Revista Crítica de Historia y Literatura (Madrid)
RE	Revista de España (Madrid)
REH	Revista de Estudios Hispánicos (Alabama)
RF	Romanische Forschungen (Köln, Germany)
RFE	Revista de Filología Española (Pamplona)
RHi	Revue Hispanique (Paris)
RHM	Revista Hispánica Moderna (New York, NY)
RIB	Revista Iberoamericana de Bibliografía (Washington, DC)
RIE	Revista de Ideas Estéticas (Madrid)
RL	Revista de Literatura (Madrid)
RLC	Revue de Littérature Comparée (Paris)
R Letras	República de las Letras
RN	Revista Nueva (Madrid)
RO	Revista de Occidente (Madrid)
Rom N	Romance Notes (Chapel Hill, NC)
RP	La Revista Popular (Oviedo)
RQ	Riverside Quarterly (Gainesville, FL)
RR	Romanic Review (New York, NY)
RUO	Revista de la Universidad de Oviedo
R y F	Razón y Fe (Madrid)
SAB	South Atlantic Bulletin (University, AL)
SAR	South Atlantic Review (University, AL)
SGym	Siculorum Gymnasium (Catania, Italy)
SPFA	Bulletin de la Société des Professeurs Français en Amérique
TB	Tempo Brasileiro (Rio de Janeiro)
UDR	The University of Dayton Review (Ohio)

OTHER ABBREVIATIONS

AC	"¡Adiós, Cordera!"
AP	Apolo en Pafos
B	Barcelona
BG	Mariano Baquero Goyanes
C or LA	Leopoldo Alas ("Clarín")
CM	Cuentos morales
CST	Cánovas y su tiempo
DB	Doña Berta
DCS	Doña Berta, Cuervo, Superchería
DS	Doctor Sutilis
EPB	Emilia Pardo Bazán
ER	Ensayos y revistas
GS	El gallo de Sócrates
LR	La Regenta
M	Madrid
MC	José María Martínez Cachero
MGS	Marino Gómez-Santos
MMP	Marcelino Menéndez y Pelayo
NC	Nueva Campaña
O	Oviedo
OC	Obras Completas
PV	Armando Palacio Valdés
RCT	Rafael Calvo y el teatro español
SDC	El Señor y lo demás son cuentos
SP	Sermón perdido
SUH	Su único hijo

STUDIES ON CLARÍN

STUDIES ON CLARÍN

A. BOOKS AND PAMPHLETS

1. Agudiez, Juan Ventura. <u>Inspiración y estética en La Regenta de Clarín</u>. Oviedo: Instituto de Estudios Asturianos, 1970. 187 pp.

     Chapters on: Génesis del tema religioso, El concepto del "alma hermana," El tema del adulterio; Flaubert, Tolstoy, Zola, y <u>LR</u>, Estructura y sentido estético de <u>LR</u>, etc. According to his "Ediciones de <u>LR</u>" (p. 177), only five appeared before 1960. Reviewed by Fernández de la Vega, García Domínguez (q.v.).

2. Alas, Adolfo, ed. <u>Epistolario a Clarín</u>. Madrid: Ediciones Escorial, 1941. 241 pp.

     Contains two letters from MMP (1891, 1898), ten from Unamuno (1895-1900), and 26 from PV (1883-1900). Topics: Unamuno's praise for <u>GS</u>, and resentment that C did not review <u>Paz en la guerra</u>; PV's report that Cortón has published a letter against C in <u>El Tribuno</u>, and that Valera's nephew has been distributing some pamphlets against C in Cádiz. The volume closes with truncated selections from several prologues, stories, and speeches by C. Reviewed by Entrambasaguas (q.v.)

3. ---. <u>Epistolario de Clarín y Menéndez Pelayo</u>. Prólogo de Marañón. Madrid: Ediciones Escorial, 1943. 234 pp.

     Contains 30 letters from C to MMP (1883-1900) and 19 from MMP to C (1885-1898), on such topics as <u>LR</u>, Cánovas, Krause, <u>Juanito Reseco</u>, Farinelli, Valbuena, and Orbón.

4. Avello, Manuel F. <u>Algo sobre Clarín y sus paliques</u>. Oviedo: Instituto de Estudios Asturianos, 1963. 40 pp.

     The "paliques" are essential to understand C. Disagrees with R. Gullón that they were written "sin importarle un bledo la calidad de lo conseguido." According to Avello, C began his journalistic career on Sunday, 8 March 1868, with his "Juan Ruyz." The "paliques" did not prevent C from writing more formal works; he did write excellent essays, stories, and novels at the same time.

1

5. Balbín Victorero, Luis. <u>De cómo desfigura el señor
    Arboleya las grandes figuras</u>.   C o v a d o n g a :
    Editorial Covadonga, 1927. 31 pp.

    A rebuttal to Maximiliano Arboleya Martínez's
    article "Alma religiosa de Clarín" in <u>Renovación
    social</u> (1926).

6. Baquero Goyanes, Mariano. <u>Una novela de Clarín</u>: <u>Su
    único hijo</u>. Murcia: Universidad de Murcia,
    1952. 55 pp.

    "Un mundo romántico, un protagonista romántico
    y un seudoespiritualismo también romántico (el ro-
    manticismo era ya cosa pasada), en choque y con-
    traste con una hiriente y actual realidad burguesa,"
    according to MC. Originally appeared in <u>Anales de
    la Universidad de Murcia</u>, X (1951-52): 125-71. Re-
    printed in BG's <u>Prosistas españoles contemporáneos</u>
    (1956). Reviewed by Helman, Muñoz Cortés (q.v.).

7. Barra Lastarria, Eduardo de la. <u>El endecasílabo
    dactílico</u>. <u>Crítica de una crítica del crítico
    Clarín</u>. Rosario, Argentina: Est. Cromo-
    Litográfico de J. Ferrazini y Cía, 1895. 85
    pp.

    A defense of Rubén Darío, who had used this
    verse form in his "Pórtico" to Salvador Rueda's <u>En
    tropel</u> (1892). C reportedly had critized Darío in a
    "palique" published in <u>LN</u>.

8. Bécarud, Jean. <u>De La Regenta al Opus Dei</u>. Versión
    española de Florentino Trapero. Madrid:
    Taurus, 1977. 136 pp.

9. ---. <u>La Regenta de Clarín y la Restauración</u>. Tra-
    ducción de Teresa García Sabell. Madrid: Tau-
    rus, 1964. 42 pp.

    Brief chapters on the clergy and three social
    classes. Originally appeared in <u>Cuadernos del Con-
    greso por la Libertad de la Cultura</u>, 69 (1963), 49-
    57. Reviewed by Pino (q.v.)

10. Beser, Sergio. <u>Leopoldo Alas, crítico literario</u>.
    Madrid: Gredos, 1968. 371 pp.

    After an overview of literary criticism in the
    second half of the 19th century, Beser presents two
    chapters on C's literary criticism and its charac-
    teristics, and separate chapters on C's ideas on
    poetry, drama, and the novel. The volume closes
    with a selective bibliography and name and title
    index. Unquestionably the best book yet written on
    the subject, even though Beser did not have access

to all of the criticism by or about C. Reviewed by
G. G. Brown, G. Davis, J. Dowling, Jackson, Kronik,
Le Bouill, López-Morillas, Mathias, Mayoral (q.v.).

11. ---. <u>Leopoldo Alas: Teoría y crítica de la novela
española</u>. Barcelona: Laia, 1972. 302 pp.

An anthology, with brief introductory remarks,
of eight pieces by C on the theory of the novel, and
11 essays on specific novels by six Spanish novelists. Nine of the selections are incomplete. Those
never before reprinted include "Del estilo en la
novela," "Del naturalismo," "<u>El sabor de la tierru-
ca</u>," and "<u>Lo prohibido</u>" (from <u>La Ilustración Ibé-
rica</u>, different from the article found in <u>NC</u>.) Reviewed by G. G. Brown, Díez Borque (q.v.)

12. ---, ed. <u>Clarín y La Regenta</u>. Barcelona: Ariel,
1982. 317 pp.

An 80-page introduction is followed by eight
essays by Durand, Weber, Serrano Poncela, Clavería,
Alarcos Llorach, and Villavicencio on the structure,
characterization, and narrative techniques of <u>LR</u>.
Of special interest are two previously unknown
reviews, by Jerónimo Vida and Luis Morote, both
reprod. in the appendix. Reviewed by Sánchez Arnosi
(q.v.)

13. Blanquat, Josette y Jean-François Botrel, <u>Leopoldo
Alas, Clarín, y sus editores (1884-1893)</u>.
Rennes: Université de Haute-Bretagne, 1981. 85
pp.

A collection of 65 unpublished letters from C
to Fernando Fé and Manuel Fernández Lasanta mailed
1884-1893, with numerous notes identifying the periodicals and personalities mentioned. Topics:
money, <u>SP</u>, Renan, <u>Pipá</u>, <u>Folletos</u>, <u>SUH</u>, Bobadilla,
etc. Reviewed by García Sarriá, Richmond (q.v.)

14. Bobes Naves, María del Carmen. <u>Teoría general de
la novela. Semiología de La Regenta</u>. Madrid:
Editorial Gredos, 1985. 395 pp.

Reviewed by García Sarriá, Martínez San Martín
(q.v.)

15. Bonafoux, Luis. <u>Tiquismiquis: Yo y el plagiario
Clarín</u>. Madrid: Administración, 1888. 74 pp.

Accuses C of plagiarizing Flaubert, Zola, and
Fernanflor. The article is signed Paris, 20 Apr
1888. Reprinted in his book, <u>Huellas literarias</u>
(Paris: Garnier Hermanos, 1894), pp. 357-415.
Studied by MC in <u>RL</u>, III (1953): 99-111.

16. Botrel, Jean-François. <u>Preludios de Clarín</u>. Ovie-
     do: Instituto de Estudios Asturianos, 1973.
     lxxiii + 244 pp.

     A collection of 82 heretofore unknown pieces
     which Alas (as "Clarín" or "Zoilito") published in
     <u>El Solfeo</u> and <u>La Unión</u> during his literary appren-
     ticeship, 1875-1880.   Included are articles on <u>Doña
     Perfecta</u>, <u>Gloria</u>, and the <u>Episodios Nacionales</u>.
     Botrel's 73-page introd. consists of five parts: El
     hombre y su circunstancia; El periodismo militante;
     LA, krausista; LA y el compromiso político; and
     Teoría y práctica de la crítica.   In addition to a
     name-title index, Botrel furnishes a useful "Indice
     biográfico" identifying some 190 names mentioned by
     C.

17. Brent, Albert. <u>Leopoldo Alas and La Regenta: A
     Study in Nineteenth Century Spanish Prose Fic-
     tion</u>. University of Missouri Studies, XXIV,
     No. 2 (1951).   135 pp.

     A study of C's novelistic theories; the role
     of literature, art, and music in <u>LR</u>; provincial
     society; morality and religion; <u>LR</u> as a novel of
     frustration; bibliography.   Quotes C's statements
     (from his book on Galdós and <u>ER</u>) that Naturalism in
     the French sense never existed in Spain.   Based on
     his doct. thesis at Princeton.   Reviewed by R.
     Avrett, R. Gullón, H. B. Hall, E. Helman, L.
     Santullano (q.v.)

18. Bull, William Emerson and Vernon A. Chamberlin.
     <u>Clarín: The Critic in Action</u>.   (Arts and
     Sciences Studies: Humanities Series, 8.)
     Stillwater: Oklahoma State University, 1963.
     64 pp.

     An exceedingly frank but perceptive and well-
     documented study of C's personality, his attitude
     towards various types of writers (established, be-
     ginners, minor, enemies), and the consequences of
     his "police criticism."   Alas was emotionally in-
     secure, aggressive, sometimes uncouth, and suffered
     from stomach upsets, tension headaches, and acute
     insomnia.   Apparently C divided the literary world
     into three classes: literary aristocracy (Galdós,
     Zorrilla, Valera, Echegaray, etc.) whom he consis-
     tently treated with great respect; lesser stars of
     recognizable talent (Pereda, EPB, Alarcón, Unamuno,
     etc.) whose individual works he praised but felt
     free to ridicule or criticize with sarcasm; and
     minor figures (Ferrari, Manuel del Palacio, Cáno-
     vas, Bonafoux, etc.) for whom he had only scorn and
     contempt.   In the treatment of the third class he

is the literary policeman dedicated not to improve-
ment but to annihilation. Reviewed by Kronik,
Pattison (q.v.)

19. Cabezas, Juan Antonio. _Clarín. El provinciano
    universal_. Madrid: Espasa-Calpe, 1936. 244
    pp.

    The earliest biography of C, written by a man
    who never met him. Remarks on C's family, Galdós,
    Castelar, and Manuel del Palacio, but nothing on
    MMP, Pereda, Valera, EPB, Bobadilla, or C's pub-
    lishers. Has no footnotes, bibliography, or list
    of C's works. Should be read with books by Posada
    and MGS. Florid and unreliable, according to
    Rutherford. Also available in Colección Austral,
    1313 (1962), 229 pp.

20. Clocchiatti, Emilio. _Leopoldo Alas Clarín. Su crí-
    tica y su estética_. Quebec: Ediciones La Crí-
    tica, 1949. 218 pp.

    A personal view of C's esthetic ideas in _LR_,
    SUH, and some stories. Clocchiatti finds "perfecta
    homogeneidad entre teoría y práctica, entre crítica
    y arte. En sus cuentos y novelas busca nuestro
    autor la expresión creadora de su mundo intelec-
    tual." Clocchiatti seems unaware of all pre-1949
    criticism on C except Barja, Cabezas, Posada, and
    Sáinz Rodríguez.

21. Espinosa Rodríguez, Ciro. _Leopoldo Alas (Clarín) y
    la novela en España del romanticismo al rea-
    lismo_. La Habana, 1928.

22. ---. _Leopoldo Alas: Matices de su personalidad li-
    teraria_. La Habana, 1929.

23. ---. _Leopoldo Alas como ensayista_. La Habana,
    1929.

24. ---. _En torno a la crítica de Leopoldo Alas_. La
    Habana, 1931.

    Fernández Rodríguez-Avello, Manuel. See Avello, M.
    F.

25. Filippo, Luigi de. _Leopoldo Alas, Clarín, critico
    letterario_. Roma: Aldo Chicca, 1964. 77 pp.

    Fray Mortero. See Miguélez, J. F.

26. García Rey, Matías. _Clarín y sus folletos_. Ma-
    drid: U. Montegrifo, 1887. 60 pp.

Prefers C's portrait of Castelar over that of MMP; agrees that Spain's only good poets are Campoamor and Núñez de Arce; regrets that C ever published <u>Cánovas</u>; and accuses C of never finding faults in his friends. Briefly reviewed in <u>RE</u>, CXIX, 472 (Enero, 1888): 311.

27. García Sarriá, Francisco. <u>Clarín o la herejía amorosa</u>. Madrid: Gredos, 1975. 301 pp.

Central to all of C's work are the interrelated themes of love and religion, occurring either separately or interrelated. Focuses on <u>SUH</u>, which recounts the way whereby, beginning with his early Romanticism, C arrived--via Naturalism--at his ideological posture of the 1890's. The title refers to the religious significance which love acquires in C's thought. The Appendix reproduces important letters to José Quevedo, presumably dated 1876-77. Reviewed by Bandera, J. Díaz, Díez Borque, Rutherford (q.v.)

28. Gener, Pompeyo. <u>El caso Clarín: Monomanía maliciosa de forma impulsiva. Estudio de psiquiatría</u>. Madrid: Fernando Fé y Barcelona: Llordachs, 1894. 31 pp.

Dr. Gener, who identifies himself as "De la Sociedad Antropológica de París," attempts to prove, through quotations from four or five foreign scientists, that C is mentally ill and in need of professional help. Signed Barcelona, 15 June 1894. C's rebuttal appeared in <u>La Publicidad de Barcelona</u>, No. 6178 (7 Enero 1896). <u>El caso Clarín</u> was reviewed by Manuel Sanguily (q.v.)

29. Gómez Santos, Marino. <u>Leopoldo Alas Clarín. Ensayo bio-bibliográfico</u>. Prólogo de Gregorio Marañón. Oviedo: Instituto de Estudios Asturianos, 1952. 255 pp.

Especially useful are the chapters on C's religious ideas, polemics, and (incomplete) index of articles which he wrote for <u>MC</u>, 1883-97. Reviewed by Cabal, Entrambasaguas, Fraga, Gich, I. S. R. (q.v.)

30. Gramberg, Eduard J. <u>Fondo y forma del humorismo de Leopoldo Alas, Clarín</u>. Oviedo: Instituto de Estudios Asturianos, 1958. 265 pp.

Gramberg distinguishes two types of humor: "humorismo de piedad" and "humorismo de desprecio (o sátira)," and three principal ingredients: "españolismo, espontaneidad estilística, visión idealista del mundo." Based on his 1957 doct.

diss. at California. Reviewed by MC, A. Muñiz (q.v.)

31. Gutiérrez Llano, Francisco. <u>Clarín, hombre de su tiempo</u>. Oviedo, 1952. 35 pp.

32. Heras, Dionisio de las ("Plácido"). <u>El besugo Clarín</u>. Madrid: Imprenta La Propaganda, 1895. 55 pp.

       A virulent attack on C and his style. According to Heras, <u>Teresa</u> closely resembles Luis de Eguílaz's three-act play, <u>La cruz del matrimonio</u> (1861). This pamphlet went on sale on 30 Apr. 1895, according to <u>La Epoca</u>. MC describes <u>El besugo Clarín</u> in "Noticia de tres folletos contra Clarín" (q.v.)

33. Iranza, Carmen. <u>La Regenta: Cultura e idiosincrasias de Clarín</u>. Valencia: Albatros, 1984. 64 pp.

       Comments on prologues to <u>LR</u> (by Galdós, MC, Sobejano), and the 1974 movie on this novel. Intelligent and humorous notes on the characters of <u>LR</u> in order of appearance; the "action" chapter by chapter; and the hundreds of errors, oversights, contradictions, and absurd elements in <u>LR</u> and <u>SUH</u>. C was anticlerical, against the working class, against women, and knew little about music or the theater.

34. Lissorgues, Yvan. <u>Clarín político</u>, I. Toulouse-Le Mirail: Institut d'Études Hispaniques et Hispano-Américaines, 1980. 377 pp.

       Subtitled "LAC, periodista, frente a la problemática política y social de la España de su tiempo (1875-1901), estudio y antología." The 72-page introd. is followed by 80 selections by C, classified into six groups: Política, Caracteres y costumbres del pueblo español, Centralismo y regionalismo, La cuestión social, Las últimas colonias, Regeneración. Reviewed by Bonet, Botrel, Valis (q.v.)

35. ---. <u>Clarín político</u>, II. Toulouse-Le Mirail: Institut d'Études Hispaniques et Hispano-Américaines, 1981. 225 pp.

       Subtitled "LAC, periodista, frente a la problemática literaria y cultural de la España de su tiempo (1875-1901), estudios y artículos." The three chapters (Periodismo y cultura, Enseñanza y educación, Literatura y sociedad) are accompanied by a total of 10 articles by C. Both volumes have a bibliography, but the name index for both volumes appears in Vol. 2. Reviewed by Belot (q.v.)

36. ---. <u>La producción periodística de Leopoldo Alas (Clarín). Indices</u>. Université de Toulouse-Le Mirail, 1981.

Apparently very few copies of this important book were printed or distributed.

37. ---. <u>La pensée philosophique et religieuse de Leopoldo Alas (Clarín)--1875-1901</u>. Paris: Editions du CNRS, 1983. 460 pp.

Undoubtedly the most exhaustive treatment of C's philosophical and religious ideas. The appendix contains C's letters to Segismundo Moret and José Victoriano de la Cuesta, and reviews of his 1897 lectures at the Ateneo de Madrid. Bibliography, pp. 428-47.

38. Martinete <Mariano Martín Fernández?>. <u>Martingalas de Martinete. La autopsia de Clarín</u>. Madrid, 1895. 90 pp.

A violent attack on C, especially his <u>Teresa</u>, which the author considers C's "literary death." MC has studied this pamphlet in "Noticia de tres folletos contra Clarín" (q.v.) MC originally suspected that Martinete might be Emilio Martín Galí (whom C had ridiculed in the 6 and 13 July 1889 issues of <u>Madrid Cómico</u>) but in 1985 he concluded that Martinete's real name was Mariano Martín Fernández.

39. Martínez Cachero, José María, ed. <u>Leopoldo Alas Clarín</u>. Madrid: Taurus, 1978. 276 pp.

An anthology of 20 articles on C by 18 different authors, divided into five sections: Vida y semblanza, Polémicas y amistades, Teatro y versos, Crítica literaria, and Novelas y cuentos. Their original publication dates range from 1902 to 1969.

40. ---. <u>Las palabras y los días de Leopoldo Alas (Miscelánea de estudios sobre Clarín)</u>. Oviedo: Instituto de Estudios Asturianos, 1984. 332 pp.

Reproduces 18 articles previously published by MC, now arranged as follows: Biografía y bibliografía; Relaciones literarias y amistosas; Obra literaria.

41. Meregalli, Franco. <u>Clarín e Unamuno</u>. Milan: La Goliardica, 1956.

42. Miguélez, Juan. <u>Cascotes y machaqueos: Pulveriza-</u>
     <u>ciones a Valbuena y Clarín</u>.   Prólogo de Damián
     Isern.   Madrid: Librería de la Viuda de Her-
     nando y Cía, 1892.   248 pp.

     A diatribe against C (pp. 181-237) and Antonio
     de Valbuena, who also used the pen names of Miguel
     de Escalada and Venancio González.   Among other im-
     pertinent remarks, the author (also known as Fray
     Mortero) satirizes two sonnets which C had pub-
     lished in <u>La Ilustración Gallega y Asturiana</u>, I (10
     Junio 1879): 189.

43. Moxhet, Albert.   <u>La composition des personnages</u>
     <u>dans les contes de Leopoldo Alas (Clarín)</u>.
     Université de Liege, 1963.

44. Ortiz Aponte, Sally.   <u>Las mujeres de Clarín.   Es-</u>
     <u>perpentos y camafeos</u>.   Prólogo de J. A. Ca-
     bezas.   Barcelona: Ed. Universidad de Puerto
     Rico, 1971.   200 pp.

     Despite the suggestive title, Ortiz studies
     the characterization of four major female figures
     (Ana, Emma, Doña Berta, Caterina Porena) and others
     by social class (maids, nuns, actresses, etc.) or
     family classification (mothers, wives, sisters,
     lovers, etc.) and their relations with other mem-
     bers of society.   Based on her thesis at the Uni-
     versity of Puerto Rico.   Her bibliography contains
     titles not mentioned elsewhere, but also some that
     do not exist.

45. Palacio, Manuel del.   <u>Clarín entre dos platos.   Le-</u>
     <u>tras a la vista</u>.   Madrid: Librería de Fernando
     Fé, 1889.   42 pp.

     Palacio's indignant reply to C's statement
     that Spain had only two and a half poets: Campoamor
     and Núñez de Arce were full poets, Palacio only
     half.   C then devoted his fifth <u>Folleto</u>, <u>A 0,50</u>
     <u>poeta,   epístola en versos malos con notas de prosa</u>
     <u>clara</u> (M, 1889) to Palacio.

46. Posada, Adolfo.   <u>Leopoldo Alas (Clarín)</u>.   Oviedo:
     La Cruz, 1946.   232 pp.

     An emotional and fragmentary, but still use-
     ful, biography by a former student who knew Alas
     for many years.   Perhaps may have been better if
     Posada had not lost many of his notes and documents
     during the Civil War.   Should be read in conjunc-
     tion with the biographies by Cabezas and MGS.   Re-
     viewed by Araujo-Costa, D'Ors, R. Gullón, Valdea-
     vellano (q.v.)

47.   Ramos-Gascón, Antonio.   Clarín, obra olvidada.   Ma-
      drid: Ediciones Júcar, 1973.   264 pp.

      A 23-page introd. precedes this anthology of
      24 "minor" paliques on Spanish authors (EPB, Sal-
      vador Rueda, Valera, Valle-Inclán, etc.), 10 on
      foreign authors (Nietzsche, Tolstoy, Zola, Ver-
      laine, etc.), and five on "crítica higiénica."
      None on Galdós, as these are available elsewhere.
      All are reprinted here for the first time, except
      the one on El sabor de la tierruca, which Beser had
      reprinted in Teoría y crítica de la novela española
      (1972).   Reviewed by D'Auria (q.v.)

48.   Ríos, Laura de los.   Los cuentos de Clarín.   Ma-
      drid: Revista de Occidente, 1965.   327 pp.

      Part I analyzes five short novels (Pipá, Ave-
      cilla, DCS) and Part II is a global study of his
      short stories.   Reviewed by Amorós, Beser, Cano,
      Gracia, Tejedor, Thompson (q.v.) Based on her doct.
      diss. at Columbia U.

49.   Rodríguez-Alcalde, José María G.   Clarín y Menéndez
      Pelayo.   Santander: Imp. y Librería Moderna,
      1932.   47 pp.

      A compilation of his articles in several 1931
      issues of La Revista de Santander (not to be con-
      fused with BBMP).

50.   Rodríguez-Moñino, Antonio.   Clarín y Lázaro: Noti-
      cia de unas relaciones literarias (1889-1896).
      Valencia: Castalia, 1951.   32 pp.

      Apparently based on his article in Biblio-
      filia, V (1951): 47-70, concerning the relations
      between C and the editor of La España Moderna.

51.   Rutherford, John.   Leopoldo Alas: La Regenta.   Lon-
      don: Grant and Cutler, 1974.   79 pp.

      A critical guide to the characterization,
      story, and setting of the novel itself, without re-
      gard to biographical or historical factors.   Does
      not quote any scholars but considers G. G. Brown's
      doct. diss., "The Novels and Cuentos of LA"
      (Oxford, 1962) as "the most complete discussion of
      Alas' literary work so far produced."   Reviewed by
      Beser (q.v.)

52.   Sáinz Rodríguez, Pedro.   La obra de Clarín.   Dis-
      curso leído en la solemne apertura del curso
      académico de 1921-22 en la Universidad de
      Oviedo.   Madrid: Gráfica Ambos Mundos, 1921.
      93 pp.

A general study, one of the earliest attempts to "resurrect" C. Briefly reviewed by R. G. de Ortega. Reprinted in his book, Evolución de las ideas sobre la decadencia española y otros estudios de crítica literaria (M: Rialp, 1962).

53.   Siboni, Luis.   Pan de compadres para Valbuena y Clarín.   Madrid: Imprenta de Pedro Ortega, 1898. xii + 112 pp.

Another diatribe against these two popular critics. Palau y Dulcet records another edition (M, 1906), with preface by Pedro Díaz Cosau.

54.   Sobejano, Gonzalo.   Clarín en su obra ejemplar. Madrid: Editorial Castalia, 1985. 206 pp.

An up-to-date evaluation of C's literary criticism and prose fiction, based on Sobejano's 1981 lectures at the Fundación Juan March. Of special interest is Chap. 4, on LR and SUH. Reviewed by Valis (q.v.)

55.   Solís, Jesús Andrés.   Vida y obra de Clarín.   Gijón: Solís, 1975. 135 pp.

56.   Tomasso, Vincenzo de.   Clarín nella narrative spagnola del segondo ottocento. Sei studi su Leopoldo Alas. Pisa: Pacini Editore, 1973.

57.   Torréndell, Juan.   Clarín y su ensayo: Estudio crítico de Teresa.   Barcelona: López, 1895. 70 pp.

Reviewed in La Ilustración Artística (B), No. 699 (20 Mayo 1895) and by Carlos Mendoza in La Ilustración Ibérica (B), 6 Junio 1895.

58.   Torres, David.   Los prólogos de Leopoldo Alas.   Madrid: Editorial Playor, 1984. 269 pp.

The complete text of 31 prefaces--nine for C's own books and 22 for works by Balzac, Carlyle, Gómez-Carrillo, Tolstoy, Zola, etc. plus his "palique" on Valbuena's Ripios aristocráticos. Reviewed by Rivkin (q.v.)

59.   Valis, Noël Maureen.   The Decadent Vision in Leopoldo Alas: A Study of La Regenta and Su único hijo. Baton Rouge and London: Louisiana State University Press, 1981. 215 pp.

While C's position toward modernismo, symbolism, and the decadent movement was essentially hostile, Valis states that "the pervasiveness of

decadent literature in France, and, even in a number of Spanish imitators, could not fail to pene-
trate and make some impression upon a highly complex and nervous spirit who already was attracted
to such decadent precursors as the Goncourts and
Baudelaire." Based on her 1975 doct. diss. at Bryn
Mawr College. Reviewed by Dial, García Sarriá,
Kronik, D. M. Rogers, Round (q.v.)

60.   Varela Jácome, Benito. Alas Clarín. Madrid: EDAF,
       1980. 383 pp.

The most useful part of this general study and
anthology are pages 70-169, devoted to LR, SUH, and
Cuesta abajo. The anthology (pp. 173-377) is of
little value because it reproduces a few pages from
LR and other works which should be read in their
entirety.

61.   Vázquez Azpiri, Héctor. Clarín. Madrid, 1971.

62.   Vilanova, Antonio, ed. Clarín y su obra en el cen-
       tenario de La Regenta (Barcelona, 1884-1885).
       Actas del Simposio Internacional celebrado en
       Barcelona del 20 al 24 de Marzo de 1984. Bar-
       celona: Universidad de Barcelona, 1985.

This 316-page volume, hereafter called Clarín
y su obra, contains articles on C by 14 different
authors, who are listed individually in Section B
of this bibliography. Vilanova's introduction
appears on pp. 9-12.

63.   Villavicencio, Laura Núñez de. La creatividad en
       el estilo de Leopoldo Alas Clarín. Oviedo:
       Instituto de Estudios Asturianos, 1974. 285
       pp.

Three chapters: Formas lingüísticas portadoras
de expresión (el sustantivo, el adjetivo, el verbo,
etc.); La expresividad y las estructuras sintácti-
cas (la composición de la frase, modalidades reite-
rativas, etc.); and La expresividad y el lenguaje
figurado. The emphasis is on LR. Based on her
1973 doct. diss. at Maryland. Reviewed by G. G.
Brown, J. Díaz, Fernández de la Vega, Rutherford,
Ullman (q.v.)

B. ARTICLES AND PREFACES

64. Abellán, Manuel L. "Clarín: La inversión de para-
     digmas ideológicos como recurso literario (A
     propósito de La conversión de Chiripa)," Na-
     rrativa de la Restauración. Ed. Juan Ignacio
     Ferreras et al. Amsterdam: Rodopi, 1984.

     Abellán's essay, the fifth of six papers read
     at the University of Amsterdam in 1982, demon-
     strates that C was "an astute observer of social
     ideologies and practices," states reviewer V. A.
     Chamberlin in Hispania, 68 (May, 1985): 304.

65. Agudiez, Juan Ventura. "Emma Bovary-Ana Ozores o
     el símbolo del amor." RR, LIV (1963): 20-29.

     Differences between the love/adultery in Emma
     and Ana. Flaubert almost completely omits Yon-
     ville's opinion about Emma's love affairs. One of
     the basic differences between the two novels is "la
     perspectiva del drama pasional; para Emma Bovary es
     la lucha constante de la realidad subjetiva con la
     Realidad; para Ana Ozores es el conflicto religioso
     y social.

66. ---. "La sensibilidad decadentista de Barbey d'Au-
     revilly y algunos temas de La Regenta." RO,
     99 (Junio, 1971): 355-65.

     It is more than probable that C was familiar
     with the satanism and sensuality depicted in Une
     vieille maîtresse (1851), L'Ensorcelée (1852), Un
     prêtre marié (1865), and Une histoire sans nom
     (1882).

67. Alarcos Llorach, Emilio. "Notas a La Regenta."
     Archivum, II, 1 (Enero-abril, 1952): 141-60.

     Studies the structure of LR, which he divides
     into two parts of approximately equal length: "pre-
     sentativa" (Chap. 1-15) which is slow and descrip-
     tive, and "activa" (Chap. 16-30), which is narra-
     tive and moves faster. The first part takes place
     in three days (Oct. 2, 3, 4) while the second part
     goes from Nov. of the following year to Oct. three
     years later. Reprinted in Alarcos' Ensayos y estu-
     dios literarios (M, 1976), pp. 99-118 and Cajón de
     sastre asturiano, I (1980), and Beser's Clarín y
     LR, pp. 227-245.

68. ---. Cajón de sastre asturiano, I. Salinas (Astu-
     rias): Ayalga Ediciones, 1980.

Contains: Introducción a la literatura en Asturias (pp. 11-67); Notas a LR (pp. 68-91); Clarín y la lengua (pp. 92-110).

69.   ---.   "Notas remozadas sobre La Regenta." Argumentos, VIII, 63-64 (1984): 8-15.

Updated notes on the structure of the novel. "La obra se muerde la cola: de octubre a octubre, de la catedral a la catedral. No ha pasado nada. Vetusta indiferente. Los que tientan a los dioses, queriendo salir de la niebla, reciben su castigo. Hay cierta moraleja de anánke de tragedia griega."

70.   ---.   "Aspectos de la lengua de Clarín." Clarín y su obra. Ed. Antonio Vilanova. Barcelona: U de Barcelona, 1985. 13-30.

71.   Alberti, Jaime.   "Apuntes de derecho natural de Leopoldo Alas (Tomados de las explicaciones de clase por el alumno José Acebal González)." CN, II, 7 (Mayo-junio, 1981): 43-49.

Brief excerpts from some of the 60 lectures (comprising 211 pages, double-spaced) given by Prof. Alas at the University of Oviedo.   These notes, taken by his student Acebal, are now owned by José Manuel Castañón.

72.   Alberto, Luis.   "La Teresa de Clarín (Carta abierta)." La Gran Vía (M), III, 98 (12 Mayo 1895): 314.

A favorable opinion, dated 12 April 1895, by "an ordinary citizen." Reprod. by David Torres in "Noticia de otro juicio . . ." (q.v.)

73.   Alonso, Luis Ricardo.   "La Regenta: Contrapunto del ensueño y la realidad." CN, V, 23 (1984): 3-9.

"Los personajes principales de la novela están perdidos en sus respectivos ensueños y paralelamente, la necesidad va tejiendo la tela de araña en que los atrapa . . . En toda esta pasión, el ensueño es el factor central. Y la necesidad física--el sexo--y social--la imposibilidad de enamorar a Ana como sacerdote--es el contrapunto."

74.   Alonso Cortés, Narciso.   Zorrilla, su vida y sus obras.   Valladolid: Librería Santaren.   1943. 1242 pp.

Includes a long letter by Zorrilla (pp. 830-33) thanking C for his article "Los poetas en el Ateneo," El Día (30 Marzo 1884), in which the critic proposed a pension and homage for the poet. Zorrilla would like to receive the pension but does not care for the crowning. He greatly appreciates the kind words of "un crítico tan independiente y tan sin respetos humanos" like C.

75.   ---. "Clarín y el _Madrid Cómico_." _Archivum_, II, 1 (Enero-abril, 1952): 43-62.

   A survey of C's numerous _paliques_ in this weekly, from 1883-1897. In addition to many light pieces, C also wrote short stories here, such as "Un viejo verde" (1893), "Don Urbano" and "El cura de Vericueto" (1894), "El caballero de la mesa redonda" (1895), etc.

76.   Altamira, Rafael. "Leopoldo Alas." _RCHL_, VI, 8-9 (Agosto-sept., 1901): 219-30.

   A favorable overview of C's works. "Clarín, que era muy sugestionable en la vida social, en el terreno de las relaciones amistosas (por lo cual se llevó muchos chascos), lo era poquísimo en el de la ciencia y el arte." Classification of the _paliques_. Quotations from three of C's students. Recalls his streetcar ride with C, to visit Galdós the day before the premiere of _Realidad_.

77.   --- _Cosas del día_. Valencia: Sempere, 1909.

   Contains: "Leopoldo Alas: I. El literato, II. El profesor," pp. 82-103. C's qualities as a writer and his ideas on education. Reprinted in MC's anthology, _LAC_, pp. 23-33.

78.   Alvarez, Carlos Luis. "Clarín va a misa." _CN_, II, 7 (Mayo-junio, 1981): 109-13.

   C's ideas on religion and tolerance. His caustic satire reminds Alvarez of Quevedo, Forner, Larra, and especially Gallardo.

Alvarez Buylla, Adolfo. See Buylla, Adolfo A.

79.   Alvarez Sereix, Rafael. "Leopoldo Alas y su folleto _Un viaje a Madrid_." _RC_, LXII (30 Junio 1886): 628-33.

   C is Spain's only literary critic because of his good taste, knowledge, and impartiality. A favorable review of C's first _folleto_, which contains articles on MMP, Castelar, Campoamor, Núñez de Arce, Echegaray, and Novo y Colson, and a perceptive essay on how literary reputations are created and destroyed in the coffee houses of Madrid.

80. Amorós, Andrés. "Doce cartas inéditas de Clarín a Jacinto Octavio Picón." CN, II, 7 (Mayo-junio, 1981): 8-20.

Reproduces 12 letters written between 1884 and 1900 to novelist Picón, about whom C wrote almost nothing. Topics: C's and Galdós' desire to publish a literary journal called La República de las Letras; C's departure from the staff of El Día; derogatory comments on Ortega Munilla; praise for Castelar, whose chair at the Academy was awarded to Picón; thanks for Picón's article on LR, the text of which Amorós reprints on pp. 17-20.

81. ---. "Contra Clarín (Algunas citas)." Argumentos, VIII, 63-64 (1984): 48-49.

Quotes several negative reviews of LR penned between 1885-1960 by Martínez Vigil, Blanco García, Ladrón de Guevara, etc. As late as the 1960's, someone objected to the inclusion of C as required reading for students in Spain.

82. Andreu Valdés, Martín. "Breve apunte para el centenario de Clarín." BIEA, VI, 16 (Agosto, 1952): 149-58.

Recalls MMP's opinion of LR as expressed in a letter to Valera ("la novela está escrita con muchísimo talento, pero es tan repugnante todo aquello que me ha costado mucho trabajo acabar su lectura") and C's praise for Luis Pastor's Historia de los Papas desde el fin de la Edad Media.

83. Aramburo y Machado, Mariano. Literatura crítica. Paris: Ollendorff, 1909.

Pages 81-91, entitled "El gallo de Sócrates," analyze C's religious philosophy as expressed in this short story, the first in a collection of 15 stories published under this title. The review is highly favorable.

Aramís. See Bonafoux, Luis.

84. Aranguren, José Luis L. Estudios literarios. Madrid: Gredos, 1976. 349 pp.

Contains: "De La Regenta a Ana Ozores," pp. 177-211. This psychological novel shows no determinism. The importance of times, locations, climate, liberation, style. LR also contains characteristics of erotic novel, novela de folletín, and black humor. C is undoubtedly a better novelist than prose writer. The novel should have been called Ana Ozores.

85. Arboleya Martínez, Maximiliano. "Alma religiosa de
    Clarín (Datos íntimos e inéditos)." La Revis-
    ta Quincenal (B), VIII, 16 (10 Julio 1919):
    328-49.

    C was a truly religious man, according to this
    priest who discussed religious matters with C on
    numerous occasions. Arboleya was the nephew of the
    Bishop of Oviedo, Martínez Vigil, with whom C had a
    "polemic" concerning LR. Reproduces four letters
    sent by C to Martínez Vigil on 28 Oct. 1892, 10
    April 1895, Sept. 1896, plus one undated. Reprint-
    ed in Renovación Social, Nos. 46-49 (1926) and in
    MC's anthology, LAC, pp. 43-59.

86. Argüelles, Juan Benito. "Nómina de personajes de
    La Regenta." CN, V, 23 (1984): 10-18.

    Using the Biblioteca Nueva ed. (M, 1966) of
    the novel, the author has compiled a descriptive
    list of all the characters, with chapter and page
    numbers in which they first appear, alphabetically
    arranged from Agapito to Zapico.

87. Arpe, C. José de. "Un libro de Clarín." RE,
    CXXXVIII, 4 (Feb., 1892): 503-06.

    A review of DCS, of which the reviewer con-
    siders DB "el mejor libro que ha salido de la pluma
    de Clarín."

    Arroyo de López-Rey, J. See López-Rey, Justa A. de

88. Asensio, Jaime. "El motivo del alarde en La Re-
    genta de Clarín." RABM, 77 (1974): 597-600.

    A closer look at the beginning of Chap. 16, in
    which Alvaro "shows off" on a beautiful white horse
    in front of Ana's balcony. Asensio had previously
    studied the topic of ostentation (in Pepita Jiménez
    and other works) in Miscelánea Hispánica (U of
    Western Ontario, 1967), pp. 217-23.

89. Ashhurst, A. W. "Clarín y Darío: Una guerrilla
    literaria del Modernismo." CHA, 260 (Feb.,
    1972): 324-30.

    C began to attack Rubén Darío as early as
    1890, probably before reading his works. Darío
    defended himself in "Pro Domo Mea," 30 Enero 1894,
    the full text of which is reprinted from E. K.
    Mapes' Escritos inéditos (NY, 1938).

90. ---. La literatura hispanoamericana en la crítica
    española. Madrid: Gredos, 1980. 132-69.

Ashhurst traces C's literary criticism of several Latin American authors, with emphasis on Darío and Rodó. C, who disliked Modernismo, was harsh on Rubén Darío and José Santos Chocano but showed respect for Rufino José Cuervo and José Enrique Rodó. Unlike Valera and MMP, C had a low opinion of many Latin American writers and made a bad impression on them.

91. Asún, Raquel. "La Regenta, un libro con larga historia." El País (M), 7 Abril 1985: 8.

During C's lifetime, LR was considerably less popular than Pequeñeces or Las ilusiones del doctor Faustino. Asún makes a list of the major editions since the first four: Barcelona, Cortezo, 1884-85; Madrid, Fé, 1901; Valencia, Maucci, 1908; Buenos Aires, Emecé, 1946. RC did not review it because its director, Cárdenas, was pro-Cánovas, and EM did not review it because of the dispute between C and the editor, Lázaro Galdeano.

92.   Avello, Manuel F.   Vida y obra literaria de Juan Ochoa Betancourt. Palabras liminares de J. M. Martínez Cachero. Oviedo, 1955. 213 pp.

A biography of a friend and admirer of C, Ochoa (1864-1899), whose novel, Los señores de Hermida (1896; 1900), has a preface by C. Contains 15 letters from PV, three from C, eight from Galdós, Pereda, MMP, Altamira, and Victoriano García San Miguel. Reviewed by MC in BIEA, X, 27 (Abril, 1956): 156-58.

93.   ---.   Tomás Tuero (La leyenda de un periodista). Oviedo: Instituto de Estudios Asturianos, 1958. 128 pp.

Numerous brief references to Tuero's intimate friendship with C. The bibliography (pp. 118-23) reproduces C's obituary on Tuero published in El Liberal (M), 27 Dec. 1892, in the form of a letter to editor Cavia. Reviewed by M. V. in BIEA, XIII, 36 (Abril, 1959): 146-48 and by J. Villa Pastor in Archivum, VIII, 1-2 (1958): 345-47.

94.   ---.   "Recuerdo de Juan Ochoa Betancourt (1864-1964)." BIEA, XIX, 54 (Abril, 1965): 139-50.

Includes an unpublished letter from C to Ochoa (with a photocopy of the original, p. 148) regarding Altamira's question whether C prefers an article on Teresa by Altamira or Ochoa. (C chose Ochoa, whose review of Teresa appeared in RCHL, I, 2, Abril, 1895: 61-62.)

95.   ---.   "Carta inédita de Clarín a Juan Ochoa."
        BIEA, XXXVI, 105-106 (Enero-agosto, 1982):
        319-24.

        Reproduces a brief letter, with facsimile,
dated Carreño, 15 Sept. 1896.   C, who is reading
and writing more, promises to visit Ochoa on Sept.
19.   Ironically, on that day C's mother, Doña
Leocadia, died suddenly.

96.   Avrett, Robert.   "The Treatment of Satire in the
        Novels of Leopoldo Alas (Clarín)."   Hispania,
        XXIV, 2 (May, 1941): 223-30.

        Satire and irony in the characterization of
Saturnino Bermúdez, Fermín, and Víctor in LR, and
Bonis and Emma in SUH.   Unfortunately Avrett does
not explain or develop this statement: "In the de-
lineation of the Magistral, Clarín presents the
tragic irony of a strong character slowly destroy-
ing himself, together with the woman he loves,
through the very strength of will that might have
proved the salvation of both" (p. 226).

97.   Azorín.   "Clarín en el Ateneo."   El Progreso (M),
        17 Nov. 1897, 5 Dic. 1897, 8 Dic. 1897, 9 Feb.
        1898.

        Not included in his OC.   The first segment was
reprinted by José María Valverde in Artículos olvidados de J. Martínez Ruiz (1894-1904), M: Narcea,
1972, pp. 121-27.   See also Lissorgues' La Pensée,
pp. 422-26.   Excerpts and comments on C's speech on
religion and charity.   In the audience were González Serrano, Benavente, and Valle-Inclán.

98.   ---.   "Avisos de Este."   El Progreso, 24 Nov. 1897.

        Criticizes C's lectures at the Ateneo, com-
pares him to Cousin, disagrees with his philosophical idealism, and quotes Echegaray as saying: "A
ver, a ver cuándo entramos en lo hondo."   Reproduced by Ramos-Gascón in his article, "Relaciones
Clarín-Martínez Ruiz."

99.   ---.   Páginas escogidas de Clarín.   Madrid: Casa
        Editorial Calleja, 1917.   390 pp.

        A brief study of C as satirist, critic, moral-
ist, novelist, and short story writer, followed by
selections of his most important and representative
works.   Azorín is particularly fond of SUH and the
stories "El sombrero del señor cura" and "Refle-
jos."   Reprinted in Azorín's OC, IX (1954): 1197-
1204.

100. ---. Prólogo a <u>Superchería</u>. Madrid: Biblioteca
         Estrella, 1918. 7-21.

101. ---. "Clarín y la inteligencia." <u>OC</u>, V (1960):
         191-94.

         C's sense of time and commitment to intelli-
      gence. High praise for <u>Superchería</u>, <u>DB</u>, and "La
      educación del rey." Originally pub. in <u>Andando y
      pensando</u> (1929).

102. ---. "De la vida de Clarín." <u>OC</u>, V (1960): 195-
         99.

         C's reply to accusations by Martínez Vigil.
      C's students denied that he had distributed free
      copies of <u>LR</u>. Originally pub. in <u>Andando y pen-
      sando</u> (1929).

103. ---. "Leopoldo Alas." <u>OC</u>, II (1959): 786-93.

         A favorable appraisal of C, originally pub.
      in <u>Clásicos y modernos</u> (1913). Two years earlier,
      Azorín had suggested to Gregorio Martínez Sierra,
      director of Casa Editorial Renacimiento, the pub-
      lication of an anthology of C's works, in order to
      show C's two styles: the detailed, realistic tech-
      nique of <u>LR</u>, etc. and the more delicate or psycho-
      logical style of <u>GS</u>, <u>CM</u>, etc.

104. ---. "Oviedo: En la biblioteca de Clarín." <u>OC</u>,
         VIII (1963): 101-07.

         At C's new home, which he occupied for only
      11 days before his death, Azorín found a notebook
      in which C had recorded the expenses of his honey-
      moon. High praise for <u>SUH</u>. Originally pub. in
      <u>Los clásicos redivivos. Los clásicos futuros</u>
      (1945). Reprinted in MC's anthology, <u>LAC</u>, pp. 60-
      65.

105. Balseiro, José A. <u>Novelistas españoles modernos</u>.
         New York: Macmillan, 1933.

         One of the earliest attempts to analyze <u>LR</u>
      and <u>SUH</u> objectively. Balseiro would have prefer-
      red to see fewer details and more morally good
      characters in <u>LR</u>; all of Chap. 20 in Part 2,
      could have easily been eliminated. In 1933 ed. of
      Balseiro, see Chap. VII, pp. 348-81. In 7th ed.
      (NY: Las Américas, 1963), see pp. 354-87.

106. Bandera, Cesáreo. "La sombra de Bonifacio Reyes
         en <u>Su único hijo</u>." <u>BHS</u>, XLVI, 3 (July,
         1969): 201-25.

The symbolic shadow on the wall reflects that caricature of a romantic, Bonis, "ajeno a sí mismo . . . buscándose en el vacío existencial de un mundo deshumanizado, hipócrita, herméticamente e-goísta." Bonis reminds Bandera of Frédéric Moreau in _L'éducation sentimentale_. Disagrees with BG and Weber; Bonifacio is, in fact, Antonio's real father. Reprod. in MC's anthology, _LAC_, pp. 212-37.

107.   Baquero Goyanes, Mariano.   "Clarín, novelista olvidado." _RUO_ (1946): 137-45.

A commentary inspired by Pérez de Ayala's ed. of _DCS_ (1942).   BG would like to see more editions of C's works.   C was a stranger in his own country, not fully appreciated by his contemporaries, because of his sincere criticism.

108.   ---.   "Clarín y la novela poética." _BBMP_, XXIII, 1 (Enero-marzo, 1947): 96-101.

An essay inspired by C's "La novela novelesca" (_ER_, 1886-1892), originally pub. in _El Heraldo_, in which he speaks of a "novela poética." _DB_ is the closest example of this type.

109.   ---.   "Clarín, creador del cuento español." _Cuadernos de Literatura_ (M), V, 13-15 (Enero-junio, 1949): 145-69.

C's stories are more psychological and less "dated" than those of his contemporaries.   A general discussion and classification of his short fiction, such as: poético (_DB_, "El dúo de la tos," etc.); religioso; tipos humildes; sátira y humor; inquietud nacional.   C does not have Maupassant's conciseness or objectivity.   "El mejor Clarín no es el crítico, ni aun el novelista, sino el creador de unos cuentos. . . ." (p. 169)

110.   ---.   _El cuento español en el siglo XIX_.   Madrid: Consejo Superior de Investigaciones Científicas, 1949.   699 pp.

Discusses C's short stories on war and military service, of which BG considers "El sustituto" the best; religious topics, of which "Cambio de luz" and "El Señor" are the most beautiful; rural themes, of which _AC_ is the most popular; social, of which "El torso" and "Un jornalero" are good examples; humorous and satirical, such as "Zurita" and "Don Ermeguncio o la vocación"; children, in which BG refutes (pp. 531-36) Bonafoux's accusation of plagiarism; animals, such as "Quin"; love;

psychological, such as "Cristales"; and tragic and dramatic, concerning DB.

111.   ---.   "Exaltación de lo vital en La Regenta." Archivum, II, 1 (Enero-abril, 1952): 189-219.

Examines the "dualidad intelectualismo-vitalismo" which BG had already studied in C's short stories. Bishop Camoirán and Frígilis represent the voice of nature as "contrafiguras de todos los vicios censurados y combatidos, tanto en la esfera clerical como en la mundana." Reprinted in BG's Prosistas españoles (1956) and in MC's anthology, LAC, pp. 157-78.

112.   ---.   Prólogo a Clarín. Cuentos. Selección de J. M. Martínez Cachero. Oviedo: Gráfica Summa, 1953. 332 pp.

Tenderness is the essential ingredient of C's short stories. He wrote two types: the tender, pleasant ones such as "La trampa" or "El dúo de la tos" and the satirical ones such as "Doctor Pertinax" or "Doctor Sutilis." A few, such as "Avecilla," combine the two styles. Similarities between the stories of Alas, Pérez de Ayala, and Aldous Huxley. Reprod. in MC's anthology, LAC, pp. 245-52.

112a. ---.   Prosistas españoles contemporáneos: Alarcón, Leopoldo Alas, Gabriel Miró, Azorín. Madrid: Rialp, 1956. 286 pp.

Reproduces his "Exaltación de lo vital en La Regenta," (pp. 127-72) and "Una novela de Clarín: Su único hijo," (pp. 33-125).

113.   ---.   "Los cuentos largos de Clarín." CN, II, 7 (Mayo-junio, 1981): 68-71.

Structure, characterization, central turning point, etc. are more important than length in determining the difference between cuento, novela corta, cuento largo, nouvelle, etc. The term cuento largo, suggested by EPB, might have solved the problem. Thus Las dos cajas, Pipá, and DB should be called cuentos largos.

114. ---.   Introducción a La Regenta. Madrid: Espasa-Calpe, 1984.

Of special interest for narrative techniques. Includes a "Guía de personajes" of some 150 names. Apparently based on the first ed. No critical notes. Reviewed by Southworth (q.v.)

115. Barbáchano, Carlos. "La Regenta y el cine." CN,
      V, 23 (1984): 77-81.

      A negative analysis of Gonzalo Suárez's movie
      version of LR, featuring Emma Penella in the title
      role.

116. Bertrand de Muñoz, Maryse. "Estudio semiológico
      del tiempo en los capítulos 3, 4 y 5 de La
      Regenta." LdD, XV, 32 (Mayo-agosto, 1985):
      103-32.

117. Beser, Sergio. "Siete cartas de Leopoldo Alas a
      José Yxart." Archivum, X, 1-2 (1960): 385-
      97.

      Reproduces seven letters dated between 27
      June 1883 and 9 Oct. 1891.   Praise for El año
      pasado (1888) and Yxart's review of Angel Guerra
      in EM. Confesses that he has trouble reading Cat-
      alan and English. Defends Castelar. Third letter
      (28 Oct. 1887) expresses disillusionment or fa-
      tigue with literature.

118. ---. "Sinfonía de dos novelas: Fragmento de una
      novela de Clarín." Insula, XV, 167 (Oct.,
      1960): 1 and 12.

      Analyzes "Sinfonía de dos novelas" (EM, Aug.
      1889), which Beser believes was going to be the
      first part of Una medianía. In Jan. 1886 C wrote
      Oller: "Yo tengo entre manos . . . una novela
      vendida a Fé, que provisionalmente se titula Una
      medianía." He again mentions it to Yxart (28 Oct.
      1887) and to MMP (6 Oct. 1891) but Una medianía
      was never published, possibly because of C's
      "tendencia hacia la abulia y la inhibición y pro-
      gresivo apartamiento de la creación y la litera-
      tura (notas que caracterizan el último decenio de
      su vida)."   Reprod. in MC's anthology, LAC, pp.
      238-244.

119. ---.   "Documentos clarinianos: Seis cartas de
      Leopoldo Alas a Narciso Oller." Archivum,
      XII (1962): 507-26.

      Part I gives the text of six letters from C
      to Oller, dated between 27 June 1885 and 13 March
      1891, concerning C's admiration for the Catalan
      novelist but difficulty in reading the language;
      the fact that the only Spanish novelists C likes
      are Galdós, Pereda, and Oller;   C's desire to read
      Zola's preface to Oller's La Papallona; an invi-
      tation for Oller to write for EM; and promises to
      write about La Papallona in El Globo. Part 2 re-
      produces the text of Fray Candil's obituary of C
      in MC.

120. ---. "La crítica de Leopoldo Alas y la novela de
          su tiempo." Homenaje a Jaime Vicens Vives,
          vol. 2. Barcelona, 1967. 57-66.

          Discerns three phases--the defense of the
          "novela tendenciosa," 1876-1880 (C's first article
          on any novel was the one on Gloria); naturalism,
          1881 (La desheredada, one of his best articles);
          and the "agotamiento del naturalismo," around
          1890. C's position during this third period was
          ecclectic; no one had taken Zola's role as model,
          but C seemed to prefer Tolstoy and Bourget.

121. ---. "En torno a un cuento olvidado de Leopoldo
          Alas." CHA, 231 (Marzo, 1969): 526-48.

          An analysis (and text, pp. 543-48) of "Kant,
          perro viejo," C's incomplete short story from La
          Publicidad (B), 2 Dec. 1880 and 2 Jan. 1881.

122. ---. "Leopoldo Alas o la continuidad de la Revo-
          lución." La revolución de 1868. Historia,
          pensamiento, literatura. Eds. Clara E. Lida
          e Iris M. Zavala. Prólogo de Vicente Llo-
          rens. New York: Las Américas, 1970: 397-
          411.

          The ideals of the revolution of Sept. 1868
          can be found throughout C's writings (not so much
          for what it achieved but for what it made pos-
          sible), especially in "El libre examen y nuestra
          literatura presente." The failure of the politi-
          cal movements of 1812, 1820, 1837, and 1854 was
          due to the lack of communication between the
          masses and the liberal minorities.

123. ---. "El lugar de 'Sinfonía de dos novelas' en la
          narrativa de Leopoldo Alas." Hispanic Stud-
          ies in Honour of Frank Pierce. University of
          Sheffield (England), 1980. 17-30.

          "Sinfonía," published in the Aug. 1889 issue
          of EM, was originally meant to be an introduction
          to SUH. Excerpts from C's correspondence with his
          publisher, Fernández Lasanta. Brief analysis of
          "Sinfonía."

124. ---. "Espacio y objetos en La Regenta." Clarín y
          su obra. Ed. Antonio Vilanova. Barcelona: U
          de Barcelona, 1985: 211-28.

125. Beser, Sergio and Laureano Bonet. "Indice de co-
          laboraciones de Leopoldo Alas en la prensa
          barcelonesa." Archivum, XVI (1966): 157-211.

A catalog, with brief annotations, of C's six articles in Arte y Letras, two in La Ilustración Artística, 41 in La Ilustración Ibérica, three in Pluma y Lápiz, 225 in La Publicidad (morning ed.) 15 in La Publicidad (evening ed.), and four in La Saeta. Each listing is preceded by a statement on the director, publisher, type of publication, etc.

126. Blanch, Antonio. "La Regenta: Vigoroso relato de dos impotencias." RyF, 209, No. 1028 (Mayo, 1984): 537-42.

127. Blanco, Mercedes. "Les personnages dans l'espace de l'histoire et dans l'espace textuel." Le Personnage en question. Toulouse: Univ. de Toulouse-Le Mirail, 1984. 241-49.

128. Blanquat, Josette. "Clarín et Baudelaire." RLC, XXXIII, 1 (Jan-March, 1959): 5-25.

Analyzes C's articles on Baudelaire in La Ilustración Ibérica (July to Nov. 1887) in response to Brunetière's article in La Revue des Deux Mondes. C's articles were reprinted in Mezclilla.

129. ---. "La sensibilité religieuse de Clarín: Reflets de Goethe et de Leopardi: RLC, XXXV, 2 (April-June, 1961): 177-96.

Approaches the subject through a little-known story by Alas, "Cuesta abajo" (Il Ib, 1890-91) and an obituary of Bishop Benito Sanz y Forés (El Imparcial, 7 Nov. 1895).

130. ---. "L'hommage de Clarín à un prélat asturien." BH, LXVIII, 3-4 (July-Dec., 1966): 216-52.

In the 29 Oct. 1894 issue of El Imparcial, C wrote a highly favorable article on Cardinal Ceferino González y Díaz Tuñón, about whom he states: "Después de Jovellanos, Fray Ceferino era para mí el gran asturiano más simpático por la índole de su talento y sus tendencias. ¡Un asturiano metafísico! . . . Está de Dios que no me conozca el asturiano ilustre más simpático entre los vivos."

131. Bobadilla, Emilio. "Baturrillo." MC, 242 (8 Oct. 1887): 6.

A favorable review of NC and AP.

132. ---. Escaramuzas (Sátiras y críticas). Prólogo de Clarín. Madrid, 1888. 331 pp.

In addition to a 23-page introd. by C, this volume contains 38 articles on C's CST, Galdós' Gloria, EPB's autobiographical notes in Los pazos de Ulloa, Echegaray's De mala raza, etc. For text by C, see David Torres' Los prólogos de Leopoldo Alas.

133.   ---.   "Un nuevo libro de Clarín."   MC, IX, 307 (5 Enero 1889): 6-7.

Favorable review of Mezclilla. Praise for C's article on Guillermo d'Acevedo. "Clarín es el escritor satírico de más ingenio y saber que ha habido en España . . . Larra valía muchísimo; pero no tenía la gracia de Clarín."

134.   ---.   Capirotazos (Sátiras y críticas).   Madrid: Librería de Fernando Fé, 1890.   420 pp.

In "Pidal, Campoamor y Clarín" (pp. 293-99), brief comments on Pidal's lecture on Balmes and Donoso Cortés; Campoamor's El Licenciado Torralba; and C's folleto on Núñez de Arce. Prefers the second part of the folleto, in which C refutes Núñez de Arce's speech on lyric poetry.

135.   ---.   "Veleidades de Clarín."   MC, XII, 464 (9 Enero 1892): 6.

As literary relations between C and Fray Candil began to sour, Fray Candil reminded C of favorable remarks made in the introd. to Escaramuzas and elsewhere.

136.   ---.   "¡Adiós, anciano!"   MC, XII, 467 (30 Enero 1892): 6-7.

Paraphrasing the title of one of C's most popular short stories, Bobadilla continues the polemic. C was 39 years old at that time.

137.   ---.   "A Clarín (Punto final)."   MC, XII, 469 (13 Feb. 1892): 6-7.

Fray Candil accepts C's offer to pay his traveling expenses, round trip, between Madrid and Oviedo in order to give C a good beating.

138.   ---.   "La última palabra."   MC, XII, 471 (27 Feb. 1892): 7.

At the end of the polemic, Bobadilla agrees to wait in Madrid for a duel with C. The same page contains a note by editor Sinesio Delgado, putting an end to the squabble.

139.   ---.   Triquitraques (Críticas de Fray Candil).
        Madrid: Librería de Fernando Fé, 1892.   240
        pp.

        Calls C's style distorted and labyrinthic
(pp. 34-35) and advises him to stick to his "paliques" and quit writing novels.   Pages 49-54,
"Clarín, histérico," purport to be a pathological
study, quoting from Jolly, Schüler, and Lombroso.
In his review of Museum (pp. 80-82), Bobadilla
agrees with C's opinion of EPB's latest novels but
considers the folleto on Cánovas original and cle-
ver, even if the style is hard and tortuous.   The
chapter on SUH (pp. 193-214) is totally hostile;
the novel is monotonous and too long, the style is
cold, the plot insipid, and there are hundreds of
grammatical errors.

140.   ---.   "Clarín."   MC, 3a época, XXI, 25 (22 Junio
        1901): 199.

        Fray Candil found out about C's death through
Ortega Munilla's obituary in El Imparcial.   C and
Bobadilla had not met until the morning of their
duel.   Bobadilla describes how they began their
correspondence (none of which, incidentally, has
been published) but cannot explain why C turned
against him.   He admired C's genius and originality of style but, unlike C, Bobadilla considers
Balart a poor poet and states that C never found
fault with MMP.   Reprinted by Beser in "Documentos
clarinianos."

141.   Bobes Naves, María del Carmen.   "Los espacios
        novelescos en La Regenta."   CN, V, 23 (1984):
        51-57.

        A perceptive and well-organized study of the
physical, social, and psychological "space" in
this novel, particularly with reference to Ana,
Fermín, and Alvaro.

142.   ---.   "Significado y función de los personajes
        secundarios, en la novela cumbre de Leopoldo
        Alas."   Argumentos, VIII, 63-64 (1984): 22-
        26.

        Comments on the characters that gather at the
Casino and at the Cathedral;   Frígilis, Ana's
aunts, doña Paula, etc.   All types of female characters appear in LR "except normal or decent
ones."

143.   ---.   "La Regenta desde la estética de la recep-
        ción."   LdD, XV, 32 (Mayo-agosto, 1985): 7-
        24.

144.   Bonafoux y Quintero, Luis.   Literatura de Bona-
        foux. Madrid, 1887.

        On pages 218-27, entitled "Novelistas tontos:
        Don Leopoldo Alas (a) Clarín," Bonafoux makes
        negative comments on LR and accuses C of plagiar-
        ism in LR, El diablo en Semana Santa, and Zurita.
        "Clarín, folletista" (pp. 228-36) contains unfav-
        orable comments on C's CST.

145.   ---.   Huellas literarias.   Paris: Garnier Herma-
        nos, 1894. 415 pp.

        Contains: "Doña Berta, Cuervo, Superchería"
        (pp. 119-27) and "Yo y el plagiario Clarín" (pp.
        357-415).   Considers Superchería the worst but
        also makes fun of Doña Berta. One can easily
        tell, according to Bonafoux, that C wrote his
        chapter in Las vírgenes locas moments after
        reading Guhl and Koner.

146.   Bonet, Laureano.   "Clarín ante la crisis de 1898."
        RO, XXV, 73 (Abril, 1969): 100-19.

        On the basis of articles which C wrote for La
        Publicidad of Barcelona between 1896 and 1901,
        Bonet attempts to interpret C's social and politi-
        cal ideas about the war in Cuba, and his coldness
        toward Pi y Margall and exaggerated respect for
        Castelar. Rather than independence, C advocated a
        "cultural unity" between Spain and Cuba. Similar-
        ities between C, Joaquín Costa, and Galdós. C's
        ideas on socialism.

147.   ---.   "Temporalidad, memoria y ensueño en la obra
        de Clarín." Clarín y su obra.   Ed. Antonio
        Vilanova.   Barcelona: U de Barcelona, 1985.
        121-43.

148.   ---.   "La música como voz callada en La Regenta:
        un rastreo léxico." CN, V, 23 (1984): 64-69.

149.   Boring, Phyllis Z.   "Some Reflections on Clarín's
        Doña Berta." Rom N, XI, 2 (Winter, 1969):
        322-25.

        Points out similarities between C's favorite
        short novel and Maupassant's Une vie (1883) and
        Cervantes' Don Quijote. Doña Berta, like Jeanne,
        is cradled in illusions and forced to take refuge
        in imaginary worlds.

150.   Botrel, Jean-François.   "Últimos ataques de
        Bonafoux a Clarín." Archivum, XVIII (1968):
        177-88.

Reproduces the text of Bonafoux's articles on C published in <u>La Campaña</u> (Paris), 29 April 1900, and <u>El Heraldo de París</u>, 18 Nov. 1900, 1 June 1901, and his obituary of C (22 June 1901). Both newspapers were edited by Bonafoux, in Spanish. The <u>Heraldo</u>, the continuation of <u>La Campaña</u> (1898-1900), began publication on 20 Oct. 1900.

151.   ---.   "Producción literaria y rentabilidad: el caso de Clarín." <u>Hommage des Hispanistes Français à Noël Salomon</u>. Barcelona: Laia, 1979. 123-33.

152.   ---.   "Clarín, el dinero y la literatura." <u>CN</u>, II, 7 (Mayo-junio, 1981): 78-82.

Facts and figures on C's salary as professor and writer; for example, some 4,000 pesetas per annum at the University of Oviedo and approx. 13,000 pesetas for books and articles published between 1881-93. His constant need of money to support his family, pay debts at billiards, and maintain his literary ego.

153.   ---.   "Un prólogo olvidado de Clarín." <u>CN</u>, II, 7 (Mayo-junio, 1981): 83.

Reproduces the text of C's preface to Querubín de la Ronda's Spanish translation of Balzac's <u>Cuentos droláticos</u> (1883). See also David Torres' <u>Los prólogos de Leopoldo Alas</u>, pp. 24 and 140-41.

154. ---.   "De periodista a periodista: Diez cartas de Clarín a Luis París." <u>LdD</u>, XV, 32 (Mayo-agosto, 1985): 171-84.

Most of these letters, dated between 16 April 1892 and 13 Dec. 1895, deal with C's attempts to find a job for Luis París. The numerous writers and editors mentioned are identified by Botrel in footnotes.

155.   ---.   "La creación y su función en la obra de Clarín." <u>Clarín y su obra</u>. Ed. Antonio Vilanova. Barcelona: U de Barcelona, 1985. 103-19.

156.   Bravo-Villasante, Carmen. <u>Vida y obra de Emilia Pardo Bazán</u>. Madrid: Revista de Occidente, 1962. 392 pp.

BV calls Alas "hombre apasionado y atrabilia-rio, pone tal pasión en sus clarinazos críticos que a veces se confunde con la grosería y el favo-

ritismo" (p. 85). On pp. 136-38 she reproduces an
unpublished letter (1890?) in which C insists he
does not consider himself a novelist, hates politics, and considers <u>Miau</u> "muy desigual; está es-
crito de prisa y sin gana ...." (p. 138) "Mi gus-
to sería tener bastante dinero para poder dedicar
toda mi vida a escribir un libro demostrando que
Jesús aunque no puede ser Dios, porque eso es una
atrocidad, será el eterno consuelo espiritual de
los buenos corazones. . . ." (p. 137)

157.   Brown, G. G.   "Leopoldo Alas, Clarín."   <u>Cuentos
      <u>escogidos</u>. Oxford: Dolphin Books, 1964. 229
      pp.

      A harsh but objective analysis (Introduction,
pp. 7-36) of C as a writer of short fiction, especially the 10 "representative" selections in this
anthology, arranged chronologically by dates of
original publication. C's short stories comprise
six volumes, published between 1886 and 1916.
"The function of his short stories is not the one
he claimed for them in the preface to <u>Cuentos mo-
rales</u>--an exploration of the psychology of volun-
tary human behaviour. The function of Alas' stories is to externalize his ideological predicament
in the lives of imaginary characters." Reprinted
in 1977. Reviewed by Cheyne, Hall, Kronik (q.v.).

158.   Bull, William Emerson. "The Naturalistic Theories
      of Leopoldo Alas." <u>PMLA</u>, LVII, 2 (June,
      1942): 536-51.

      C believed in free will and never accepted
the definition of naturalism in the French sense
insofar as it included positivistic doctrine and
scientific determinism. A profoundly religious
man, he was also very squeamish about frank language and certain subjects.

159.   ---. "The Liberalism of Leopoldo Alas." <u>HR</u>, X, 4
      (Oct., 1942): 329-39.

      "So dominant was his tendency to obscure is-
sues and so well-developed his knack for saying
one thing while implying quite the opposite that
his articles reveal a continuous pattern of con-
tradiction." A comparison between <u>LR</u> and <u>Doña
Perfecta</u> shows that C was not fighting clericalism
but certain members of the clergy; he attacked the
corruption of the clergy, their materialism, their
addiction to the pleasures of the flesh . . .
Despite his reputation as a liberal, republican,
and free-thinker, down underneath he was something
quite different. "Alas was not an atheist, nor a
skeptic, nor a free-thinker . . . He denied the

philosophy of naturalism, refused to accept scientific determinism, was skeptical about evolution, objected to the introduction of scientific courses into education . . . denied equal rights to women . . . disliked the social novel, feared the spread of democracy in the American sense."

160.　---.　"Clarín's Literary Internationalism."　HR, XVI, 4 (Oct., 1948): 321-34.

Taking 3,300 pages of literary criticism into account, Bull compiles statistics on C's familiarity with foreign authors. Although a professor of Roman law and a fervent defender of the classics, Alas mentions modern French writers more frequently than all the Latin authors combined. French, German, and English literature were evidently more important in his thinking. The writers most often mentioned by C were: Flaubert (90 times) Shakespeare (86), Hugo and Zola (76 times each), Goethe (64), Renan (50), and Balzac (48).

161.　---.　"Clarín and His Critics."　MLF, XXXV, 1-2 (March-June, 1950): 103-11.

C as seen by critics from his contemporaries to 1923, when the bookseller Palau y Dulcet wrote: "Clarín después de muerto resta casi olvidado. Sus obras se venden poco." In his praise C always gave more than he received in return; only Echegaray and Galdós wrote introductions for his works. Opinions expressed by Cuéllar, Ruiz Contreras, González Blanco, Azorín, Aramburu, Bobadilla, Fitzmaurice-Kelly, Blanco García, González Serrano, and Cejador. In 1911-12 C's son found little enthusiasm among publishers for the reprinting of C's critical essays.

162.　Buylla, Adolfo A.　"Necrología y significación de Leopoldo Alas. Discurso de apertura del curso 1901-1902 en la Universidad de Oviedo." Anales de la Universidad de Oviedo, I (1902): 359-71.

A highly favorable overview of C as teacher, comparable only to Francisco Giner de los Ríos, by a close friend and colleague. Reprinted in MC's anthology, LAC, pp. 15-22.

163.　Cabezas, Juan Antonio.　"Prólogo" a Obras selectas de Leopoldo Alas Clarín. Madrid: Biblioteca Nueva, 1947.

Mostly biographical and novelistic; does not add anything new to his 1936 biography of C. Superficial, according to Martínez-Torrón. The deluxe binding made this volume too expensive for students at that time. The second ed. appeared in 1966. Reviewed by Baquero Goyanes, Fernández Almagro, Ledesma Miranda (q.v.)

164.   ---. "Clarín vivo. La casa de Guimarán y Oviedo. Su vida y su crisis moral." <u>IAL</u>, VII, 51 (15 Mayo 1952): 5-6.

Cabezas recalls his arrival in Guimarán in 1934 to write his biography of C for Espasa-Calpe's "Vidas Españolas del Siglo XIX" series. He interviewed some 300 persons, from the Bishop to the porter at the train station. Alas began to sign his name "Clarín" in <u>El Solfeo</u> on 2 Oct. 1875 (which Kronik states should be 11 April) because the periodical required each contributor to choose the name of a musical instrument. Anecdote about a city councilman who resigned because Alas had corrected an "haiga" in a speech. Clarín wrote <u>LR</u> at 34 Uría Street, in Oviedo. The <u>crisis moral</u> occurred during the summer of 1892. After spending several days alone in the woods of Carbayeda, Clarín "ya sabe que aquel intruso, aquel otro yo es su personalidad original, despojada de lo que era cultura, maquillaje filosófico, <u>pose</u> intelectual."

165.   ---. "Cómo nació la primera biografía de Clarín. Memorias de <u>El provinciano universal</u>." <u>CN</u>, II, 7 (Mayo-junio, 1981): 98-103.

The idea of writing the first biography of C was suggested by Benjamín Jarnés during the summer of 1933. Cabezas makes a list of the few bibliographical sources available, and of some of the hundreds of persons he interviewed in 1934. His book was placed on sale in the autumn of 1936, but Cabezas himself did not see it until 1939 because of the Civil War.

166.   ---. "<u>La Regenta</u> y sus enemigos." <u>Argumentos</u>, VIII, 63-64 (Enero-feb., 1984): 44-47.

Reproduces the full text of C's reply to the Bishop of Oviedo (11 May 1885) denying that Clarín had distributed free copies of his novel among his students; explaining the purpose of <u>LR</u>; and requesting a public retraction. The two men later became good friends.

167.   Canals, Salvador. "Sobre el estreno de <u>Teresa</u>." <u>El Diario del Teatro</u>, 84 (7 y 21 Abril 1895).

An unfavorable review, reprinted by MC in his article "Noticia del estreno . . . y de algunas críticas periodísticas," <u>Archivum</u>, XIX (1969): 256-60 and also in his book, <u>Las palabras y los días</u>, pp. 278-81.

168.   ---.   "Después de la lectura. Clarín y el martirio de <u>Teresa</u>, o berrinches mal reprimidos." <u>El Diario del Teatro</u>, No. 92 (7 Abril 1895): 1, and No. 94 (21 Abril 1895): 1.

Reprinted in his book, <u>El año teatral</u> (1896) and by MC in <u>Archivum</u>, XIX (1969): 260-70 and <u>Las palabras y los días</u>, pp. 282-89.

168a.   ---.   <u>El año teatral: Crónicas y documentos</u>. Con un artículo preliminar sobre <u>El Público</u> por Jacinto Octavio Picón. Madrid: Establecimiento Tipográfico de El Nacional, 1896. xiv + 269 pp. 150 grabados.

Pages 97-102, dated 21 March 1895, explain why <u>Teresa</u> failed the two nights it was staged. It failed not because of the "select public" or C's enemies, but "por culpas y defectos de la obra misma; defectos inexplicables y culpas increíbles. . . ." Pages 102-04, dated 7 April 1896, consist of Canals' reply to Alas' article in <u>El Imparcial</u>; Canals confirms the same negative opinion after reading the play several times, and adds: "Antes creía que Clarín no había sabido hacer un drama; ahora creo que no ha sabido hacer lo que sabe el más vulgar noticiero: decir lo que quería decirnos y demostrarnos" (p. 104).

169.   ---.   "Tribuna libre (Polémica literaria): ¡Al maestro . . .psh!" <u>HM</u>, 28 Oct. 1896.

The polemic on <u>Teresa</u> continues. Canals' book, <u>El año teatral</u>, had gone on sale on 3 Oct. 1896.

170.   Cañizal de la Fuente, Luis.   "Antonio Gala trasplanta una situación de <u>La Regenta</u>." <u>Insula</u>, XXXV, 406 (Sept., 1980): 3 y 14.

Several conversations and descriptions "transplanted" from <u>LR</u> (especially Chap. 15 and 25) to Gala's <u>Los buenos días perdidos</u> (Tarragona, 1976).

171.   Cardenal Iracheta, M.   "Seis cartas inéditas de Clarín a Castelar." <u>BBMP</u>, XXIV, 1 (Enero-marzo, 1948): 92-96.

Six letters dated between 20 May 1893 and 7 June 1898, in which C writes about his support for Castelar, his mother's death (on 19 Sept. 1896),

asks for Castelar's (and, if need be, Cánovas')
help for his brother Adolfo Alas who is unem-
ployed; sends him a copy of SUH, and reminds Castelar to write the article for Carlyle's Heroes,
translated by "an old Californian" who is now
destitute.

172.   Carnicer, Ramón.   "La etapa de Leopoldo Alas en la
       Universidad de Zaragoza."   Insula, XXV, 284-
       85 (Julio-agosto, 1970): 27.

       Prof. Alas' appointment, signed by J. F. Ria-
       ño on 10 July 1882, called for an annual salary of
       3,500 pesetas.   The University of Zaragoza posses-
       ses 43 documents relative to Alas, some of which
       Carnicer describes or reproduces here.

173.   Carreño, Orlando.   "Clarín, el escritor y el
       público."   CN, V, 23 (1984): 48-50.

       According to the 1877 census, only 60% of the
       population of Asturias knew how to read or write.
       C wrote mostly for newspapers, to educate the gen-
       eral public and to supplement his university sal-
       ary.   After 1891, he received 15,000 pesetas per
       article.

174.   Castro, José P.   "Un epistolario y unas eleccio-
       nes.   Menéndez Pelayo-Martínez Vigil.   La
       Universidad de Oviedo."   BBMP, XXVIII (1952):
       7-29.

       In a biographical sketch of MMP written for
       La Publicidad de Barcelona (19 Feb. 1894), C re-
       calls that MMP failed to write the introduction
       requested for a book on Percy B. Shelley.

175.   Champsaur, Baltasar.   "Su único hijo, por Leopoldo
       Alas."   RC, LXXXIV, 6 (30 Dic. 1891): 615-32.

       C has talent, but his novel is too cold and
       lifeless, except for the final scene between Boni-
       facio and Serafina.   "A Clarín le falta la intui-
       ción artística de los conjuntos; no puede crear un
       ambiente de belleza que dé vida a los episodios y
       a los personajes; observa mucho, pero no anima
       nada."

176.   Chichón, Rafael.   "Revista crítica."   RE, XCIII,
       370 (Julio, 1883): 280-81.

       According to Chichón, C's violent remarks in
       El Progreso demonstrate that something is wrong
       with his liver or viscera.   Alas replied with
       "Chichones personales" in MC, III, 3 (7 Oct.
       1883), pp. 3 and 6, in which he calls Chichón "un

cursi" and resents that Chichón had called Campoamor a "zapatero."

177. Cifo González, Manuel. "La ironía y la sátira en
       La Regenta: variantes narrativas." CHA,
       CXXXIX, 415 (Enero, 1985): 13-23.

178. Clavería, Carlos. "Flaubert y La Regenta." HR, X
       (1942): 116-25.

       Echoes of Flaubert's portrayal of bêtise
       humaine. "¡Cuántas veces no esconde Ana sus idea-
       lismos o su hastío por temor a que los vetustenses
       la llamaran romántica!" Clavería calls LR "la me-
       jor novela acaso del siglo XIX español." Re-
       printed in Clavería's Cinco estudios, pp. 11-28;
       Beser's C y LR, pp. 165-83, and MC's anthology,
       LAC, pp. 179-93.

179. ---. Cinco estudios de literatura española moder-
       na. Salamanca: Consejo Superior de Investi-
       gaciones Científicas, 1945. 118 pp.

       "Clarín y Renan" (pp. 31-45) points out the
       importance of Renan in C's spirit and works. Cla-
       rín saw in Renan "un ejemplo viviente y un caso de
       conciencia en el que creyó encontrar la imagen de
       muchas de sus dudas y de sus problemas . . . pa-
       rece indiscutible que Renan entró en el alma de
       Clarín por la gran puerta del idealismo profesado
       toda la vida." Briefly reviewed by E. Allison
       Peers in BSS, XXIII, 92 (Oct., 1946): 291.

180. ---. "Una nueva carta de Clarín sobre Teresa."
       HR, XVIII, 2 (April, 1950): 163-68.

       Quotes two brief paragraphs from a letter
       written by C (Oviedo, 6 April 1895) to the empre-
       sario Luis París of Madrid, about two weeks after
       the performance of Teresa. The letter came from
       the archives of Arturo Sedó of Barcelona. For
       full text and other letters to Luis París, see
       Botrel's "De periodista a periodista."

181. ---. "La Teresa de Clarín." Insula, VII, 76 (15
       Abril 1952): 1 y 4.

       Considers this play an attempt to reform the
       Spanish theater, as Galdós had tried to do at
       about the same time. Reprinted in MC's anthology,
       LAC, pp. 101-04.

182. Clementi, Silvia Ferroni. "Introducción" a Dos
       cuentos de Clarín: ¡Adiós, Cordera! y Pipá.
       Padova: CEDAM, 1967. 75 pp.

182a. Clocchiatti, Emilio. "Clarín y sus ideas sobre la
        novela." RUO, IX, 53-54 (Mayo-agosto, 1948):
        5-28.

            The first two chapters of a study in pro-
        gress. These deal with C's life and his literary
        relations with PV, MMP, Valera, and Unamuno.
        Chap. 3 and 4 (Clarín's novelistic art; naturalism
        and idealism) appeared in Vol. IX, No. 57-58
        (Sept-dic., 1948): 41-78. See also book section
        of this bibliography.

182b. ---. "Menéndez Pelayo y Clarín." Hispania,
        XXXIII (1950): 328-32.

            Friendship between the two critics, based on
        Adolfo Alas' Epistolarios and Artigas Ferrando's
        Epistolario de Valera y MMP. MMP's letters to C
        are "corteses, afables, dignas; pero rara vez pe-
        netran en la intimidad . . . En cambio, Alas es
        todo nervio y entusiasmo." From Clocchiatti's
        book on C.

183. ---. "Miguel de Unamuno y sus cartas a Clarín."
        MLJ, XXXIV, 8 (Dec., 1950): 646-49.

            Comments on Unamuno's letters to C as pub-
        lished in a 1941 Epistolario, presumably the one
        compiled by Adolfo Alas. Unamuno looked up to C
        for guidance but was disappointed because the mas-
        ter did not review Paz en la guerra (1896) and his
        criticism of Tres ensayos (1900) was "demasiado
        hábil e insincera."

184. Comas, Antonio. "Introducción" a Su único hijo.
        Barcelona: Taber, 1968.

185. Cortón, Antonio. Pandemonium: Crítica y sátira.
        Palencia, 1889.

            In ";Sépase quién es Clarín!" (pp. 549-69)
        Cortón describes meeting Alas at the home of
        Rafael María de Labra, one day after Bremón had
        written an article against Alas in La Ilustración
        Española y Americana. Cortón refers to Alas as
        "García, the author of the pornographic La Re-
        genta." The host did not know that Cortón had
        attacked Alas in El Buscapié (Puerto Rico), and
        that Alas had ridiculed Cortón's introd. to Abe-
        lardo Morales Ferrer's poem, La religión del amor.
        In front of all the guests, Clarín reportedly made
        this statement about Núñez de Arce's Maruja: "Es
        muy malo, muy malo . . . pero tengo que darle un
        bombo. . . ." (p. 557)

186. Cossío, José María de. "Correspondencias litera-
      rias del siglo XIX en la Biblioteca de Menén-
      dez y Pelayo." BBMP, XII, 3 (Julio-sept.,
      1930): 248-73.

      Includes an undated letter from C to Cañete
(pp. 253-54) in which Alas agrees that La Pasio-
naria is a poor drama.

187. Cruz Rueda, Angel. Armando Palacio Valdés. Su
      vida y su obra. 2a ed. aum. Madrid:
      S.A.E.T.A., 1949. 221 pp.

      Chapter 11, entitled "La amistad con Tuero y
Clarín" (pp. 68-76), describes C's friendship with
PV and Tomás Tuero. C and PV wrote a book of literary criticism together (La literatura en 1881)
but PV soon decided to devote himself to the
novel. Quotes a letter from Bobadilla to Gómez-
Carrillo describing the duel between C and Fray
Candil. PV gave C a few lessons in fencing to
prepare him.

188. Cuéllar, José de. Lo palpitante. Dioses caídos
      (Clarín, Pardo Bazán, Galdós). M a d r i d :
      Imprenta de la viuda e hijos de la Riva,
      1895. 31 pp.

      Declares war on these three "fallen gods" who
have not provided guidance or hope for the new
generation. C has published some good stories
(Pipá, AC, La conversión de Chiripa) but as a critic, he is "un eterno fracasado" (p. 24).

189. Custodio, Alvaro. "La escenificación teatral de
      una novela densa." Argumentos, VIII, 63-64
      (Enero-feb., 1984): 50-52.

      With a cast of 20, Custodio directed the
stage version of LR on 1 Sept. 1983. Rafael
Lapesa wrote him a congratulatory letter, part of
which is quoted here.

190. Damonte, Mario. "Funzione dei referimenti musi-
      cale de La Regenta de Clarín." Omaggio a
      Guerciri Crocetti. Genoa, 1971. 5-47.

191. Darío, Rubén. "Pro Domo Mea." LN, 30 Enero 1894.

      The poet defends himself against C's attacks.
Reprinted in E. K. Mapes' Escritos inéditos de
Rubén Darío (NY, 1938) and in A. W. Ashhurst's
article.

192. Davis, Gifford. "The Literary Relations of Clarín
      and Emilia Pardo Bazán." HR, XXXIX (1971):
      378-94.

Studies the quarrel between C and EPB, who never met socially. C wrote about her "from the time of her first article throughout that of her naturalistic novels, showing his early hopes and doubts, his momentary enthusiasm, his disillusion with her and with naturalism, and his anger at her attempted direction of his work . . . One perceives C's jangled nerves, need for appreciation, and essential honesty; Pardo's patrician incomprehension and proud resentment."

193. Delogu, F. M. "Note su Leopoldo Alas (Clarín) 1852-1901." SGym, XIV, 2 (July-Dec., 1961): 212-19.

194. Díaz Dufóo, Carlos. "Sobre Teresa de Clarín." Revista Azul (México), III, 16 (18 Julio 1895): 241-42.

Teresa reminds the author of Tolstoy's Poder de las tinieblas. Analysis of the main character. The public's rejection of the socialist worker and brutal scenes. The failure of Teresa can be explained only by the formidable success of Cura del regimiento. Reprinted in Romero's ed. of Teresa, pp. 185-88.

195. Díaz Plaja, Guillermo. Modernismo frente a Noventa y ocho. Madrid: Espasa-Calpe, 1979.

Pages 46-50 present a rapid overview of C's polemic with Darío and Maeztu, which began about 1893. C made fun of Darío, Benavente, Maeztu, and Martínez Sierra, mostly because of what he considered their extravagant style.

196. Dicenta, José Fernando. Luis Bonafoux, la víbora de Asnieres. Madrid: CVS - Videosistemas, 1974. 286 pp.

Chap. 4 (pp. 87-134), entitled "Aramís contra Clarín," consists mostly of excerpts (unfortunately without exact dates or sources) from the disputes between Bonafoux and C. The last two pages reproduce the text of Bonafoux's obituary on C.

197. Donahue, Moraima de Semprún. "La doble seducción de la Regenta." Archivum, XXIII (1973): 117-33.

The spiritual and sexual downfall of Ana Ozores, who is "de los tres culpables la única que sufre el castigo de su pecado, y sólo por debilidades muy naturales, haber caído dos veces en las redes sensuales que su creador ha ido tramando a su alrededor."

198.   Durand, Frank.   "Structural Unity in Leopoldo
          Alas' La Regenta."   HR, XXXI, 1 (Jan., 1963):
          324-35.

          Vetusta is "the force of gravity which holds
          the themes and action together and gives the work
          unity." The first volume of the novel consists of
          three major parts, each of which corresponds to
          one day. The second volume falls naturally into
          three parts, each corresponding to one year.

199.   ---.   "Characterization in La Regenta: Point of
          View and Theme."   BHS, XLI (1964): 86-100.

          C believed that the author, not the charac-
          ter, was best qualified to interpret the thoughts
          and acts of a character. Durand attempts to point
          out some of the relations between point of view,
          theme, characterization, and the ironic presenta-
          tion of diametrically opposed perspectives. One
          of the most important themes is the interaction of
          life and literature, especially in Víctor and Sa-
          turnino. The use of mirrors and multiple perspec-
          tives: "A sees A as A thinks B sees A." Reprod.
          in Beser's C y LR, pp. 249-70.

200.   ---.   "Leopoldo Alas, Clarín: Consistency of
          Outlook as Critic and Novelist."   RR, LVI
          (1965): 37-49.

          C's aim was to raise the cultural and lit-
          erary level of his country; his attacks on medi-
          ocre writers was also a defense of the best ones.
          C's ideas on naturalism. All of his literary
          theories were put into practice in LR. Reprinted
          in Beser's C y LR, pp. 97-115.

201.   ---.   "El crimen religioso y ético de Ana de Ozo-
          res."   CN, V, 23 (Enero-feb., 1984): 19-24.

          Most of the characters in LR have a cynical
          or distorted idea of religion and morality. Ana's
          "sin" does not result from adultery but rather
          from her inability to accept the moral conventions
          of Vetusta. The influence of the environment on
          Ana is one she reacts against; her personality and
          adultery should be viewed from an antinaturalistic
          perspective.

202.   ---. Dimensiones irónicas y estéticas en el estilo
          de La Regenta."   Clarín y su obra.   Ed. An-
          tonio Vilanova.   Barcelona: U de Barcelona,
          1985.   145-61.

203.   Elizalde, Ignacio.   "Ideología religiosa de
          Clarín."   LdD, XV, 32 (Mayo-agosto, 1985):
          45-68.

          C's religious ideas from adolescence to LR.
       Alas and Renan.   C believed firmly in God but
       questioned the divinity of Jesus.

204.   Endress, Heinz-Peter.   "La Regenta von Leopoldo
          Alas Clarín und Madame Bovary: Von der An-
          klage der Flagiats zum Nachweis der Origi-
          n a l i t ä t . "   Beiträge zur vergleichenden
          Literaturgeschichte: Festschrift für Kurt
          Wais zum 65. Geburtstag.   Eds. Johannes Hösle
          and Wolfgang Eitel.   Tübingen: Max Niemeyer
          Verlag, 1972.   225-46.

205.   Entrambasaguas, Joaquín de.   "Una semblanza de
          Menéndez Pelayo, por Clarín."   Archivum, II,
          1 (Enero-abril, 1952): 23-32.

          A commentary on C's Un viaje a Madrid (1886).

206.   Eoff, Sherman H.   The Modern Spanish Novel.   New
          York: New York UP, 1961.   280 pp.

          For Alas, see pp. 67-84.   LR and Madame
       Bovary center on essentially the same subject: the
       heaviness of the material world and the failure of
       love as a means of liberation.   A major distinc-
       tion is the preponderance, in LR, of the comic
       element over the tragic.   De Pas is a more solid
       psychological portraiture than Ana.   In the tug of
       war between De Pas, Ana, and Mesía, Alas conducts
       "a prolonged cat-and-mouse game which . . . ser-
       iously taxes the reader's patience."   The major
       dramatic force of C's novel "originates in a con-
       ception of an impassive God out of reach of human
       love."   Translated by Rosario Berdagué as El pen-
       samiento moderno y la novela española (B: Seix y
       Barral, 1965).

207.   Esquer Torres, Ramón.   "Las luchas del siglo XIX:
          El Padre Blanco García y Leopoldo Alas
          Clarín."   BSCC, XXXVIII (1962): 241-55.

208.   Estruch Tobella, Joan.   "La Teresa de Clarín, un
          intento fracasado de renovación del teatro
          español."   Segismundo (M), 37-38 (1983): 99-
          111.

          All of C's ideas on the theater can be found
       in Teresa.   It failed partly because it was so
       different from the Echegaray-type drama of its
       time.   One aspect of the natural dialog can be
       seen in the use of incomplete sentences and
       leaders.

209.   Feal-Deibe, Carlos. "La anunciación a Bonis:
       Análisis de <u>Su único hijo</u>." <u>BHS</u>, LI, 3
       (July, 1974): 255-71.

       Maternal/paternal symbolism; possible latent
       homosexuality in the two principal characters;
       woman as a lascivious being. "Clarín se mantiene
       en el fondo, en materia sexual al menos, muy adic-
       to a la doctrina católica que le inculcaron en su
       infancia. La concepción del matrimonio como re-
       medio contra la sensualidad, y no como lugar donde
       la sensualidad se manifiesta, es en efecto carac-
       terística del catolicismo."

210.   Fedorchek, Robert M. "En torno a una imagen de <u>La
       Regenta</u>." <u>Horizontes</u> (Puerto Rico), XIX, 38
       (Abril, 1976): 71-75.

       The "bird" image is evident in the depiction
       of Fermín de Pas as an "ave de rapiña" and Ana de
       Ozores as an imprisoned "tórtola" before and after
       her marriage. Her husband, Víctor de Quintanar,
       is in fact an ornithologist who keeps many birds
       in cages.

211.   ---. "Clarín y Eça de Queirós." <u>Archivum</u>, 29-30
       (1979-1980): 69-82.

       Similarities and differences between <u>LR</u> and <u>O
       Crime do Padre Amaro</u> (1876) and <u>O Primo Basilio</u>
       (1878).

212.   Fernández Almagro, Melchor. "Crítica y sátira en
       Clarín." <u>Archivum</u>, II, 1 (Enero-abril,
       1952): 33-42.

       The differences and similarities between
       these two forms, as they pertain to C. Throughout
       his literary career, C was able to write serious
       criticism (on Galdós, for example) at the same
       time as lighter pieces on second-rate authors.
       Reprinted in MC's anthology, <u>LAC</u>, pp. 147-53.

213.   Fernández Larraín, Sergio. <u>Cartas inéditas de
       Miguel de Unamuno</u>. Santiago de Chile:
       Empresa Editora Zig-Zag, 1965. 455 pp.

       In a letter to Pedro de Mugica (Salamanca, 31
       Oct. 1901), Unamuno writes: "Estaba en relación
       con Clarín aunque estas relaciones eran un tanto
       frías . . . Fue el pobre Clarín un tejido de bue-
       nas y malas cualidades, un hombre que se empeñaba
       en ser bueno y no lo conseguía. Era adulador y
       envidioso y poco sincero. Se pasó los últimos
       años adulando a unos cuantos viejos (Valera, Gal-

dós, Menéndez Pelayo) y torciendo el gesto a los jóvenes. Mía es una frase acerca de él que por ahí corre: Era injusto cuando atacaba, muy injusto cuando elogiaba y soberanamente injusto cuando callaba. Con todo y con ello gran sembrador de ideas y el espíritu más alto y movido de fines de nuestro siglo XIX español" (p. 307).

214.   Fernández Miranda, Torcuato.   "Actitud ante Clarín." CHA, XIV, 37 (Enero, 1953): 33-48.

A speech delivered at the University of Oviedo on 23 May 1952 and published in La Nueva España (O), 27 to 31 May 1952. The author, president of the university, calls LR "radicalmente disolvente" but recognizes C's greatness as a writer. DB reminds him of Stefan Zweig.

Fernández Rodríguez-Avello, Manuel.   See Avello, Manuel F.

215.   Fernández Silvestre, Marta.   "Entrevista con el profesor Martínez Cachero."   Argumentos, VIII, 63-64 (Enero-feb., 1984): 60-66.

The distinguished specialist (born Oviedo, 1924) answers questions on the initial reaction to LR; Alas' influence on other writers; intellectual and spiritual values, style, techniques, etc. Clarín may not rank as high as Galdós but could hardly be accused of being garbancero. LR could well be a "desahogo" in which C lashed out at everything he disliked. It is not certain whether or not C experienced a "spiritual crisis." The university is absent in the novel because it was the most valuable element in Oviedo. The project to publish C's complete works in six large volumes, edited by five specialists, has encountered financial difficulties.

Fernández Villegas, Francisco.   See Zeda.

216.   Ferreras, Juan Ignacio.   "La Regenta ante un nuevo método."   LLNL, 169 (June-July, 1963):   15-41.

Following Lucien Goldmann's theories, Ferreras divides his analysis into three sections: El texto (delimitación, argumento temático, argumento intencional); el autor; la sociedad. The three "problems" in this novel (love, religion, liberty) and the manner in which C treats them. Reprinted in Ferreras' book, Introducción a una sociología de la novela española del siglo XIX (M: Edicusa, 1973): 197-223.

217. Fishtine, Edith. "Clarín in His Early Writings."
      RR, XXIX, 4 (Dec., 1938): 325-42.

      C's points of view as expressed between 1875-
      1881, mostly in El Solfeo, La Unión, and La lite-
      ratura en 1881. Among the early victims of his
      literary persecution were all contemporary drama-
      tists except Tamayo, Ayala, Echegaray, and Sellés.
      His praise for Sellés' El nudo gordiano is one of
      C's most appalling errors of judgment. In gener-
      al, C paid more attention to the meaning of a work
      than to its form or style, except when dealing
      with inferior works. At no time does he question
      the reality of religious experience or attack the
      Catholic religion; it is only obscurantism and
      fanaticism that he combats. His political arti-
      cles are a vehement plea for a dynamic, progres-
      sive political policy and a passionate onslaught
      on Cánovas' quietismo. Toward the end of his life
      he seemed to repent his torturing of worthless
      writers (MC, 30 Oct. 1897): "Estoy cansado de ser
      maleante. A veces, me entran tentaciones de man-
      dar telegramas a mis periódicos diciendo: 'Clarín
      ha muerto. Se ha pegado un tiro en el seudónimo.
      Ya no hay Clarín' y dedicarme exclusivamente a la
      filosofía. Con firma entera."

      Frézals, G. de. See Navarro, Felipe B.

218. Fuentes, Víctor. "Los límites del naturalismo de
      Clarín en La Regenta." Arbor, III, 434
      (Feb., 1982): 29-36.

      While LR is symbolically naturalistic, it
      contains very little or nothing of the social con-
      flicts, of the tensions and struggles of the real
      Oviedo of that period.

219. Gamallo Fierros, Dionisio. "Campoamor, Zorrilla y
      Valera escriben a don Leopoldo Alas. Tres
      cartas inéditas del epistolario de Clarín."
      EstLit, 2 (20 Marzo 1944): 3.

      Campoamor tells Clarín (3 April 1883) to
      advise EPB to publish her articles in book form
      "siendo escritores tan descarados con los demás,
      como usted, ella, y yo." Zorrilla says (1 Jan
      1893) that he reads everything he receives written
      by C. Valera (23 Jan. 1896) thanks C for his ar-
      ticle on Juanita la Larga in El Imparcial, com-
      ments on MMP's anthology of Latin American poets,
      and advises C not to have so much "academifobia."

220. ---. "Páginas abandonadas de Clarín. Sus 400 co-
      laboraciones en El Solfeo." Imperio (Zamo-
      ra), 7 Enero 1949.

221. ---. "Aportaciones al estudio de Valle-Inclán."
     RO, IV, 2a época, 44-45 (Nov.-dic., 1966):
     343-66.

     Reproduces the text of three letters from
     Valle-Inclán to C (9 May 1895, 29 Sept. 1897, 18
     Oct. 1897) and two "paliques" (MC, 25 Sept 1897;
     HM, 9 Oct. 1897), the first one a negative review
     of Epitalamio, the second one on latest trends in
     general: "Cuantos han dicho que soy enemigo de la
     gente nueva, así como suena, o mienten o se enga-
     ñan. Yo también he sido nuevo y he tenido pruri-
     tos que he dejado después." Gamallo Fierros
     claims to possess 800 letters, presumably by many
     different writers, addressed to Clarín.

222. ---. "En el centenario de un malogrado gran
     escritor, Francisco Navarro Ledesma. Una
     carta que dirigió a Clarín. . . ." Arriba
     (M), 5 Sept. 1969.

     (The literary relations between C and Navarro
     Ledesma began about 1889 and ended in 1897 when NL
     struck C with his walking cane at the Ateneo de
     Madrid.)

223. ---. "Las primeras reacciones de Galdós ante La
     Regenta." La Voz de Asturias (Oviedo), 30
     Julio y 6, 10, 13, y 27 Agosto 1978.

     Discusses and reproduces the text of five
     letters from Galdós to C, dated between Feb. and
     Dec. 1885. It is regrettable that Prof. Gamallo
     Fierros did not publish these articles (and the
     one on El Solfeo) in a literary journal with
     worldwide circulation.

224. Garagorri, Paulino. Unamuno, Ortega, Zubiri en la
     filosofía española. Madrid: Editorial Pleni-
     tud, 1968.

     In Chap. VI, entitled "Dos precursores" (pp.
     229-44), Garagorri states that Clarín rejected
     Comte's positivism, Spencer's evolution, and
     Hegel's idealism in favor of Dilthey, Carlyle,
     Bergson, and other "new currents." C's philo-
     sophical thought can be found in "Cartas a Ham-
     let," Un discurso, Cuervo, and several short
     stories such as "El doctor Pértinax," "Cuento
     futuro," "Viaje redondo," etc.

225. García Alvarez, María Teresa Cristina. "Eça de
     Queiroz y Clarín (Cotejo entre El primo Ba-
     silio y La Regenta." Estudios ofrecidos a
     Emilio Alarcos Llorach, IV, Oviedo, 1979.
     419-27.

A clear, well-organized comparison between <u>LR</u> and <u>El Primo Basilio</u> (1878).

226.   García Blanco, Manuel.   "Clarín y Unamuno."
        <u>Archivum</u>, II, 1 (Enero-abril, 1952): 113-40.

The appendix (pp. 136-40) reproduces the article on Unamuno's <u>Tres ensayos</u> which C published in <u>Los Lunes de El Imparcial</u>, 7 Mayo 1900. Although C and Unamuno never met, they shared many points in common, as can be seen in the Unamuno letters published by Adolfo Alas.   Unamuno was greatly disappointed that C did not write a review of his first novel, <u>Paz en la guerra</u> (1897).   Numerous brief references to C by Unamuno.   Reprod. in MC's anthology, <u>LAC</u>, pp. 82-97, without the appendix.

227.   García de Cortázar Ruiz de Aguirre, Fernando.
        "Iglesia y religión en la España de <u>La
        Regenta</u>."   <u>LdD</u>, XV, 32 (Mayo-agosto, 1985):
        25-44.

The organization and role of the Church in Oviedo since the Concordato of 1851.   The bishop portrayed in <u>LR</u> (Camoirán) was Benito Sanz y Forés in real life.

228.   García Domínguez, Elías.   "Los cuentos rurales de
        Clarín."   <u>Archivum</u>, XIX (1969): 221-42.

An examination of C's rural short stories published between 1891-1896, especially <u>Boroña</u>, <u>DB</u>, and <u>AC</u>.

229.   García Lorenzo, Luciano.   "De Clarín y Unamuno."
        <u>Prohemio</u> (M), III, 3 (Dic., 1972): 467-72.

The influence of "Cambio de luz" on Unamuno's <u>La venda</u> and <u>San Manuel Bueno, mártir</u>.   Both authors experienced a so-called "crisis religiosa," C in 1892 and Unamuno in 1897.   García Lorenzo suspects that C did not review <u>Paz en la guerra</u> because he saw in Unamuno a rival novelist, essayist, and professor "que podía hacerle sombra."

230.   García Mercadal, José.   "Clarín, Pérez de Ayala,
        Ortega Munilla, y <u>Los Lunes de El Imparcial</u>."
        <u>Destino</u> (B), XXVI, 1300 (7 Julio 1962): 31-
        33.

Reproduces Pérez de Ayala's first article on C, with comments on their literary relations.   "La generalidad de los españoles conocen al Clarín de los paliques, al desparramador de sales y picar-

días a granel, pero muy pocos se paran a mirar
. . . a escudriñar la riqueza cristalina de su espíritu de filósofo místico." Reappears in García
Mercadal's preface to OC de Pérez de Ayala (1964),
pp. xi-xxxiv.

231. García Pavón, Francisco. "Crítica literaria en la
     obra narrativa de Clarín." Archivum, II, 1
     (Enero-abril, 1952): 63-68.

     Quotes several examples of literary criticism
     in "El hombre de los estrenos," "El poeta buho,"
     LR, etc. Clarín was above all a literary critic,
     and examples of this style can be found in almost
     all of his prose fiction.

232. ---. "Clarín, crítico en su obra narrativa." In-
     sula, VII, 76 (Abril, 1952): 5 y 11.

     C was primarily a critic, at several levels.
     The italicized words in many of his works usually
     refer to "incorrecciones fonéticas, sintácticas o
     galicismos de sus personajes, amén de frases he-
     chas, reticencias, tópicos, etc. Hay en él una
     oscura delectación . . . en crear criaturas ajenas
     al bien hablar." García Pavón cites examples from
     LR and several stories.

233. ---. "Gentes humildes en la obra narrativa de
     Clarín." Arbor, XXII, 78 (Junio, 1952): 186-
     97.

     Distinguishes three types of characters: pí-
     caros (Pipá, Chiripa, El Rana); lovers (El dúo de
     la tos); and intellectuals, such as those in "Dos
     sabios," "Doctor Pértinax," and "La mosca sabia."
     Reprinted in MC's anthology, LAC, pp. 263-71.

234. ---. "El problema religioso en la obra narrativa
     de Clarín." Archivum, VI, 2-3 (Mayo-dic.,
     1955): 319-49.

     After surveying what five commentators (Arbo-
     leya, Azorín, Barja, Cabezas, Sáinz Rodríguez)
     have written on this subject, García Pavón exam-
     ines the religious problem as reflected in LR and
     several stories such as "El Señor," "Cambio de
     luz," "Viaje redondo," "Un grabado," "El cura de
     Vericueto," etc. Apparently C believed in a God
     not associated with any particular denomination,
     and he had a critical, rationalistic attitude to-
     ward the Church and its priests. One cannot speak
     of specific dates or crisis, because his religious
     feelings had their ups and downs.

235. García Sarriá, Francisco. "<u>Su único hijo</u> en la obra de Clarín." <u>Actas del Cuarto Congreso Internacional de Hispanistas (Salamanca, Agosto, 1971)</u>. Salamanca, 1982.

See Vol. 2, pp. 599-609. Topics discussed: Religion and love; woman as "mujer-madre-Virgen"; pagan love; love and religion in <u>SUH</u>. Female characters practically disappear in C's last stories.

236. García Valero, Vicente. <u>Dentro y fuera del teatro</u>. Madrid: Victoriano Suárez, 1913.

See chapter entitled "Romea y Clarín," pp. 21-33. According to Valero, Julián Romea insisted that he wanted to have Alas express an opinion on his zarzuela <u>El señor Joaquín</u>. When Clarín did so (in a letter published in <u>MC</u>, 3 Sept. 1898), Romea was offended. C's letter is reprod. on pp. 28-31 of <u>Dentro y fuera del teatro</u>.

237. García Venero, Maximiano. <u>Melquíades Alvarez: Historia de un liberal</u>. Prólogo de Azorín. Madrid: Editorial Alhambra, 1954. 390 pp.

His friendship with C, pp. 59-65. Reproduces (pp. 91-92) a letter dated 12 May 1898 from C to Antonio Maura, recommending Melquíades; this letter was previously published by Maura's secretary, Prudencio Rovira y Pita, in <u>Cartas son cartas</u> (M: Espasa-Calpe, 1949).

238. Gil, Ildefonso Manuel. "Un verso de Garcilaso disimulado en la prosa de Clarín." <u>Insula</u>, XVII, 190 (Sept., 1962): 4.

In Chap. 13 of <u>SUH</u> (<u>Obras selectas</u>, 1947, p. 655) C uses verse 380 of Garcilaso's first <u>Egloga</u>, perhaps to tease the reader's cultural background, just as he had called Moratín by his pen name, Inarco Celenio, in <u>LR</u> (<u>Obras selectas</u>, 1947, p. 30.)

239. Gil Cremades, Juan José. <u>Krausistas liberales</u>. Madrid: Seminarios y Ediciones, 1975. 320 pp.

See especially pp. 181-99 for an analysis of C's best known Krausist stories: "El Doctor Pértinax," "La mosca sabia," Doctor Angelicus," "Zurita," "Don Ermeguncio o la vocación," and "Ordalías."

240. Gil de Muro, Eduardo T. "El anticlericalismo de Clarín." <u>Ciclo de Conferencias sobre Oviedo</u>, VI-VII (Oviedo), 1973: 101-18.

Clarín was profoundly Christian. His anticlericalism was sincere and alert, and directed at
hypocrisy, fanaticism, and ignorance rather than
the Church. He was never a "clerófobo."

241.   ---.   "Clarín, un cristiano en la balanza."   CN,
II, 7 (Mayo-junio, 1981): 114-19.

C's ideas on religion, particularly in the
"political Catholicism" of his times. The author
quotes from C's reviews of Gloria and El nudo gor-
diano, and from the stories "El cura de Vericueto"
and "El frío del Papa," etc. but there are no
footnotes.

242.   Gilman, Stephen.   "La novela como diálogo: La Regenta y Fortunata y Jacinta."   NRFH, XXIV, 2
(1975): 438-48.

C's influence on Galdós, through Cervantes
and Flaubert. "Después de leer La Regenta, Galdós
ya no vio en don Quijote un modelo de caricatura
política y social; en vez de ello, en la singular
amalgama de aventura y experiencia del caballero,
vislumbró nuevos caminos inesperados y altamente
emocionantes para la exploración novelística."

243.   ---.   Galdós and the Art of the European Novel,
1867-1887.   Princeton UP, 1981.   154-86.

In studying the "inter-novel dialogue" between LR and Fortunata y Jacinta, Gilman detects
the tacit presence of Cervantes, Flaubert, Balzac,
and, at one remove, Zola.

244.   Giner de los Ríos, Francisco.   Ensayos y cartas.
Edición de homenaje en el cincuentenario de
su muerte. México: Tezontle, 1965.   188 pp.

Contains three letters to C (pp. 109-116),
all of which had appeared in the Boletín de la
Institución Libre de Enseñanza; dated 6 Jan. 1888,
18 Aug. 1891, and 28 Sept. 1896. Topics: EPB's
and Castelar's Catholicism, the pessimistic tone
of SUH, the death of Clarín's mother.

245.   Glendinning, Nigel.   "Some Versions of Carnival:
Goya and Alas."   Studies in Modern Spanish
Literature and Art Presented to Helen F.
Grant.   London: Tamesis, 1972. 65-78.

Goya's use of carnival in his later "Dispa-
rates" as the embodiment of dark forces in human
nature, and C's use of carnival in Pipá and "El
entierro de la sardina" as an inversion of normal

moral values and as the expression of emotions deeply rooted in man.

246. Gómez Carrillo, Enrique. <u>Treinta años de mi vida:</u> <u>La miseria de Madrid</u>. Madrid: Sociedad Española, 1921. 220 pp.

This is Vol. 26 of his <u>OC</u>. Reproduces a letter from C (pp. 121-25) and on pp. 191-92 recalls a conversation with Bobadilla regarding the Alas-Bobadilla duel. In his letter, C disagrees with Carrillo that Lemaître has more substance than Brunetière, and repeats four paragraphs, verbatim, from his preface to <u>Almas y cerebros</u> (1898), expressing his disappointment that so many Latin American writers follow the latest French authors indiscriminately. A 1945 ed. of <u>Treinta años</u> exists, published by Editorial Victoria of Buenos Aires.

247. Gómez de Baquero, Eduardo. "<u>Cuentos morales</u>, por Clarín." <u>RCHL</u>, I (Marzo, 1896): 129-31.

A favorable review; the reviewer especially likes "El cura de Vericueto," "Dúo de la tos," "Snob," and "Viaje redondo." C's preface reminds him of Renan. C is difficult to judge because of the way he has treated other writers. In this book C is too harsh on those who do not follow today's "neo-misticismo" or "renacimiento idealista."

248. Gómez de la Serna, Ramón. <u>Azorín</u>. Buenos Aires: Losada, 1948.

In "El espaldarazo" (pp. 42-46) Ramón reprints the entire text of C's Jan. 1897 "palique" from <u>La Saeta</u> (B). C considers Martínez Ruiz "un anarquista literario" and deplores the horrible things he writes about Pereda, Balart, and others, but admits that the young critic shows talent. "Yo no me he atrevido a escribir un prólogo para su libro <u>Pasión</u>, próximo a publicarse. González Serrano lo va a escribir." Azorín began his correspondence with C soon thereafter, addressing his letters to the offices of <u>El Progreso</u>. In his letters, C offers advice and calls Bonafoux a "chisgarabís." This <u>palique</u> also appeared in <u>MC</u>, XVII, 742 (8 Mayo 1897): 158.

249. Gómez Santos, Marino. "Dos cartas del Clarín íntimo: La religiosidad de Leopoldo Alas." <u>BIEA</u>, V, 13 (Agosto, 1951): 240-44.

Two letters addressed by C to the bishop of Oviedo, Ramón Martínez Vigil--one concerning the recent death of C's mother, the other (28 Oct. 1892) accompanying the shipment of <u>DB</u> and <u>ER</u>.

250. ---. "Clarín, poeta (Dos composiciones en verso, inéditas, y una bibliografía." <u>BIEA</u>, V, 14 (Dic., 1951): 396-401.

Quotes a few verses by C and lists 16 poems published between 1876-1943 in <u>RC</u>, III (30 Abril 1876): 194; <u>La Revista de Asturias</u>, II, 29 (15 Julio 1878): 362; <u>LL</u> (1907): 162; and local periodicals.

251. Gómez-Tabanera, José M. y Esteban Rodríguez Arrieta. "La 'conversión' de Leopoldo Alas Clarín: Ante una carta inédita de Clarín a Don Francisco Giner (20-X-1887)." <u>BIEA</u>, XXXIX, 115 (Mayo-agosto, 1985): 467-82.

Reproduces the text (with facsimile) of a long letter from C to his former teacher, mostly on an article on agnostics by the Belgian philosopher, Tiberghien. C briefly describes his new novel, "Una medianía," the female character of which is based on Carlyle's wife. Clarín states that Ana Ozores resembled Georges Sand in her youth.

252. González Aurioles, Norberto. "Sobre el estreno de <u>Teresa</u>." <u>El Correo</u> (M), No. 5447 (21 Marzo 1895): 2.

A favorable review, reprinted by MC in his article, "Noticia del estreno de <u>Teresa</u> . . . y algunas críticas periodísticas."

253. González Blanco, Andrés. "El espíritu de Clarín." <u>NT</u>, XIII, 169 (Enero, 1913): 67-74.

In an article dated Madrid, 8 Dec. 1912, the author announces that C's oldest son has finally persuaded reluctant editors to publish C's <u>OC</u>. Alas' best works were his short stories and novelettes and should be published first: <u>CM</u>, <u>GS</u>, <u>SDC</u>, etc., followed by <u>SUH</u> and <u>LR</u> in the 6th and 7th volumes, and none of his "paliques" since <u>ER</u>, <u>Siglo pasado</u>, and <u>Folletos</u> are better. "No fue justo e imparcial Clarín en los últimos años de su vida."

254. ---. "Leopoldo Alas (Clarín): Juicio crítico de sus obras." <u>La Novela Corta</u>, V, 250 (2 Oct. 1920).

A 48-page overview of <u>LR</u>, <u>Pipá</u>, <u>Solos</u> (stories only), <u>SDC</u>, and <u>CM</u>, with their plots. The introd. repeats many statements made in his <u>Historia de la novela</u> (1909). Calls <u>LR</u> "novela cruda y triste," the most truly intensive chapter of which is Vol. 2, Chap. 17. The walk with Petra down the boulevard reminds him of <u>O Primo Basilio</u>, while "El diablo en semana santa" recalls Eça de Queiroz's "O senhor Diablo."

255.   ---. "Clarín como crítico." <u>NT</u>, XXIII, 298 (Oct., 1923): 5-18.

Gives exact dates in C's professional career. "No fue hombre de mundo ni de sociedad." Alas wrote too much on too many things ("fue un libertino de las ideas") and his "paliques" in <u>MC</u> will not survive. As a critic he was alert, well-informed, restless, and at times virulent, but never frivolous or superficial. He was profoundly religious, even though at the beginning of his career there was "un instante de irreverencia y de frivolidad . . . Es la irreligiosidad irreflexiva y ligera tan propia del astur."

256.   González Herrán, José Manuel.   <u>La obra de Pereda ante la crítica literaria de su tiempo</u>. Santander: Estudio, 1983. 525 pp.

Contains at least 140 references to C and his reviews of Pereda's novels. González Herrán wonders (p. 173) why C bothered to ask Galdós for a "prólogo" to <u>LR</u>, if he thought so little of Galdós' "prólogo" to <u>El sabor de la tierruca</u>. C wrote articles on all 13 books published by Pereda between 1878 and 1896, except <u>Esbozos y rasguños</u> (1881) and <u>Al primer vuelo</u> (1891).

257.   González Llana, Félix. "Solos de Clarín." <u>La Iberia</u> (M), XXVIII, 7588 (8 Julio 1881): 3.

Considers "De la comisión" worthy of Larra and "la más severa crítica de los tiempos presentes." Galdós and others included "son objeto de un examen tan imparcial como concienzudo, porque el crítico al poner de manifiesto las brillantes condiciones que reunen no se ha olvidado de señalar sus defectos."

258.   González Ollé, Fernando.   "Prosa y verso en dos polémicas decimonónicas: Clarín contra <u>Núñez</u> de Arce y Campoamor contra Valera." <u>BBMP</u>, XXXIX, 1-3 (1963): 208-27.

A study of C's <u>Folleto literario</u> IV, a reaction to Núñez de Arce's speech at the Ateneo on 3 Dec. 1887, and to the debate between Valera and Campoamor, <u>La metafísica y la poesía</u> (1891).

259.   ---. "Del Naturalismo al Modernismo: Los orígenes
del poema en prosa y un desconocido artículo
de Clarín." RL, XXV (1964): 49-67.

The unknown article by C, reproduced and studied here, was entitled "Pequeños poemas en prosa.
Prólogo," and appeared in Revista del Antiguo Rei-
no de Navarra, 15 Mayo 1888.

260. González Serrano, Urbano. "La crítica en España."
Il Ib, VIII, 407 (18 Oct. 1890): 662-63.

A commentary on C, MMP, and PV as critics, by
C's philosophy professor, who considered Taine the
outstanding critic. Alas, who calls himself an
"albañil literario," has made considerable progress from the pages of El Solfeo to Paliques,
except for his tendency to worship certain "gods"
such as Núñez de Arce. C's obsession for Zola has
resulted in a "carga de inmensa pesadumbre." Reprinted in his Estudios críticos (1892).

261.   ---. Estudios críticos. Madrid: Escuela Tipo-
gráfica del Hospicio, 1892. 155 pp.

Contains "La crítica en España" (pp. 123-32)
and "Museum" (pp. 149-55). Admits that Alas' criticism of Núñez de Arce's speech is a reply to
those (including UGS himself) who had accused C of
"triturar a las medianías y embotar sus flechas
cuando iban dirigidas contra las reputaciones ya
hechas." Alas criticizes Campoamor and EPB with a
certain air of admiration and respect.

262.   ---. Siluetas. Madrid: Rodríguez Serra, 1899.
93 pp.

This rare little volume contains vignettes of
ten contemporaries. The text on Clarín (pp. 47-
50) states that C tends to combine the profound
with the humorous and superficial. Also, he tends
to show too much respect for major writers; for
example, "apenas si se ha atrevido con Núñez de
Arce."

263.   ---. La literatura del día. Barcelona: Henrich,
1903. 254 pp.

Contains "Un día de luto" (pp. 141-47), a
flattering obituary except for one brief paragraph: "Conservaba Clarín íntegra su perspicacia
crítica, pero la obscurecía y aun ponía en difu-
mino con un mariposeo intelectual que le conducía
a veces a un infantilismo incomprensible." In his
last letter of an extensive correspondence (as yet

unpublished), the author would have liked to ask his friend and former student to explain how he was able to admire Giner and Castelar, two entirely different personalities, at the same time.

Gracián, Baltasar. See Maínez, R. L.

264.   Gramberg, Eduard J.   "Su único hijo, novela incomprendida de Leopoldo Alas."   Hispania, XLV, 2 (May, 1962): 194-99.

Believes that SUH is not as strange or different as some critics think. Explores four problems: "la total ausencia de ambientación concreta; el enjuiciamiento satírico del seudorromanticismo; el tratamiento eufemístico-naturalista de los personajes; el tema fundamental de la obra, sobre todo en relación a su desenlace." Reprod. in MC's anthology, LAC, pp. 204-11.

265.   ---.   "Tres tipos de ambientación en la novela del siglo diecinueve."   RHM, XXVIII, 2-4 (April-Oct., 1962): 315-26.

Descriptive techniques in the milieu of LR, AC, Sotileza, and Cañas y barro.

266.   Green, O. H.   "Blanco-Fombona, Pérez Galdós, and Leopoldo Alas."   HR, X (1942): 47-52.

Points out the similarities between SUH, Blanco-Fombona's novel, El hombre de hierro (1905), and between LR and La mitra en la mano (1925).

267.   Griswold, Susan C.   "Rhetorical Strategies and Didacticism in Clarín's Short Fiction."   KRQ, XXIX, 4 (1982): 423-33.

Limiting herself to CM, the author studies C's "artistic strategies, the manipulation of point of view . . . The central and informing characteristic of Clarín's short fiction is his very conscious and deliberate effort to engage and influence the reader, for the most part by means of the authoritative persona whose voice is a dominant, and didactic, presence in the fictions."

268.   Guastavino, Guillermo.   "Algo más sobre Clarín y Teresa."   BH, LXXIII, 1-2 (Jan.-June, 1971): 133-59.

After a brief description of the circumstances surrounding C's play, the Director of the Biblioteca Nacional reproduces 17 letters written by C to María Guerrero between 8 Oct. 1894 and 4

Jan. 1896. Topics: Admiration for Shelley's <u>Los Cenci</u>; props and rehearsals for <u>Teresa</u>; plans to write other plays; Múgica's translation of Sudermann's <u>Magda</u>, etc.

269. Guenoun, Pierre. "À propos de l'entrée en scène d'Ana Ozores dans <u>La Regenta</u> de Clarín." <u>Mélanges offerts a Charles Vincent Aubrun</u>, I. Paris: Editions Hispaniques, 1975. 341-49.

270. Guillén, Claudio. "Apuntes para un estudio de la diégesis en <u>La Regenta</u>." <u>Clarín y su obra</u>. Ed. Antonio Vilanova. Barcelona: U de Barcelona, 1985. 265-91.

271. Gullón, Germán. <u>El narrador en la novela del siglo XIX</u>. Madrid: Taurus, 1976. 186 pp.

Chap. VII, entitled "Clarín o la complejidad narrativa" (pp. 133-48) studies narrative techniques in <u>SUH</u>. Rev. by Maurice Hemingway, <u>BHS</u>, LV, 2 (April, 1978): 163-64.

272. ---. <u>La novela como acto imaginativo (Alarcón, Bécquer, Galdós, Alas)</u>. Madrid: Taurus, 1983. 151 pp.

"El estudio se cierra con un capítulo dedicado a la imaginación autorial y contextual en <u>LR</u>. Representa la mejor sección del libro y uno de los más penetrantes ensayos existentes sobre la obra de Alas. Gullón detalla aquí la manera en que Clarín parece dialogar con su propio texto, releyéndolo en múltiples maneras y otorgándole sucesivas capas de significación paradógica. Así el novelista va creando un realismo velado en el cual los elementos del mundo social se izan a un nivel discursivo que le permite al narrador subrayar su presencia en el texto," says reviewer T. R. Franz in <u>HR</u>, LIII, 1 (Winter, 1985): 107-08. Also reviewed by Antonio Ferraz Martínez in <u>RL</u>, XLVI, 92 (Julio-dic., 1984): 220-23.

273. Gullón, Ricardo. "Clarín, crítico literario." <u>Universidad</u> (Zaragoza), XXVI, 3 (1949): 389-431.

A detailed examination of C as literary critic, even though R. Gullón believes C's fame will rest on his novels and short stories, especially <u>LR</u> and <u>Pipá</u>. Greatest weakness: C's praise of Campoamor and Núñez de Arce. C's opinion of MMP, Valera, EPB, Pereda, Alarcón, and Cánovas was justified. Reprinted in MC's anthology, <u>LAC</u>, pp. 115-46.

274.   ---.   "Aspectos de Clarín."   Archivum, II, 1 (Ene-
       ro-abril, 1952): 161-87.

       Alas' "crítica de policía" had a patriotic
incentive to improve Spanish literature.   Friendship with Pereda, MMP, and others with opposing
views.   Moral preoccupation, tenderness, the psychological novel.   C is a "provinciano europeo"
rather than "universal."   Two anecdotes by R.
Gullón's father, who studied under Prof. Alas.

275.   ---.   "Las novelas cortas de Clarín."   Insula,
       VII, 76 (15 Abril 1952): 3.

       Of all his contemporaries, only C excelled in
all three forms--novela, novela corta, cuento.   R.
Gullón considers Cuervo a failure, and El Señor
perhaps his best novela corta.   "La capacidad de
invención está restringida en Clarín . . . Su invención es imaginativa y no fantástica; por eso,
propiamente novelesca."

Gutiérrez Abascal, José.   See Kasabal.

276.   Hafter, Monroe Z.   "Heroism in Alas and Carlyle's
       On Heroes."   MLN, XCV, 2 (March, 1980): 312-
       34.

       Alas' interest in this book seems remarkable
considering that most of his characters are "a
sorry lot" which he seems to take "a perverse
pleasure in humiliating."   His interest in Carlyle
probably began in 1888.   Hafter traces influence
in "Cuesta abajo" (1890-91), SUH (the problem of
mediocrity), and through Renan.   Carlyle's work
helped Clarín to see his own efforts in a heroic
light.

277.   ---.   "A Goncourt Clue to a Clarín Plot."   Compar-
       ative Literature Studies, XIX, 3 (Fall,
       1982): 319-34.

       The influence on C's "Una medianía" of Edmond
and Jules Goncourt's roman à clef, Charles Demailly (1868), which originally appeared as Les
Hommes de lettres (1860).   Clarín himself wrote to
Oller: "Si se parece algo es, remotamente, a
Charles Demailly, de los Goncourt, pero sólo por
el asunto" (11 Jan. 1886).

278.   Hatzfeld, Helmut.   "La imitación estilística de
       Madame Bovary (1857) en La Regenta (1884)."
       Thesaurus, XXXII, 1 (Enero-abril, 1977): 40-
       53.

A stylistic comparison, supported by dozens of textual examples and divided into: Personificaciones, Parangones, Ritmo ternario, Impresionismo, Discurso indirecto libre, Repetición insistente, Bastardillas, Retórica crítica, and Leitmotif.

279.   ---.   "Two Stylizations of Clerical Tragedy: O Crime do Padre Amaro (1875) and La Regenta (1884)," The Two Hesperias: Literary Studies in Honor of Joseph G. Fucilla. Ed. Americo Bugliani. Madrid: Porrúa Turanzas, 1977. 181-95.

A comparison of the two priests (Padre Amaro and Don Fermín) divided into: The setting of the stage, Growing temptations, The factor of jealousy, Explosion of scandal, The turn to crime. There are no other novels serious enough, either by Balzac, Galdós, or Zola, from which such a clerical tragedy would be extricable.   Queiroz's novel is more brutal and cynical. LR has an "open end" fitting for a novel written in a minor tone.

280.   Heredero, Carlos F.   "Gonzalo Suárez frente a Clarín. La Regenta en el cine." Argumentos, VIII, 63-64 (Enero-feb., 1984): 54-55.

Although film director Suárez's version of LR disappointed many people, Heredero considers the movie "una obra interesante y sugerente, muy bien interpretada."

281.   Horno Lirio, Luis.   "Lo aragonés en Clarín." Zaragoza, XIII (1961): 107-30.

281a.   ---.   Lo aragonés en algunos escritores contemporáneos. Zaragoza, 1978.

Chap. 4 (pp. 93-119) points out the Aragonese elements in LR.

282.   Hurtado i Arias, E. G.   "Leopoldo Alas (Clarín)." La Revista Nueva (Santiago de Chile), Año 2, IV, 15 (Junio, 1901): 259-67.

Portions of this article were reprinted in the "Revista de revistas" section of NT, I, 9 (Sept., 1901): 366-68.   Clarín exerted enormous influence upon young Latin American writers even though he underrated them and cast doubt on Valera's sincerity when he praised them.   Among C's accomplishments was his desire for Hispanic readers to become familiar with Taine, Renan, Carlyle, Zola, Baudelaire, and Tolstoy.   LR is too long but contains "many good things."   He was not always just, but the fact remains that the authors he condemned to oblivion have not been resurrected. (The "i" in the name is correct; throughout the volumes of this journal, which I have examined, "i" is consistently used instead of "y.")

283. Ibargüengoitia, Jorge. "Prólogo" a La Regenta. México: Porrúa, 1972. ix-xix.

284. Ibarra, Fernando. "Clarín-Galdós: Una amistad." Archivum, XXI (1971): 65-76.

Clarín, who idolized Galdós, wrote a biography of him (1889) and maintained correspondence from 1879-1901. Yet Galdós never really confided in him (as he did in Pereda or Dr. Tolosa Latour) and took more than a year to write the preface to LR.

285. ---. "Clarín y el teatro político." Rom N, XIII (1971): 266-71.

C proposed the theme of politics, and especially that of the politician, as a good subject to deal with in the renovation of the stage. But he worked to make the stage a platform for moral and philosophical teaching, instead of changing the esthetic structure of the Spanish theater. Since neither he nor the playwrights of the time were suited for that endeavor, his ideas never materialized and his attempt to removate and revitalize the theater of Spain failed.

286. ---. "Clarín y Azorín: El matrimonio y el papel de la mujer española." Hispania, LV (1972): 45-54.

In Teresa, C presented his social ideas about women in relation to marriage. Dominated by a not very well defined kind of religious mysticism, he presents women as subject to their husbands' often brutal demands. Against the Catholic idea of an indestructible contract, C had previously championed separation and even divorce, when love and trust are absent in marriage. Azorín attacked Clarín as an enemy of the idea of liberty and dignity for women. Years later, Azorín defended what he had previously attacked. Both writers follow a similar emotional and ideological development in their careers.

287. ---. "Clarín y algunos escritores portugueses." LBR, X, 1 (June, 1973): 52-67.

C's admiration for Portuguese writers, especially Eça de Queiroz, Antero de Quental, Joaquim de Araújo, and Guilherme de Azevedo. The emphasis

here is on Quental's <u>Sonetos</u> (1881), which C discussed in <u>NC</u>, and D'Acevedo, about whom he wrote
in <u>SP</u>.

288.   ---.   "Clarín y Rubén Darío: Historia de una in-
comprensión."   <u>HR</u>, XLI (1973): 524-40.

C was too blind to see and appreciate the
value and transcendental literary significance of
Darío.   Blinded by minimal details of the new po-
etical expression, C failed to see the lyrical
revolution that Darío was bringing to the Hispanic
world of literature.

289.   ---.   "Clarín y la liberación de la mujer."   <u>His-
pano</u>, 51 (Mayo, 1974): 27-33.

An analysis of an article which C wrote (perhaps with tongue-in-cheek) at the age of 27, "El
amor y la economía" (<u>La Unión</u>, 14 Julio 1879) urg-
ing women to demand their rights.   But C, like Valera, was a man of his times; both objected to women in politics, literature, or academies.   "Clarín quiere buenas esposas y buenas madres de fami-
lia, pero no quiere ver una <u>caballera femenina</u> fi-
gurando en los centros de la cultura."

290.   ---.   "El dios de Clarín."   <u>Actas del Quinto
Congreso Internacional de Hispanistas</u>.   Eds.
Maxime Chevalier et al.   Bordeaux, 1977.

Ibarra believes (Vol. II, pp. 467-79) that
all of C's writings are of an autobiographical
nature.   Until more of Alas' correspondence comes
to light, it is difficult to ascertain his personal, private definition of God.   C was greatly
disappointed to learn that two of his favorite
teachers, Salmerón and González Serrano, thought
little of religion.   Poetic and mystical, C always
felt attracted to a spiritual interpretation of
life and was "fiel a ese amor imposible, su Dios
desconocido, siempre entrevisto, soñado, nunca alcanzado."   Unlike Renan, he felt "la insaciable
sed . . . de una relación íntima y amorosa con
Dios."

291.   Ife, Barry W.   "Idealism and Materialism in Clarín's <u>La Regenta</u>: Two Comparative Studies."
<u>RLC</u>, XLIV, 3 (July-Sept., 1970): 273-95.

The purpose of Ife's article is to examine
C's "presentation of the nature of personality and
its functioning within society and to go on and
use this analysis to determine Clarín's attitudes
to the most frequently recurring debate of his
time: spiritual transcendentalism versus scien-

tific materialism." LR and George Eliot's The Mill on the Floss (1860) seem to be "the result of a common approach to a common problem," but Ife does not suggest any influence.

292. Jackson, Robert M. "Cervantismo in the Creative Process of Clarín's La Regenta." MLN, LXXXIV, 2 (March, 1969): 208-27.

The influence of Cervantine techniques (literature within literature, imagination and reality, multiple perspectives, autonomous characters, etc.) "Clarín has created an entire city of people who inhabit a world created in turn by their own imagination, to a great extent as a result of contact with literature, that is, the interpretation of literature and the personal lives of Vetustans."

293. ---. "La Regenta and Contemporary History." REH, XI, 2 (Mayo, 1977): 287-302.

Alas' first novel is truly a study of its times. The characters act out in microcosm C's view of the social history of Spain, and their personal struggles are charged with allegorical transcendence.

294. Junceda Avello, E. "Análisis sexológico de la novela de Clarín: Su único hijo." BIEA, XXXVIII, 111 (Enero-abril, 1984): 187-203.

295. Juretschke, Hans. España ante Francia. Prólogo de Antonio Tovar. Madrid: Editora Nacional, 1940. 243 pp.

See pp. 90-109. For C, contemporary Paris was the spiritual center of Europe. Alas' perception of France and French literature, especially Zola, Renan, Hugo, and Baudelaire. C represents the spiritual bridge between the 19th century and the Generation of 1898.

296. Kasabal. "Sobre Teresa de Clarín." Il Ib, XIII, 639 (30 Marzo 1895): 194-95.

The premiere of Teresa at El Teatro Español did not receive a single applause partly because it was presented after Lope's La niña boba and partly because the setting and theme of Teresa was in sharp contrast with the elegant audience in attendance. Reprod. in Romero's ed. of Teresa, pp. 178-80. Kasabal's real name was José Gutiérrez Abascal.

297.   Kronik, John W.   "Un cuento olvidado de Clarín."
        <u>CHA</u>, 136 (Abril, 1961): 27-35.

        Gives the full text of "La guitarra," origin-
        ally published in <u>Los Lunes de El Imparcial</u>, XXX,
        10.617 (23 Nov. 1896): 3, and not reprinted in any
        anthology since that date.

298.   ---.   "The Identification of Clarín."   <u>Rom N</u>, II,
        2 (Spring, 1961): 87-88.

        Leopoldo Alas first used the signature
        "Clarín" in <u>El Solfeo</u> of Madrid on 11 April 1875,
        not 2 Oct. as reported in Cabeza's biography.
        Alas belonged to the paper's editorial staff from
        the time of its founding (by Antonio Sánchez
        Pérez) in Feb. 1875, not 5 July. A note in the 13
        June 1875 edition clearly identifies Clarín as
        being Leopoldo Alas.

299.   ---.   "Censo de personajes en los cuentos de
        Clarín." <u>Archivum</u>, XI (1961): 323-406.

        Names and descriptions of characters which
        appear in six collections. Divided into six cat-
        egories: Protagonistas, Otros personajes prin-
        cipales, Personajes secundarios importantes, Per-
        sonajes secundarios de menos importancia (acceso-
        rios), Personajes secundarios insignificantes (in-
        cidentales), Grupos. Done by collections (<u>Pipá</u>,
        <u>DB</u>, <u>SDC</u>, etc.) rather than alphabetically.

300.   ---.   "Clarín and Verlaine." <u>RLC</u>, XXXVII, 3
        (July-Sept., 1963): 368-84.

        Describes and analyzes a little-known article
        by C, "Paul Verlaine (<u>Liturgias íntimas</u>)," <u>La
        Ilustración Española y Americana</u>, XLI, 36 (30
        Sept. 1897): 191, 194, and No. 37 (8 Oct. 1897):
        214-15, the complete text of which Kronik
        reproduces on pp. 372-84.

301.   ---.   "The Function of Names in the Stories of
        Alas." <u>MLN</u>, LXXX, 2 (March, 1965): 260-65.

        Classifies names in the following categories,
        which often overlap: Humoristic, thematic, charac-
        ter portrayal (profession, physical trait, person-
        ality). "The fictional being already character-
        ized through his name is in danger of being typed
        before he appears, of not being able to unveil
        himself on his own initiative or to develop into
        his own personality.. . . <Nevertheless> The tech-
        nique does not testify to creative weakness or
        lack of imagination in Alas. Pleasing or not, it
        is an intrinsic esthetic manifestation of a pur-
        posefully constructed artistic creed."

302.   ---.   "La modernidad de Leopoldo Alas."   PSA, Año
        XI, Vol. XLI, 122 (Mayo, 1966): 121-34.

        Alas' narrative techniques are similar to
        those of the generation of 1868, but he appealed
        to the generation of 1898 because of his ideolog-
        ical preoccupations and his subjective identifi-
        cation with characters in his short stories.   C
        reacted with greater intensity to the conflict
        between what he saw and what he felt.

303.   ---.   "Unamuno's Abel Sánchez and Alas' Benedic-
        tino: A Thematic Parallel."   Spanish Thought
        and Letters in the 20th Century.   Nashville:
        Vanderbilt UP, 1966.   287-97.

        Benedictino was originally published in El
        Imparcial, XXVII, 9370 (19 Junio 1893): 3, and in-
        cluded that same year in SDC.   "Unamuno uses the
        Cain-Abel myth to point to the presence of envy
        and hatred as a trait of human nature (and especi-
        ally of Spanish human nature), and he exalts the
        individual who fends against this spiritual op-
        pression.   Alas, using the same raw materials,
        paints a portrait of injustice as the basic ingre-
        dient of social existence.   Both thus evoke the
        tragedy of man's concurrent need and inability to
        be loved and to love."

304.   ---.   "Sesenta y ocho frente a noventa y ocho: La
        modernidad de Leopoldo Alas."   Actas del Se-
        gundo Congreso Internacional de Hispanistas.
        Eds. Jaime Sánchez Romeralo y Norbert
        Puolussen.   Nijmegen, Holland: Inst. Español
        de la U de Nimega, 1967.   371-76.

        An abbreviated version of Kronik's article in
        PSA.

305.   ---.   "Leopoldo Alas, Krausism, and the Plight of
        the Humanities in Spain."   MLS, XI, 3 (1981):
        3-15.

306.   Labanyi, Jo.   "City, Country and Adultery in La
        Regenta."   BHS, LXIII, 1 (Jan., 1986): 53-66.

307.   Laffitte, G.   "Madame Bovary et La Regenta."   BH,
        XLV, 2 (1943): 157-63.

308.   Landeira, Ricardo.   "Pipá: Maniqueísmo, ironía y
        tragedia en un relato de Leopoldo Alas."
        Studies in Honor of Sumner M. Greenfield.
        Ed. Harold L. Boudreau and Luis T. González
        del Valle.   Lincoln, NE: Soc. of Span. and
        Span-Amer. Studies, 1985.   129-44.

See also under López Landeira.

Lara y Pedraja, Antonio.   See Orlando.

309.   Laso Prieto, José María.   "La religión en la obra
cumbre de Leopoldo Alas."   Argumentos, VIII,
63-64 (Enero-feb., 1984): 38-43.

Briefly examines the Church of Leo XIII (when
LR was published), religion during the Restauración, C's religious ideas, and religion in C's
masterpiece.

310.   Lissorgues, Yvan.   "España ante la guerra colonial
de 1895-1898; Leopoldo Alas (Clarín), periodista y el problema cubano."   Cuba, Les
étapes d'une libération   (Hommage à Juan
Marinello et Noël Salomon), Actas del Co-
loquio Internacional sobre Cuba, 22-24-XI-
1978.   France-Ibérie Recherche, Université de
Toulouse-Le Mirail, 1979.   47-76.

Clarín did not begin to write on the colonial
problem until 30 Sept. 1895.   From that date until
his death in 1901, he wrote some 42 articles and
stories on the subject, which Lissorgues analyzes
here.

311.   ---.   "Concepción de la historia en Leopoldo Alas
(Clarín): Una Historia artística al servicio
del progreso."   CN, II, 7 (Mayo-junio, 1981):
50-55.

C felt that history should be not only positivistic (accumulated facts, with impartiality and
objectivity) but also philosophical and artistic,
hence his admiration for Castelar, MMP, Carlyle,
Renan, etc. and his affinity with Unamuno.   History is progress, but it is also the struggle between good and evil.   His 1886 lecture on Alcalá
Galiano is his only writing of a historical nature.   A sentence from Palique best summarizes his
ideas: ". . .una historia filosófica, artística,
documentada y pintoresca, sin el andamiaje de la
erudición, pero no sin sus frutos, sin la falsedad
de la leyenda y de la novela, pero no sin sus
atractivos y su verdad sentimental y sintética."

312.   ---.   "La autenticidad religiosa de Leopoldo
Alas."   Insula, XXXIX, 451 (Junio, 1984): 3.

For C religion was always "otra cosa que un
conjunto de dogmas o de preceptos, muy otra cosa
que una institución."   He was critical of the
Spanish Church throughout his life.   He greatly

respected Moreno Nieto, Ceferino González, and
Sanz y Forés for their ideas on Christianity. In
1893 Alas wrote: "El cristianismo es la santa
idealidad humana en busca de lo divino." Antonio
Machado, himself a student of Giner, seems to have
agreed with Clarín.

313. ---. "Idée et réalité dans _Su único hijo_ de
      Leopoldo Alas Clarín." _LLNL_, LXXVI, 243
      (1984): 47-64.

314. ---. "Unamuno y Clarín: ¿Una amistad frustrada?"
      LdD, XV, 32 ((Mayo-agosto, 1985): 87-101.

      Disagrees with García Blanco concerning an
      "honda y trascendente amistad" between these two
      writers. Unamuno's pride and vanity made commu-
      nication impossible. C admired Unamuno's intel-
      ligence but did not concede aptitude as novelist
      or poet. Alas' silence on _Paz en la guerra_. The
      appendix reproduces C's "Como gustéis," originally
      published in Blasco Ibáñez's newspaper, _El Pueblo_
      (Valencia, 9 July 1900), in which C praises Rodó
      very highly and reviews Unamuno's _Tres ensayos_.

315. ---. "Etica y estética en _Su único hijo_ de Leo-
      poldo Alas Clarín." _Clarín y su obra_. Ed.
      Antonio Vilanova. Barcelona: U de Barcelona,
      1985. 181-210.

316. Little, William y Joseph Schraibman. "Notas sobre
      el motivo de la paternidad en _Su único hijo_
      de Clarín." _BIEA_, 93-94 (1978): 21-29.

317. Lope, Juan M. y Huberto Batis. "Introducción" a
      La Regenta. México: Universidad Nacional
      Autónoma de México, 1960. 2 vols.

      Lope's introd. appears in Vol. 1, pp. vii-
      xxvii, and Batis' on pp. xviii-xxviii. Reprinted
      in 1972.

317a. López Landeira, Ricardo. "_Pipá_: maniqueismo,
      ironía y tragedia." _Archivum_, 29-30 (1979-
      80): 83-106.

      Examines "la desmitificación del cosmos reli-
      gioso mediante el uso de los tres factores anun-
      ciados en el título." _Pipá_, Clarín's earliest and
      longest _novelette_, was first published in the Ma-
      drid newspaper, _La Unión_, in 1879.

318. López-Rey, Justa Arroyo de. "_La Regenta_ de Cla-
      rín: Justicia, verdad, belleza." Eds. Rizel
      Pincus Sigele y Gonzalo Sobejano. _Homenaje a_
      Casalduero: Crítica y poesía. Madrid: Gre-
      dos, 1972. 325-39.

Symbol and metaphor in LR: "Leopoldo Alas
actúa en LR en su triple papel de crítico, educador y artista. Como crítico tiene por fin la justicia; como educador, la verdad; como artista, la
belleza." Dozens of quotations but only one
footnote.

319.   López Sanz, Mariano. "Punctualizaciones en torno
al naturalismo literario español." CA,
XXXVII, 1 (Enero-feb., 1978): 209-25.

Spanish naturalism as perceived and practiced
by Galdós, EPB, and C. Alas' ideas from the journal La Diana (1882), his preface to La cuestión
palpitante, and his book Galdós (1912).

320.   Lorda Alaiz, F. M. "Descripción científica de la
obra literaria ¡Adiós, Cordera! de Leopoldo
Alas." BRAE, 52, cxcvii (Sept.-dic., 1972):
503-10.

321.   ---. "Morphématique litteraire (sur le chapitre
VIII de La Regenta de Leopoldo Alas." Han-
delingen van het tweundertigste Nederlands
Filologencongres: Gehouden te Ultrecht op
woensdag 5, donderdag 6 en vrijdag 7 april
1972. Amsterdam: Holland UP, 1974. 217-20.

322.   Lott, Robert C. "El estilo indirecto libre en La
Regenta." Rom N, XV (1973): 259-63.

C was aware of the presence in Galdós of the
naturalistic Zolaesque style feature of free indirect style. In LR Alas used this essentially
ironic-mimetic device in four ways--the ironical-
critical blending of the author's narrative style
and the characters' thoughts and words, the use of
many words and phrases in italics to emphasize the
characters' speech mannerisms, the reporting of
real or imagined dialogues, and the psychologic-
ally revelatory, often dramatic, flashbacks.

323.   Maeztu, Ramiro de. "Clarín, Madrid Cómico and Co.
Limited." RN, I, 25 (15 Oct. 1899): 49-54.

A defense of Modernismo and a merciless attack on Clarín, whom Maeztu considers too negative, sarcastic, and insolent. C replied with a
"palique" in MC, 21 Oct. 1899. The entire RN was
recently reprinted in facsimile.

324.   Maínez, Ramón León. "Las sandeces de Clarín." El
Eco Montañés (Cádiz), 1891-92.

A series of six negative articles signed "Baltasar Gracián," four published in 1891 and two in 1892. See MC's "Un ataque a Clarín . . ." in RUO and "La Regenta y Clarín en sus días . . ." in Insula.

325.   Marañón, Gregorio.   "Prólogo" a Epistolario de Clarín y Menéndez Pelayo.   Madrid: Ediciones Escorial, 1943.   5-17.

C greatly admired MMP as a scholar and as a man, even though these two friends represented opposite ideologies.   C was to the 19th century what Feijoo was to the 18th and Unamuno to the 20th.   Despite C's constant attacks on Cánovas, Dr. Marañón considers Cánovas the great Spanish historian of the 19th century, second only to MMP.

326.   ---.   "Prólogo" a Marino Gómez-Santos, Leopoldo Alas Clarín.   Oviedo, 1952.

Alas, Feijoo, and Jovellanos were equals in three essential qualities: "la sabiduría, la generosidad tolerante, y la pulcritud moral."   As for C's so-called religious doubts, Dr. Marañón asks: "Pero estas dudas, ¿qué otra cosa son que resaca de una profunda, y no externa y acomodaticia religiosidad?"

327.   Marcos, Balbino.   "El catalejo del magistral de Vetusta."   LdD, XV, 32 (Mayo-agosto, 1985): 69-85.

The various characters and social classes as seen through the telescope by the canon, who in turn is being observed by Celedonio and Bismark.

328.   Marías, Javier.   "La Regenta en inglés."   CN, V, 23 (Enero-feb., 1984): 38-39.

Comments on John Rutherford's introd. to his translation, published simultaneously by Penguin Classics and the University of Georgia Press. Rutherford spent seven years translating it, at the risk of not being read or being accused of translating because he was not capable of anything else.

329.   Marrero, Vicente.   Historia de una amistad.   Madrid: Novelas y Cuentos, 1971.   319 pp.

The correspondence and literary relations between Pereda, Rubén Darío, Clarín, Valera, MMP, and Galdós, with an occasional reference to Laverde.   For C, see especially pp. 134-43, 152-62, 165-79, 262-66.   Topics: Valera's and MMP's opin-

ion of C; C's rejection of Marxist ideas; C's idea
of Christianity; C's death. There is no bibliography or index, but Marrero is obviously very
well-informed.

330.   Marrone, Nila. "Hacia un análisis lingü"ístico
comparativo del estilo de Clarín en La Regen-
ta, Juan Rulfo en Pedro Páramo, y Gabriel
García Márquez en Cien años de soledad."
Eds. Mary Ann Beck, Lisa E. Davis, José Her-
nández, Gary D. Keller, and Isabel C. Terán.
The Analysis of Hispanic Texts: Current
Trends in Methodology. Jamaica: Bilingual P,
York College, 1976. 170-90.

331.   Martín Galí, Emilio. "Mirón . . . y errarla."
Barcelona Cómica, 18 Agosto 1889.

A reply to C's articles "Martingalicismos,"
in MC, IX, 333 (6 Julio 1889): 3 and 6; and No.
334 (13 Julio 1889): 3.

332.   Martín-Gamero, Sofía. "Introducción" a Leopoldo
Alas, Juan Ruiz. Madrid: Espasa-Calpe, 1985.
489 pp.

The brief introd. by Martín-Gamero (Adolfo
Posada's granddaughter) is followed by the text of
all 50 issues of this handwritten "périodico humorístico" by Alas, composed in 1868-69.

333.   Martínez Cachero, José María. "La Condesa de
Pardo Bazán escribe a su tocayo, el poeta
Ferrari (Ocho cartas inéditas de doña Emi-
lia)." Revista Bibliográfica y Documental
(M), I, 2 (Abril-junio, 1947): 249-56.

Of special interest is the letter dated Venta
de Baños, 26 July 1901, in which EPB writes:
"¿Quién nos desgarrará como aquel perro? Mire
usted que yo pasé cuatro o seis años de mi vida
sin que un solo instante dejasen de resonar en mis
oídos ladridos furiosos del can."

334.   ---.   "Salvador Rueda escribe a Clarín." RUO,
XLIX-L (1948): 137-40.

335.   ---.   "Un ataque a Clarín: Seis artículos de Ramón
León Maínez." RUO, XI (Sept.-dic., 1950):
247-73.

Using the nom de plume "Baltasar Gracián,"
Maínez tried to discredit Alas and defend the poetry of Ferrari, which Alas had criticized in MC,
30 May 1891, and elsewhere. C found out when PV
informed him that he had seen Valera's nephew dis-

tributing these "stupid leaflets" at a bar.   Two
letters reproduced here, from Manuel Castrillo y
Sanromá to Emilio Ferrari, warn the poet about the
forthcoming "paliques" by Chirimía (as Manuel del
Palacio called Clarín) in MC, and that a "friend"
is printing hundreds of copies of the six pamphlets against C.   The sixth pamphlet, "La renova-
ción de nuestro teatro," disagrees with C's high
opinion of Galdós' drama Realidad and Echegaray's
El hijo de don Juan, both coolly received by the
public.

336.   ---.   "Los versos de Leopoldo Alas."   Archivum,
       II, 1 (Enero-abril, 1952): 89-111.

       An overview of C's poetry since childhood,
and a description of two unpublished notebooks
("Flores de María") written by C as an adolescent
and preserved by his granddaughter.   Reprinted in
MC's anthology, LAC, pp. 105-11, without the five
poems reprod. in the appendix of the Archivum
article.

337.   ---.   "Silencio sobre Clarín."   La Nueva España
       (Oviedo), 27 Abril 1952.

338.   ---.   "Un dato para la fortuna de Víctor Hugo en
       España."   Archivum, II, 2 (Mayo-agosto,
       1952): 314-18.

       Reproduces an unknown article by C, "Lec-
turas," on Hugo's posthumous book, Toda la lira,
from Il Ib, XI (1893): 739 y 742.

339.   ---.   "Una opinión sobre El señor y lo demás son
       cuentos, de Leopoldo Alas."   Archivum, II, 2
       (Mayo-agosto, 1952): 312-13.

       Reproduces Alfredo Opisso's brief review from
Il Ib, II (2 Sept. 1893): 558.

340.   ---.   "Adiciones a una bibliografía sobre Leopoldo
       Alas, Clarín."   Archivum, II, 3 (Sept.-dic.,
       1952): 408-20.

       Adds 49 entries on C prior to 1951, not in-
cluded in MGS' book.

341.   ---.   "Luis Bonafoux y Quintero, 'Aramís,' contra
       Clarín: Historia de una enemistad literaria."
       RL, III, 5 (Enero-marzo, 1953): 99-111.

       In April of 1887, Bonafoux launched a series
of attacks on C, probably because C had not written a word about Mosquetazos de Aramís (1885).   MC
studies Bonafoux's articles in El Español, El

Pueblo, La Regencia; and C's replies in MC and Mis plagios.

342.   ---. "Clarín y Azorín: Una amistad y un fervor."
Archivum, III, 2 (Mayo-agosto, 1953): 159-80.

C wrote on Azorín in La Saeta (B), No. 320 (1 Enero 1897) and on Charivari in MC, XVII, 742 (8 Mayo 1897): 158, reprinted by MC on pp. 169-72. Reproduced are three letters (26 Oct. 1897, 19 April 1898, and 12 May 1898) from Azorín to Alas. The two authors met at the offices of El Progreso in Nov. 1897.

343.   ---. "Clarín, crítico de su amigo Palacio Valdés." BIEA, VII, 19 (Agosto, 1953): 401-12.

A scholarly study of the friendship between C and PV, with references to Alas' criticism of El señorito Octavio (El Mundo Moderno, 1881), Marta y María (El Día, 1883), El idilio . . . Aguas fuertes, Riverita, Maximina (which Clarín did not like), La hermana San Sulpicio (MC, 11 Mayo 1889), La fe. Martínez Cachero states that he does not know where C's "complete" reviews, if any, of La fe and La hermana San Sulpicio were published.

344.   ---. "Crónica y bibliografía del primer centenario de Leopoldo Alas, Clarín; años 1951 y 1952." Archivum, III, 1 (1953): 79-112.

Describes some 85 books, articles, reviews, and short "noticias" on C, many published in local newspapers.

345.   ---. "Introducción" a Cuentos de Clarín. Oviedo: Gráficas Summa, 1953.

Selects 14 stories from CM, one from Pipá, three from GS, one from Doctor Sutilis. None from SDC, since this book has been reprinted in recent years. Also contains the three known chapters of C's first (unfinished) novel, "Speraindeo." Drawings by Sra. Cristina Alas de Tolívar, C's granddaughter. Reviewed by Alarcos Llorach, Caso González, Moreno Baez (q.v.)

346.   ---. "Menéndez Pelayo y Clarín: Historia de una amistad." BIEA, X, 28 (Agosto, 1956): 169-96.

A study of their literary relations, with numerous references to C's articles on MMP, and the 55 letters published by Adolfo Alas in 1943. Another letter from MMP to C appears in Avello's Vida y obra literaria de Juan Ochoa Betancourt (1955), pp. 187 and 190.

347. ---. "Noticia de tres folletos contra Clarín."
BIEA, XIII, 37 (Agosto, 1959): 225-44.

A detailed description of literary attacks by
Fray Juan de Miguélez (Fray Mortero), Dionisio de
las Heras (Plácido), and Martinete. Martinete's
pamphlet, although mentioned by Martínez Cachero
and Alonso Cortés in 1952, was practically unknown
until now. Reprod. in MC's anthology, LAC, pp.
69-81.

348. ---. "El temido y odiado Clarín." ABC, 6 Dic.
1959.

349. ---. "Oviedo en dos novelas del siglo XIX."
BIEA, XV, 43 (Agosto, 1961): 381-90.

The city of Oviedo as depicted in LR and PV's
El Maestrante.

350. ---. "Dos fragmentos narrativos de Leopoldo
Alas." Archivum, XII (1962): 479-506.

Gives the text (on pp. 483-99) of C's con-
tribution (Chap. 6) to a novel entitled Las vírgenes locas (1886), and on pp. 500-06 the text of
"Mosquín," the first and only chapter of C's incomplete novel, "Palomares" (1887).

351. ---. "Introducción" a La Regenta. Barcelona:
Planeta, 1963.

Follows the text of the first ed. The preface is divided into three parts: brief biography, Alas' writings other than LR, and a study
of LR. Includes a complete study of the "incident" between C and the bishop of Oviedo. Good
analysis of C's stories. Contains only 19 footnotes, some of which are unnecessary, according to
reviewer Beser. Not scholarly, and deletes entire
paragraphs, according to Sanz Villanueva's article. See also Martínez Torrón's comments.
Reprinted in 1967.

352. ---. "13 Cartas inéditas de Leopoldo Alas a Rafael Altamira, y otros papeles." Archivum,
XVIII (1968): 145-76.

The letters are dated between 13 June 1887
and 21 Nov. 1897. The "other papers" consist of
the text of Fedon's review (La Justicia, 11 Abril
1888) of G. A. Cesáreo's article, "El naturalismo
en la novela española," published in La Nueva
Antología), concerning LR; and the text of C's
preface to Altamira's Mi primera campaña (1893).

353.   ---.   "Leopoldo Alas, narrador (Sus cuentos, sus novelas, _Su único hijo_)."   _EstLit_, 402-404 (15 Sept. 1968): 21-26.

354.   ---.   "Noticia del estreno de _Teresa_ (ensayo dramático en un acto y en prosa, original de D. Leopoldo Alas, 1895) y de algunas críticas periodísticas."   _Archivum_, XIX (1969) 243-73.

Reproduces full text of articles by González Aurioles, Canals, and Bustillo.   Reprinted in MC's book, _Las palabras y los días_, pp. 267-91.

355.   ---.   "Introducción" a _Doña Berta y otros cuentos._ Barcelona: Ed. Salvat-Alianza Editorial de Madrid, 1969.   188 pp.

356.   ---.   "Introducción" a _Palique_.   Barcelona: Editorial Labor, 1973.   309 pp.

See pp. 7-40 for a brief description of C's literary criticism from _La literatura en 1881_ to _Ensayos y revistas_, with emphasis on _Palique_.   The bibliography on pp. 41-55 includes an annotated list of 67 items.   Reviewed by Díez Borque, Kronik (q.v.)

357.   ---.   "Noticia de más críticas periodísticas sobre el estreno de _Teresa_."   _BEIA_, 95 (1978): 459-81.

Reprinted in his book, _Las palabras y los días_, pp. 293-317.   Comments on reviews of _Teresa_ by Zeda, Don Cualquiera, Sánchez Pérez, and Arimón.

358.   ---.   "Doña Berta de Rondaliego en Madrid: Leopoldo Alas: _Doña Berta_, VIII."   _El comentario de textos_, 3: _La novela realista_.   Ed. Andrés Amorós.   Madrid: Castalia, 1979. 255-78.

An analysis of section 8 of this short novel. Reprinted in his book, _Las palabras y los días_, pp. 235-52.

359.   ---.   "Necrologías sobre Clarín."   _CN_, II, 7 (Mayo-junio, 1981): 2-7.

Describes the obituaries and memorials published in _El Progreso de Asturias_ and also those by Bonafoux, Bobadilla, Bremón, Navarro Ledesma, and González Serrano.   In footnote 8, MC wonders if Jove y Bravo, who published poems as "Luis del Carmen," may have served as model for Trifón Cármenes in _LR_.

360.   ---.   "La actitud anti-modernista del crítico
       Clarín."   <u>ALE</u>, 2 (1983): 383-98.

361.   ---.   "El crítico Clarín a través de sus comenta-
       rios al poeta Emilio Ferrari."   <u>Homenaje a
       José Manuel Blecua</u>.   Madrid: Gredos, 1983.
       433-42.

       C's opinion of Ferrari's poetry was con-
       sistently negative, as can be seen in <u>La litera-
       tura en 1881</u>, <u>SP</u>, and <u>MC</u> No. 432 of 30 May 1891
       and No. 732 of 27 Feb. 1897.   He was particularly
       harsh on <u>Pedro Abelardo</u>.   Ferrari was defended by
       the Conde de las Navas in <u>Cultura Española</u>, XVI
       (Nov. 1909): 880-900.

362.   ---.   "Noticia de otras novelas largas del autor
       de <u>La Regenta</u>."   <u>CN</u>, V, 23 (Enero-feb, 1984):
       87-92.

       The fragments in question are "Speraindeo"
       (1880), "Las vírgenes locas" (1886), "Palomares"
       (1887), "Una medianía" (1889), "Cuesta abajo"
       (1890-91) and "Tambor y gaita" (1905).

363.   ---.   "<u>La Regenta</u> y Clarín en sus días: noticia de
       una crítica negativa."   <u>Insula</u>, XXXIX, 451
       (Junio, 1984): 7.

       Excerpts from Ramón León Maínez's third ar-
       ticle or "repaso" on Clarín, entitled "Sus cuentos
       y sus cuentecillos.   Sus novelas y sus noveluchos"
       (<u>El Eco Montañés</u>, 1891).   Maínez considered some
       of the characters of <u>LR</u> false and improbable,
       especially Don Víctor.

364.   ---.   "Vetusta: Los <u>seudos</u> de una sociedad provin-
       ciana."   <u>LdD</u>, XV, 32 (Mayo-agosto, 1985):
       159-70.

       Gives examples of "seudo-política, seudo-
       cultura, seudo-religión" and other "inautenti-
       cidades" in <u>LR</u>.   The university is not mentioned
       in the novel because it was "lo poco agradable que
       tenemos" as C himself said in a letter to MMP.

365.   ---.   "Polémicas y ataques del Clarín crítico."
       <u>Clarín y su obra</u>.   Ed. Antonio Vilanova.
       Barcelona: U de Barcelona, 1985.   83-102.

       Concerning Ferrari, Suárez Bravo, Bonafoux,
       Maínez, Fray Mortero, Heras, and Martinete.   MC
       has now learned that Martinete's real name was not
       Emilio Martín Galí, as originally suspected, but
       rather Mariano Martín Fernández.

366.   Martínez Cachero, José María y Enrique Sánchez
       Reyes, <u>Menéndez Pelayo y Asturias</u>.   Oviedo:
       Instituto de Estudios Asturianos, 1957.

       Chap. 3 contains a little-known letter from
       C, and Chap. 4 describes in detail the friendship
       between C and MMP.   Reviewed by Jesús Neira in
       <u>BIEA</u>, XI, 30 (1957): 152-54 and by Rafael Benítez
       Claros in <u>Archivum</u>, VI, 3 (Sept.-dic., 1956): 334-
       35.

       Martínez Ruiz, José.   See Azorín

367.   Martínez Torrón, Diego.   "El naturalismo en <u>La
       Regenta</u>."   <u>CHA</u>, CXXVIII, 380 (Feb., 1982):
       257-97.

       "El objetivo de este trabajo es estudiar los
       aspectos de <u>LR</u> a propósito del naturalismo
       francés."   Naturalism was and still is misunder-
       stood in Spain, even by literary critics.   The
       social commentary in <u>LR</u> has "una intencionalidad
       ideológica mucho más demoledora que el entreteni-
       miento sensualista zolesco."   Surveys previous in-
       terpretations of <u>LR</u> by García Sarriá, Brent, and
       BG.   "Personalmente creo que no es fácil encontrar
       novela propiamente naturalista en España."

368.   ---.   "Ediciones recientes de <u>La Regenta</u>."   <u>CHA</u>,
       CXXXIX, 415 (Enero, 1985): 64-74.

       A perceptive comparison of the editions pre-
       pared by Cabezas (1947, 1966), Martínez Cachero
       (1963, 1967), Sobejano (1981), Baquero Goyanes
       (1984), and Oleza (1984).   Believes that someone
       ought to compare the first and second editions of
       <u>LR</u> (1884-85, 1900) to study the changes made by
       Clarín.

369.   Masip Acevedo, Julio.   "Alrededor de <u>La Regenta</u>:
       Don Fermín de Pas y Don José María de Cos."
       <u>BIEA</u>, XXXVIII, 113 (Sept.-dic., 1984): 845-
       58.

       After furnishing biographical data on Dr.
       José María de Cos y Macho (1838-1919), Archbishop
       of Valladolid and later Cardinal, the author sug-
       gests the possibility that Cos may have inspired
       Fermín de Pas, but only physically and intellec-
       tually.   Cos spent the years 1865-86 in Oviedo.

370.   Matamoro, Blas.   "Magas, niñas, adúlteras y tra-
       vestis."   <u>CHA</u>, CXXXIX, 415 (Enero, 1985): 25-
       36.

371. Mayoral, Marina. "Clarín y Valera, críticos lite-
      rarios." RO, XXXVIII, 2a época, 82 (Enero,
      1970): 97-103.

      A review of Beser's and Bermejo Marcos' books
      on C and Valera, respectively, both published by
      Gredos in 1968. Valera, in his correspondence,
      could be as harsh as C, even though publicly he
      was benevolent or evasive, in order not to make
      any enemies. Valera favored Renaissance poetry to
      medieval poetry, and denied any French influence
      since the 18th century. Contrary to popular be-
      lief, C did find defects in Zola, Galdós, Eche-
      garay, and Campoamor. Comparison between EPB,
      MMP, C, and Valera as the top Spanish critics of
      the 19th century.

372. Mazzeo, Guido E. "La voluntad ajena en Los pazos
      de Ulloa y La Regenta." DHR, IV (1965): 153-
      61.

      A study of the influence exerted upon Ana
      Ozores and Víctor Quintanar by doña Camila, Ana's
      two aunts, Tomás Crespo (Frígilis), Visitación,
      don Fermín, Alvaro Mesía, and even don Víctor's
      servants. Among the secondary characters, doña
      Paula dominates her son Fermín; Clarín's anger at
      this type of domineering person can be seen in Dr.
      Somoza's words to Fermín in LR, 1947, pp. 182-83.

373. ---. "The Banquet Scene in La Regenta, A Case of
      Sacrilege." Rom N, X, 1 (Autumn, 1968): 68-
      72.

      The banquet honoring don Pompeyo Guimarán,
      the town atheist in LR, is seen by Mazzeo as a
      decidedly irreverent and sacrilegious caricature
      of the Last Supper.

374. McBride, Charles A. "Afinidades espirituales y
      estilísticas entre Unamuno y Clarín." CCU,
      XIX (1969): 5-15.

      Ideological and stylistic similarities be-
      tween Unamuno and Clarín (autobiographical fea-
      tures, the child figure, search for faith, cosmo-
      logical rather than sociological framework, etc.),
      particularly as reflected in Superchería, DB,
      "Cambio de luz," etc.

375. ---. "Alienation from Self in the Short Fiction
      of Leopoldo Alas, Clarín." Homenaje a Casal-
      duero: Crítica y poesía. Ed. Rizel Pincus
      Sigele y Gonzalo Sobejano. Madrid: Gredos,
      1972. 379-87.

Self-alienation as portrayed by the characters in "Zurita," "Las dos cajas," "El entierro de la sardina," "La Reina Margarita," and Supercheria. For social alienation, see Thompson's article, "Egoism and Alienation . . ."

376. ---. "Literary Idealism in Clarín's Creation and Setting." CH, II, 2 (1980): 149-56.

Doña Berta, Supercheria, and other stories reveal C's tendency "to temper the realistic-naturalistic doctrine of the faithful reproduction of reality with a propensity to follow the dictates of the subjective realm of imagination and feeling."

377. Medina, Jeremy T. Spanish Realism: The Theory and Practice of a Concept in the Nineteenth Century. Potomac, Maryland: José Porrúa Turanzas, 1979. 374 pp.

The most ambitious attempt in English to study this subject in eight major novelists and their masterpieces. For Clarín, see especially pp. 189-221. Reviewed by Kay Engler in Sym, XXXVI (1982): 187-89; J. H. Hoddie in REH, XVII, 2 (Mayo, 1983): 317-18; R. B. Klein in Hispania, 65 (March, 1982): 144-45; Stephen Miller in Anales Galdosianos, XVIII (1983): 153-55.

378. Melcón, Mary Luz. "La Regenta: contrafigura de Carmen." CHA, CXXXIX, 415 (Enero, 1985): 5-11.

379. Melón Fernández, Santiago. "La generación del Carbayón y la Revista de Asturias." CN, II, 7 (Mayo-junio, 1981): 104-08.

In 1879 this generation (Alas, Aramburu, PV, Buylla, Fermín Canella, etc.) founded the Revista de Asturias, which could be divided into four thematic sections. Among the contributors were Clarín, Galdós, and PV. The "carbayón" refers to the symbolic tree of Asturias. Illustrations in Melón's article include photos of Aramburu and Canella.

380. Melón Ruiz de Gordejuela, Santiago. "Clarín y el Bovarysmo." Archivum, II, 1 (Enero-abril, 1952): 69-87.

Flaubert's novel is based on an actual case. The meaning of bovarysmo. The psychosomatic story of Ana Ozores. Psycological differences between Emma and Ana, Charles and don Víctor, and the lovers.

381.   Mendoza, Carlos. "Bibliografía: Su único hijo."
        Il Ib, IX, 448 (1 Agosto 1891): 482-83.

    The reviewer detects "a river of bitterness
and deepest sorrow" between the lines of this novel about provincial life and morals. A highly
favorable review of this novela de salón describing the decrepit, paralyzed soul of fin de siècle
Spain.

382.   Menéndez Arranz, Juan. "Clarín y don Marcelino."
        IAL, X, 95-96 (Nov.-dic., 1956): 8-9.

    Possibly the same article which appeared in
Cultura (El Salvador), IX (1956): 128-41.

383.   ---. "Documentos para la historia de la litera-
        tura: Unamuno juzgado por Clarín." IAL, XI,
        105-06 (Oct.-Nov., 1957): 8-9.

    After a brief introduction, Arranz reproduces
the full text of C's "Revista literaria" on Tres
ensayos from the 7 May 1900 issue of Los Lunes de
El Imparcial.

384.   ---. Clarín y Valle-Inclán." IAL, XIII, 127
        (Agosto, 1959): 20 y 10.

    Reproduces the text of C's "palique" on Epi-
talamio (MC, 24 Sept. 1897), which had escaped
Melchor Fernández Almagro's attention in Vida y
literatura de Valle-Inclán. Clarín recognized
Valle's talent but called him "un muchacho extraviado, decidor, de fantasía," while Navarro
Ledesma was "un gazmoño."

385.   Menéndez y Pelayo, Marcelino. Epistolario. Ed.
        Manuel Revuelta Sañudo. Madrid: Fundación
        Universitaria Española, 1982- .

    These invaluable volumes, still in progress,
contain MMP's private opinion of C. Example from
Vol. 4, p. 332: "He leído la insulsa crítica de
Clarín. Y no porque él sea tonto, sino porque la
pasión política le ciega. Es un condiscípulo mío
. . . discreto y gracioso a veces; pero demagogo e
impío como un diablo, y muy aficionado a carne de
clérigo" (27 Agosto 1880).

386.   Meregalli, Franco. "Da Clarín a Unamuno." Annali
        di Ca'Foscari (Venecia), IV (1965): 77-85.

    Reprinted in his book, Parole nel tempo: Stu-
di su scrittori spagnoli del novecento (Milano,
1969), pp. 11-24.

387. ---. Clarín and Unamuno: Parallels and Divergencies." <u>Unamuno, Creator and Creation</u>. Ed. José Rubia Barcia and M. A. Zeitlin. Los Angeles: U of California P, 1967. 156-70.

Clarín's influence on Unamuno can be seen in <u>Amor y pedagogía</u> and <u>El espejo de la muerte</u>. Unamuno was particularly impressed by "La conversión de Chiripa." Both men were congenial and shared several characteristics in common--fear of death, individualism, love for family, deep-rooted provincialism, absolute need for sincerity, etc., but Unamuno had a stronger personality.

388. Milazzo, Elena. "Modernità ed esemplarità di Clarín (Leopoldo Alas)." <u>Cenobio</u>, IV (1956): 461-66.

389. Miller, Martha LaFollette. "Oppositions and Their Subversion in Clarín's <u>La rosa de oro</u>." <u>MLS</u>, XII, 3 (Summer, 1982): 99-109.

Structure, treatment of duality, opposition, in this short story.

390. Miquel y Badía, Francisco. "<u>Teresa</u>, ensayo dramático por D. Leopoldo Alas." <u>Diario de Barcelona</u>, 18 Junio 1895.

<u>Teresa</u> lacks dramatic emotion. Most of its scenes are brutal and repugnant, as if taken from a socialist newspaper calling for a clash between social classes. Reprinted in Romero's ed. of <u>Teresa</u>, pp. 180-85.

391. Miralles, Andrés. "Clarín." <u>El Correo</u> (M), Nov. 1887.

Attacks C for praising mediocre authors, such as PV. C's reply and defense of PV appeared in <u>MC</u>, VII, 248 (19 Nov. 1887): 6.

392. ---. <u>De mi cosecha</u>. Madrid: Sáenz de Jubera, 1891. 276 pp.

In "La revista de Clarín" (pp. 161-75), signed Agosto de 1890, Miralles comments on C's disagreement with <u>La España Moderna</u>, his "folleto" on Campoamor's <u>Poética</u>, and EPB's latest novels (<u>Morriña</u>, <u>Insolación</u>, <u>Una cristiana</u>), which Miralles considers "tres latas de primer orden." According to Miralles, Alas was too soft on EPB this time.

393.   Miralles, Enrique. <u>La novela española de la Restauración (1875-1885): Sus formas y enuncia-
dos narrativos</u>. Barcelona: Puvill, 1979.
331 pp.

Arranged by topics (el galán, la dama, el
obstáculo en el asunto político, diálogos, cartas,
descripción del objeto, etc.) for 36 novels by
seven major authors. Unfortunately, the absence
of an index makes it difficult to locate specific
references to <u>LR</u>. Does not take <u>SUH</u> into con-
sideration.

394.   Miranda García, Soledad. <u>Religión y clero en la
gran novela española del siglo XIX</u>. Madrid:
Ediciones Pegaso, 1982. 281 pp.

Contains: "La crítica del misticismo en
Palacio Valdés y Clarín," pp. 51-55; "Personaliza-
ción y praxis del mensaje religioso: La postura de
dos asturianos: Palacio Valdés y Clarín," pp. 106-
116; and "Un regeneracionismo original, Clarín,"
p. 164. The second segment examines the subject
through the stories "El frío del Papa," "Viaje
redondo," "Un grabado," and "Cambio de luz."

395.   Montes Huidobro, Matías. "Riqueza estilística de
<u>La Regenta</u>." <u>REH</u>, III, 1 (Abril, 1969): 43-
59.

A well-organized study of various tecniques:
"Disolvencias, desdoblamientos, saltos en el espacio y en el tiempo, los objetos (tacto y sonido
también) como vehículos de las emociones y expresión de estados subjetivos . . . haciendo uso
evidente de su humor satírico." Ana Ozores is one
of the great feminine characters of the Spanish
19th century. "<u>La Regenta</u> podría ser en sí misma
un curso de civilización. Allí aparecen reunidos:
misticismo, ascetismo, realismo, idealismo, romanticismo, naturalismo, catolicismo, paganismo . . .
Es la novela de un hombre culto que revierte en la
ficción todas las integrantes literarias que hay
dentro de él."

396.   ---. "Leopoldo Alas: El amor, unidad y pluridad
en el estilo." <u>Archivum</u>, XIX (1969): 207-20.

An analysis of C's style in <u>AC</u>, which Montes
believes can be divided into three parts. Reprinted in MC's anthology, <u>LAC</u>, pp. 253-62.

397.   ---. "<u>Su único hijo</u>: Sinfónico avatar de Clarín."
<u>Archivum</u>, XXII (1972): 149-209.

A 61-page interpretation of the sensual and sexual. "Lo erótico-musical es clave esencial de la obra . . . Su juego novelesco (de Bonifacio Reyes) es un constante _avatar_, nombre, en la India, de las encarnaciones del Visnú . . . Lo musical, lo teatral, lo humorístico, lo disonante, lo sensorial, todo funciona en múltiples ocasiones en relación con las ambigüedades del sexo que resultan inquietantes y que, al parecer, mucho inquietaban al novelista."

398.   Morote, Luis. "_La Regenta_." _La Opinión_ (Palma de Mallorca), 16 Oct. 1885.

C's portrait of a provincial town is quite accurate and complete. Ana should have fallen into the arms of Fermín, not Alvaro. As a psychological study of a woman, as a social study of a city, Alas may not have an equal among contemporary Spanish novelists. Reproduced in Beser's _Clarín y La Regenta_, pp. 303-09.

399.   Navarrete, Rosina D. "Análisis algebraico de un retrato." _ExTL_, I, 2 (1973): 125-28.

An "algebraic analysis" of José Ronzal, the "Trabuco" of _LR_, with the use of numerals, letters, and arrows in different directions.

400.   Navarro, Felipe Benicio. "_La Regenta_: Roman de Léopold Alás." _Revue Britannique_ (Paris), LXII, 9 (Sept., 1886): 139-51.

A favorable review, translated into French by G. de Frézals. Clarín himself made a brief reference to this article in a letter to Picón; see Amorós' article, "Doce cartas . . ." Apparently Navarro published the same article in _Le Temps_ (Paris), 11 Oct. 1886, p. 3.

401.   Navarro Adriaensens, José M. "Leopoldo Alas y su actitud ante la lengua." _ALE_, II (1983): 399-407.

402.   Navarro y Ledesma, Francisco. Cartas abiertas, I. Al señor Clarín en Vetusta." _El Globo_ (M), 1 Feb. 1889.

See the 6 Feb. 1889 issue for the second "Carta." Reportedly Navarro also wrote on C in the 14 Aug. and 25 Sept. issues.

403.   ---. "Batir de alas." _Gedeón_ (M), No. 69 (4 Marzo 1897), No. 70 (11 Marzo 1897), No. 72 (25 Marzo 1897), No. 73 (1 Abril 1897), y No. 76 (23 Abril 1897).

The references to Clarín had begun in "De ojeo," No. 63 (21 Enero 1897). In the 4 March 1897 issue, Navarro denies Clarín's statement that Urrecha had rejected several of Navarro's articles for El Imparcial. For brief description of this polemic, see Zulueta's Navarro Ledesma, pp. 128-31.

404.   ---. "Clarín: Apuntes para un estudio psicográfico." LL, II, 9 (Sept., 1901): 361-70.

C was restless, impulsive, sad; a man who wanted to know about everything. He was wrong in his judgment of Cánovas and Zola. C thought that literature was or ought to be everything in life; he could never have befriended a person who could not write well. Errors of grammar and syntax, according to C, should be punishable under the Penal Code. He either had not read Gustave Planche's study on hatred in literature, or paid no attention to it.

405.   Neira Martínez, Jesús. "La función del disparate lingüístico y del dialectalismo en La Regenta." CN, V, 23 (Enero-feb., 1984): 60-63.

The linguistic element in the characterization of Ronzal, Alvaro, Frígilis, Visita, Bismarck, Celedonio, etc. Clarín did not write the novel in bable because Spanish was the language of Clarín and most of his characters.

406.   Nelson, Jeanne P. "Développement du thème en fonction de la structure dans El sustituto de Leopoldo Alas (Clarín)." Rom N, XIII (1971): 262-65.

This story is divided into two distinct temporal spheres--the narrative past in which Eleuterio remembers what he has done to Ramón, and the narrative future in which he goes to find Ramón in order to absolve his guilt. These two spheres are divided by a narrative present in which we see Eleuterio remembering his past injustices. This same division can be applied to the antitheses egotism/abnegation and cowardice/ courage which mark the evolution of Eleuterio's character.

407.   Nimetz, Michael. "Eros and Ecclesia in Clarín's Vetusta." MLN, LXXXVI, 2 (March, 1971): 242-53.

Vetusta is a city in which sex and religion occupy the same shrine and neutralize one another in the process. Sexual ambiguity in Ana, Celedo-

nio, Obdulia, De Pas, Saturnino, etc. Except for
Ana, the women of LR seem to be innately perverse.

408.   Noval Fernández, Francisco. "Vetusta, Clarín,
       Frígilis (Aproximación a La Regenta)." BIEA,
       XXVI, 77 (Sept.-dic., 1972): 743-63.

       "Vetusta" would have been a more appropriate
       title for this novel. Frígilis, a secondary char-
       acter, becomes more important in the last two
       chapters; everybody considers him crazy, but he is
       the only one who manages to "escape."

409.   Ochoa, Juan. "Teresa." RCHL, I, 2 (Abril, 1895):
       61-62.

       The characterization of Teresa and Roque was
       good, but the audience sensed the absence of "a-
       rrequives y artificios exigidos en el teatro."
       Reprod. in David Torres' article, "Juan Ochoa
       escribe . . ."

410.   O'Connor, Dolores Jeanne. "The Telescoping of
       Time in Clarín's Su único hijo." Rom N,
       XXIII, 2 (Winter, 1982): 134-39.

       The problem of the imprecise location and
       time of this novel. The explanation probably lies
       in Alas' desire to "sum up the experience under-
       gone, in fact, by two generations in one indi-
       vidual's experience, again in consideration of the
       likelihood that the dramatic impact of such tele-
       scoping would be more intense."

411.   Oleza, Juan. "Introducción" a La Regenta. Ma-
       drid: Cátedra, 1984. 2 vols.

       Follows the text of the second (1900) edi-
       tion. Discusses realism/naturalism from a Marxist
       ideology. Well-documented, lengthy study of C's
       thought since early years. For comparison with
       editions by BG, MC, and Sobejano, see Martínez-
       Torrón's article.

412.   ---. La novela del XIX: Del parto a la crisis de
       una ideología. Barcelona: Editorial Laia,
       1984. 246 pp.

       For Clarín, see Chap. 7, pp. 147-235; for LR,
       pp. 186-235. Nothing on SUH. No bibliography.

413.   ---. "La Regenta y el mundo del joven Clarín."
       Clarín y su obra. Ed. Antonio Vilanova.
       Barcelona: U de Barcelona, 1985. 163-80.

414.   Oller, Narcís. <u>Memòries literàries: Història dels
       meus llibres</u>. Pròleg de Gaziel. Barcelona:
       Editorial Aedos, 1962. 434 pp.

       C had always urged Oller to write in Spanish
       because Catalan "le crispaba los nervios." Oller
       describes to José Lázaro his displeasure at seeing
       his "Novenari d'ànimes" published in <u>El Imparcial</u>
       and in a volume called <u>Novelas y caprichos</u>, even
       though he had sent the manuscript to Clarín two
       years before, for translation into Spanish and
       publication in <u>La España Moderna</u>. Pages 126-28
       reproduce a "palique" by C on Catalan writers and
       the story in question, "La novena de las ánimas,"
       translated into Spanish by Pereda and published in
       <u>EM</u>. Reviewed by Albert Manent in <u>Insula</u>, XVII,
       188-89 (Julio-agosto, 1962): 21.

415.   Opisso, Alfredo. "Bibliografía: <u>El señor y lo de-
       más son cuentos</u>." <u>Il Ib</u>, XI, 557 (2 Sept.
       1893): 558.

       A brief and favorable review, reprod. by MC
       in his article, "Una opinión sobre <u>El Señor</u> . . ."

416.   ---. "Bibliografía: <u>Teresa</u>, ensayo dramático
       . . . por Leopoldo Alas." <u>Il Ib</u>, XIII, 644
       (4 Mayo 1895): 282-83.

       This play should have had three acts. Other
       defects: insistence on hunger, triteness of the
       character named Roque and the drunkenness scene,
       and the improper ending. The characterization of
       Teresa is good, but the audience probably expected
       a class struggle or social problem instead of a
       <u>Mater Dolorosa</u>.

417.   Orlando. "Revista literaria: <u>La Regenta</u>, por D.
       Leopoldo Alas." <u>RE</u>, CVI, 421 (Sept.-oct.,
       1885): 124-43.

       <u>LR</u> is both a psychological and a social
       study. Analysis of Ana and Fermín. Psychologic-
       ally, Fermín is the best character. While some
       readers may find the second volume tedious, it is
       probably because of "la poca costumbre que existe
       entre nosotros de leer libros de este género, se-
       rios, concienzudos, cuyo interés no radica princi-
       palmente en hechos y escenas llenas de luz y co-
       lor, sino más adentro, en el corazón y en la mé-
       dula del individuo y de la sociedad." Of the mi-
       nor characters, doña Paula is the best. This no-
       vel "por su fondo y por su forma es la mejor de
       nuestra literatura contemporánea." Reprod. by N.
       M. Valis in "Dos artículos olvidados . . ."

418.   Ortega, José.   "Don Fermín de Pas: De superbia et
       concupiscentia catholicis."   <u>REH</u>, IX, 3
       (Oct., 1975): 323-42.

       The treatment of this character reflects
       Spain's late 19th century religious crisis as it
       related to krausismo, rationalism, Catholicism,
       and especially the conflict of liberal and bour-
       geois conceptions.   Fermín is a study of a member
       of the Church, his ambition, and his neurosis and
       psychosis in relation to the sexual problem pos-
       ited by his counterpart, Ana.

419.   Ortega, Soledad.   <u>Cartas a Galdós</u>.   Madrid: Revis-
       ta de Occidente, 1964.   454 pp.

       Pages 209-96 reproduce the text of 75 letters
       from C to Galdós dated between 27 March 1879 and
       17 May 1901, on such subjects as <u>Tormento</u>, <u>Lo pro-
       hibido</u>, Galdós' high praise for <u>LR</u>, Pereda (whom C
       met in June, 1885), derogatory remarks on Luis Al-
       fonso, favorable opinion of Felipe B. Navarro, <u>Re-
       alidad</u>, and <u>Los condenados</u>.

420.   Ortega Munilla, José.   "<u>Doña Berta</u>, por Leopoldo
       Alas (Clarín)."   <u>El Imparcial</u> (M), 29 Feb.
       1892.

421.   Pabst, W.   "Clarín: Naturalismus und irrationales
       Weltbild."   <u>Die Neueren Sprachen</u> (Marburg-
       Frankfurt), XLI, 4 (May-June, 1933): 202-11.

422.   Padrós de Palacios, Esteban.   "Introducción" a <u>La
       Regenta</u>.   Col. Círculo de Lectores.   Barce-
       lona, 1968.

423.   Palls, Byron P.   "El naturalismo de <u>La Regenta</u>."
       <u>NRFH</u>, XXI, 1 (1972): 23-39.

       "No se muestra seguidor del naturalismo sino
       en el empleo del tema del adulterio, en el pante-
       ísmo de Frígilis . . . y en la idea de que el me-
       dio ambiente es el causante de una vida estancada
       y frustrada . . . es naturalista pero no desde el
       punto de vista filosófico . . . sino por su técni-
       ca estética."

424.   Palmerín de Oliva.   "Palabras y plumas."   <u>RC</u>,
       LXXVI (30 Dic. 1889): 647-50.

       According to Palmerín, <u>RCT</u> consists of 10 ar-
       ticles published in <u>MC</u>, difficult to judge until
       the second part appears.   He disagrees with the
       "dictator" Clarín that Luis Eguilaz, Florentino
       Sanz, and Gil y Zárate were fools or "calamities."
       The author's real name was Luis Ruiz Contreras

(q.v.); he also wrote about C in his Memorias de un desmemoriado.

425.   ---.   "Palabras y plumas: Importancia literaria de Clarín." RC, LXXVII (15 Feb. 1890): 307-17.

Palmerín was writing a seven-chapter study on EPB when he read C's "Revista mínima" in La Publi-cidad de Barcelona, 30 Oct. 1889.   Clarín, like EPB, has awakened an interest in new books. Since Daniel Cortezo's plan for a series called "Nove-listas Españoles Contemporáneos" was not too suc-cessful, Palmerín proposes a series of French translations in which EPB would translate the Gon-court brothers, and C would translate Zola. (EPB had already worked on Los hermanos Zemganno, but C's translation of Travail did not appear until 1901).

426.   Panebianco, Candido.   "Personaggi e problematica ne La Regenta."   SGym, XXIII, 1-2 (1970): 158-74.

427.   Pardo Bazán, Emilia.   "Nota bibliográfica: Mez-clilla." EM, I (Feb., 1889): 185-90.

Points out the dual character (serious and humorous) of C's style and calls him "un alma tan dolorida y . . . una complexión tan neuro-bilio-sa."   C's attacks on Cánovas are unjust. Praises "A muchos y a ninguno," "Lecturas," "Baudelaire," and "Quintilius."   Notices C's pessimism, and his unconditional admiration for the maestros such as Zorrilla.   May Clarín continue to stop Zola's me-diocre imitators, but his nerves probably will not allow it.

428.   Pedraza Jiménez, Felipe B. y Milagros Rodríguez Cáceres.   Manual de literatura española, VII: Epoca del Realismo.   Tafalla (Navarra): Cénlit Ediciones, 1983.

The section on Clarín (pp. 784-839) discusses in great detail his life and works, taking into account the latest major studies.   Included are segments on narrative techniques, style, and ideas of LR, SUH, and numerous novelettes and short stories.

429.   Pelegrín, Benito.   "Doña Ana en la cama, la regen-ta en el diván." Cahiers d'Etudes Romanes, V (1979): 139-66.

430.   Peña, Vidal.   "Algunas retóricas de La Regenta." CN, II, 7 (Mayo-junio, 1981): 36-42.

431. Peña M., Nicolás. "Leopoldo Alas (Clarín)." La
     Revista de Chile (Santiago), VI (Enero-junio,
     1901): 246-48.

     A previously unreported obituary calling Alas
     a good stylist even though Clarín "andaba a trope-
     zones con la frase castellana" in his preface to
     Resurrección and in his article on Trabajo in La
     Lectura. Peña quotes from his own review of Ica-
     za's Examen de críticos in La Libertad Electoral.
     C's defects: the virulence of his language, his
     constant attacks on Cánovas and the Academy, his
     excessive use of italics, and his ill-will toward
     Latin American writers.

432. Penzol, Pedro. "Parentescos." Archivum, II, 3
     (Sept.-dic., 1952): 421-26.

     Suggests a parallel between LR, Hugo's Notre-
     Dame de Paris (1832), and Zola's La faute de
     l'abbé Mouret (1875).

433. Percival, Anthony. "Sexual Irony and Power in Su
     único hijo." La Chispa. Ed. Gilbert Paoli-
     ni. New Orleans: Tulane U, 1983. 221-29.

434. Perés, R. D. "Un drama de Clarín." La Vanguardia
     (B), 13 Abril 1895: 4.

     This long article by the Catalan poet and
     critic, Ramón Domingo Perés y Perés, has never
     been mentioned by clarinistas. The audience of
     Teresa was "un público refractario en parte y, en
     parte también, insuficientemente preparado para
     saborearla," but the play in book form seems to be
     better appreciated. The Spanish public apparently
     is not ready for innovations such as those intro-
     duced by Maeterlinck and Hauptmann. Clarín's ob-
     jective seems to be "presentar el amor-egoísmo co-
     mo inferior al amor-deber, y a éste último como
     ideal de la vida y consuelo de la infinita mise-
     ria, del infinito dolor humano." Teresa and her
     husband are more impressive characters than Rita
     or Fernando. The public probably misinterpreted
     Fernando's intentions. The style, theme, and set-
     ting remind Perés of Hauptmann as well as Guime-
     rá's María Rosa.

435. Pérez de Ayala, Ramón. "El paisaje en Clarín."
     Obras completas. Madrid: Aguilar, 1964.

     See Vol. I, pp. 1113-17, for this piece dated
     1906, with no indication of where it first ap-
     peared. Page 1153 contains a shorter piece enti-
     tled simply "Clarín." The poet and novelist Pérez
     de Ayala was a student of Prof. Alas in Oviedo.

436.   ---. "Clarín y D. Leopoldo Alas." Prólogo a <u>Doña Berta, Cuervo, Superchería</u>. Buenos Aires: Emecé, 1942. 7-26.

C's naive interpretation of Renan. Echegaray and C were among the first to introduce Nietzsche into Spain. According to Ayala, C was small and thin, all bones and nerves, with blondish, almost reddish hair. Reprod. in <u>Archivum</u>, II, 1 (1952): 5-21 and in his book, <u>Amistades y recuerdos</u> (Barcelona, 1961), pp. 11-30. Also found in the Taurus 1970 ed. of <u>Superchería</u>, pp. 9-30.

437.   ---. "Los novelistas españoles y Clarín." <u>ABC</u>, 3 Junio 1952.

Of Spain's seven major novelists in the 19th century, only C had to write for a living. He would have preferred to write only novels and short stories, instead of hundreds of newspaper articles. Reprinted in Ayala's <u>Amistades y recuerdos</u>, pp. 30-34.

438.   ---. "Clarín, Valera y Menéndez Pelayo." <u>ABC</u>, 12 Sept. 1957.

According to Ayala, Clarín took his pseudonym from Calderón's <u>La vida es sueño</u>. C used to spend his summers in Carrió or Candás. At that time Madrid had two serious critics (Valera, MMP) and two minor ones (Revilla, Valbuena). Reprinted in his <u>Amistades y recuerdos</u>, pp. 9-11.

439.   Pérez de Castro, José Luis. <u>Huella y presencia de Asturias en el Uruguay</u>. Montevideo: Centro Asturiano de Montevideo, 1960. 110 pp.

Literary relations between Clarín, Rodó, and Pérez Petit. C's imitator in Montevideo, Jorge Carbonell, known as Valbuenita, wrote some "paliques gramaticales" for <u>El Ideal</u> during 1921.

440.   ---. "El magisterio de Clarín en la literatura uruguaya." <u>Archivum</u>, XIII (1963): 234-76.

C as seen by Rodó, Torrendell, and Pérez Petit. Reproduces correspondence between C and Rodó. Criticism of <u>Ariel</u>. C's influence on Rodó and Pérez Petit.

441.   Pérez Galdós, Benito. "Prólogo" a <u>La Regenta</u>. Madrid: Librería de Fernando Fé, 1900.

Galdós' 15-page introd. to the second edition, dated Madrid, Enero de 1901, considers <u>LR</u>

"muestra feliz del Naturalismo restaurado . . .
Picaresca es en cierto modo . . . lo que no ex-
cluye en ella la seriedad, en el fondo y en la
forma, ni la descripción acertada de los más gra-
ves estados del alma humana . . . de una lengua
que no tiene semejante en la expresión equívoca ni
en la gravedad socarrona." Ana de Ozores' problem, according to don Benito, "no es otro que dis-
cernir si debe perderse por lo clerical o por lo
laico," a national symbol.   Among the best pages
of LR is the presentation of Fermín de Pas' youth
and his mother.

442.   Pérez Gutiérrez, Francisco.   El problema religioso
       en la Generación de 1868.   Madrid: Taurus,
       1975.   378 pp.

       See pp. 269-338 for an exhaustive study of
       Clarín's religious ideas, gleaned from all his
       published novels, stories, essays, and letters.

443.   Pérez Minik, Domingo.   Novelistas españoles de los
       siglos XIX y XX.   Madrid: Ediciones Guadarra-
       ma, 1957.   348 pp.

       See "Revisión de Leopoldo Alas, Clarín" (pp.
       131-55) for a brief survey of criticism on Alas
       from Azorín, who never read LR ("con sus mil pági-
       nas, intolerables para un escritor impresionista")
       to Valbuena Prat, who devotes less than 20 pages
       to Clarín.   LR is much more than costumbrismo or
       novela regional.   How C's humor differs from that
       of Dickens or major French novelists.

444.   Pérez Petit, Víctor.   Lecturas.   Montevideo: Clau-
       dio García Editores, 1942.   343 pp.

       Chap. 3, entitled "A propósito de los pa-
       liques de Clarín" (pp. 107-43) describes the ar-
       ticles as humorous but intellectual, and agrees
       with Clarín's low opinion of Cavestany, Retes,
       Grilo, Suárez Bravo, Rubí, etc.   This article ap-
       peared originally in La Revista Nacional of Monte-
       video.   Lecturas is Vol. 4 of his OC.

445.   Phillips, Allen W.   "Nueva luz sobre Clarín y Gó-
       mez Carrillo."   RABM, LXXXI, 4 (Oct.-dic.,
       1978): 757-79.

       Although Clarín was very severe with Rubén
       Darío and other new authors, he wrote favorably
       about Carrillo's Esquisses (1892) and Sensaciones
       de arte (1893), and wrote an introd. to Almas y
       cerebros (1898).   Clarín admired Carrillo's ef-
       forts to propagate foreign literature in Spain but
       questioned some of his literary tastes.

446.   Picón, Jacinto Octavio.   "La Regenta."   El Correo
        (M), 15 Marzo 1885.

        Describes the setting, plot, and character-
        ization of Vol. 1 of LR.   Reprinted by Amorós in
        "Doce cartas inéditas . . ." and by Valis in "Dos
        artículos olvidados . . ."

447.   Polo de Bernabé, José Manuel.   "Mito y símbolo en
        la estructuración narrativa de La Regenta."
        PSA, Año 17, LXVIII, 203 (Feb., 1973): 121-
        40.

        C uses "a lo largo de la obra el símbolo y el
        mito literario como un juego de reflejos o espe-
        jismos por medio de los cuales nos hace penetrar
        en las conciencias de los personajes y en el tiem-
        po síquico de la acción."

448.   Posada, Adolfo.   "Escritos inéditos de Clarín."
        LL, VI, 3 (1906): 211-16.

        Posada, who knew Alas for 20 years, takes a
        look at the incomplete manuscript of "Juanito
        Reseco" (begun around 1875), three pages of "Tam-
        bor y gaita," and several pages of "Una medianía,"
        "El infame burgués," "Quijada," "El libro y el ve-
        rano," "Esperaindeo," "Meeting monstruo (novela
        idealista)," "Cánovas Malaparte," "Exámenes," "La
        millonaria," and a novel without title.   Also, two
        small volumes of "Juan Ruiz, periódico humorís-
        tico," written between 8 March 1868 and 14 Jan.
        1869.

449.   ---.   Autores y libros.   Valencia: Sampere, 1909.
        256 pp.

        Contains: "El Quijote y Clarín," pp. 164-67;
        "Escritos inéditos de Clarín," pp. 168-76; and "De
        Alas adentro," pp. 235-38.

450.   ---.   España en crisis.   La política.   Madrid: Ca-
        ro Reggio, 1923.   216 pp.

        Clarín as thinker and educator, pp. 185-99.
        Reproduces an unpublished letter of 22 July
        (1894?) in which C discloses that Galdós and María
        Guerrero had encouraged him to write a play.   He
        finished Teresa in 12 days (based on a girl he
        knew) and sent a copy to Echegaray before telling
        anyone else about the play.   Reprinted in MC's
        anthology, LAC, pp. 34-42.

451.   ---.   Fragmentos de mis memorias.   Prólogo de
        Emilio Alarcos Llorach.   Oviedo: U de Oviedo,
        1983.   363 pp.

For notes on how Posada met Clarín, see pp. 103-04; C and Ihering, pp. 116-17; C as teacher, pp. 178-81; C's influence, pp. 189-91; C and Ordóñez, pp. 210-04; C and Sela, pp. 207-08; C and real-life Zurita, pp. 212-14; C and LR, pp. 215-19; C's death, pp. 264-65.

452.   Prat de la Riba y Sarrá, Enric.   Per la llengua catalana. Barcelona, 1918.   9-46.

453.   Proaño, Franklin.   "Ascesis y misticismo en Ana Ozores."   BIEA, XXVI, 77 (Sept.-dic., 1972): 765-82.

454.   ---.   "Presencia y problemática del 'yo' en los personajes de Clarín."   BIEA, XXVII (1973): 549-75.

455.   ---.   "Cambios de identidad en Ana Ozores."   NRFH, XXIII, 1 (1974): 115-21.

456.   ---.   "Tricotomías del 'yo' en los personajes de Clarín."   BIEA, XXVIII (1974): 313-21.

This plurality can be found only in Ana Ozores, Bonifacio Reyes, and Doña Berta.

457.   ---.   "Dicotomías en los personajes de Leopoldo Alas."   BIEA, XXIX, 84-85 (Enero-Agosto, 1975): 65-75.

The analysis of "the other self" can be formulated on the basis of four mental restrictions: intellectual, spiritual, moral, and imaginative.

458.   ---.   "Religious and Secular Aspects of Leopoldo Alas, Clarín."   UDR, XIII, 3 (Spring, 1979): 27-31.

Describes C as "a religious and secular man, a writer full of reticence, opposition, and innovation." His originality consisted of trying to unite and synthesize new and traditional elements.

459.   ---.   "El Yo y su doble en los personajes de Leopoldo Alas."   BIEA, XXXV, 104 (Sept.-dic., 1981): 723-31.

460.   Rabassa, Gregory.   "Padrões de frustração e impotência em La Regenta."   TB, IV, 7 (Oct., 1965): 107-118.

Frustration and impotence can be found in almost all of the characters. Quintanar and Mesía have "interior limitations," while Fermín is limited by "external elements." The "amortajada" Doña Paula may well represent the Church and tradition. The Germán incident, which serves as leit-motiv of frustration, reminds Rabassa of Asdrúbal in Rómulo Gallegos' Doña Bárbara.

461.   Ramos-Gascón, Antonio.   "Clarín y el primer Unamuno."   DHR, X (1971): 129-38.

Comments on Unamuno's 10 letters (1895-1900) from Epistolario a Clarín. Calls attention to Unamuno's indirect references to Alas in "Sobre el marasmo actual" (En torno al casticismo).

462.   ---.   "Introducción" a Clarín, obra olvidada. Madrid: Ediciones Júcar, 1973. 264 pp.

A 23-page introd. precedes this anthology of 24 "minor" paliques on Spanish authors (EPB, Salvador Rueda, Valera, Valle Inclán, etc.), 10 on foreign authors (Nietzsche, Tolstoy, Zola, Verlaine, etc.), and five on "crítica higiénica." None on Galdós, as these are available elsewhere. All are reprinted here for the first time, except the one on El sabor de la tierruca, which Beser had reprod. in Teoría y crítica de la novela española (1972). Reviewed by D'Auria.

463.   ---.   "Relaciones Clarín-Martínez Ruiz, 1897-1900."   HR, XLII, 4 (Autumn, 1974): 413-26.

A scholarly study tracing their literary relations from Martínez Ruiz's days as "anarquista literario" to "liberal prometedor." Says Ramos-Gascón: "La publicación de Alma castellana vino a colaborar las palabras de Clarín; su autor va dejando de ser enfant terrible para convertirse en persona seria y ponderada."

464.   ---.   "Prólogo" a Pipá.   Madrid: Ediciones Cátedra, 1976. 355 pp.

The introd. covers: "Vida y obra de Clarín: Entorno social y mundo estético" (pp. 11-70); a study of "Pipá, colección de cuentos" (pp. 71-97); and "Bibliografía" (pp. 99-102).

465.   Reiss, Katherine.   "Valoración artística de las narraciones breves de Leopoldo Alas desde los puntos de vista estético, técnico y temático."   Archivum, V, 1 (Enero-abril, 1955): 77-126 y Nos. 2-3 (Mayo-dic., 1955): 256-303.

Selections from her doctoral thesis, "Las narraciones breves de Leopoldo Alas Clarín," University of Heidelberg, 1953-54.

466.   Rice, Miriam Wagner.   "The Meaning of Metaphor in
          La Regenta."   REH, XI, 1 (Enero, 1977): 141-
          51.

          The metaphors (implicit or explicit) which
          appear most frequently are those dealing with na-
          ture and the struggle for survival. Birds, ani-
          mals, and the hunt are among the metaphorical com-
          ponents most basic to LR's meaning. Ana is often
          compared to a bird, and the toad is "a recurring
          symbol of a loathsome material reality to which
          Ana is attracted whenever the ideal fails to sus-
          tain her."   C's view of life as "a struggle in
          which any form of spirituality is a weakness like-
          ly to be defeated."

467.   ---.   Vetusta Invertebrada: El particularismo en
          su contexto asturiano."   SAB, XLII, 2 (1977):
          67-75.

          Ortega's ideas in España invertebrada are
          found in LR, where an extremely superficial and
          materialistic society ignores or denies the few
          superior beings such as Ana Ozores, Fortunato Ca-
          moirán, and Frígilis.   "Espiritualmente muerto
          Fermín, invisibles Frígilis y Camoirán, destruída
          Ana, termina la novela sin mejores. ¡Qúe ironía
          de título! La Regenta no reina en esta sociedad
          moral y espiritualmente invertebrada. Reinaba y
          sigue reinando la masa--indócil, hermética, parti-
          cularista."

468.   ---.   "Metaphorical Foreshadowing in La Regenta."
          Hispano, 71 (Enero, 1981): 41-52.

          "One poetic use of setting and action in La
          Regenta is the foreshadowing of major conflicts
          and situations . . . Setting is used poetically to
          foreshadow theme . . . as well as to provide a
          structure for conflicts and states of mind that
          the characters are destined to face and experi-
          ence." Examples: the weather, church buildings,
          the boat incident, Celedonio's kiss, the tele-
          scope, Fermín's constant thirst, etc.

469.   Richmond, Carolyn.   "La polémica Clarín-Bonafoux y
          Flaubert."   Insula, XXXII, 365 (Abril, 1977):
          1 y 12.

          Bonafoux's accusations of plagiarism probably
          grew out of a "palique" (MC, 26 Marzo 1887) in
          which C in general terms severely criticized se-
          veral inferior novelists. The opera scene in SUH
          may be a parody or challenge stemming from this
          polemic. Parallels between Bonifacio Reyes and

Bonafoux, and between Bonifacio and Frédéric Moreau of L'Education sentimentale.

470.   ---.   "A Peristyle without a Roof: Clarín's Su único hijo and its Unfinished Trilogy." Studies in Honor of Ruth Lee Kennedy.   Ed. Vern G. Williamsen and A. F. Michael Atlee. Chapel Hill: Estudios de Hispanófila, 1977. 85-102.

The story of, and the relationship between, SUH and the trilogy ("Una medianía," "Esperaindeo," and "Juanito Reseco") which was supposed to follow it. Alas himself had used the architectural term "peristyle," a range of roof-supporting columns around a building or an open court, to describe the relationship of SUH to "Una medianía." Richmond's article has also appeared in Spanish as "Un peristilo sin techo: Su único hijo de Clarín y su trilogía inacabada" in LT, XXVII, 103-06 (1979): 113-40.

471.   ---.   "La ópera como enlace entre dos obras de Clarín: Amor è furbo y Su único hijo." Insula, XXXIII, 377 (Abril, 1978): 3.

Similarities and differences between the story published in Pipá (1892) and Clarín's second long novel.

472.   ---.   "Introducción" a Su único hijo.   Madrid: Espasa-Calpe, 1970. xi-lxiii.

Discusses the novel's themes and preoccupations. Her presentation of time in the novel makes clear Azorín's interest. The appendices include the extant chapters of "Una medianía" and "Speraindeo," which together with "Juanito Reseco" (a trilogy C never completed) were to present "la vida de una especie de tres mosqueteros psicológicos." Illustrations include a photo of C's wife, Onofre García Argüelles. Reviewed by Bonet, Jackson, Sobejano (q.v.)

473.   ---.   "Clarín y el teatro: El cuento de un crítico." CN, II, 7 (Mayo-junio, 1981): 56-67.

C was very fond of the theater, throughout his life, especially as a boy and after 1890, when he wrote RCT. The second part of Richmond's article consists of a detailed analysis of "La Ronca" (El Liberal, 19 Junio 1893), which was later included in SDC.

474.   ---.   "Un documento (vivo, literario y crítico). Análisis de un cuento de Clarín." BIEA, XXXVI, 105-106 (Enero-agosto, 1982): 367-84.

This story about love, disillusion, and ven-
geance was completed in June, 1882, and included
in Pipá.

475.   ---.   "Un eco de Maupassant en Clarín: El desenlace de Su único hijo."   CN, III, 16 (Nov.-
dic., 1982): 28-33.

476.   ---.   "Prólogo" a Leopoldo Alas Clarín: Treinta
relatos. Madrid: Espasa-Calpe, 1983.   445
pp.

See "Prólogo" (pp. 9-15), "Bibliografía" (pp.
16-22), and "Apéndice" (pp. 444-45.)   The 30 stories are classified into four groups: El escritor
(five stories); Las relaciones interpersonales (14
stories); La religiosidad (six stories); and La
muerte (five stories).   Each group begins with a
brief analysis of the stories included in that
section.   The appendix gives the exact dates of
publication, if known.   Reviewed by Bonet, Thompson (q.v.)

477.   ---.   "El heroísmo irónico de Vetusta."   CN, V, 23
(Enero-feb., 1984): 82-86.

The ironic treatment of "heroism" begins with
the first line of LR ("La heroica ciudad dormía la
siesta") and is most evident in Víctor, Mesía, and
Fermín.

478.   ---.   "Gérmenes de La Regenta en tres cuentos de
Clarín."   Argumentos, VIII, 63-64 (Enero-
feb., 1984): 16-21.

The three stories are: "El diablo en Semana
Santa" (La Unión, 24 Marzo 1880), "El doctor Pértinax (La Publicidad, 8 y 29 Julio 1880), and "Mi
entierro" (La Ilustración Artística, 26 Marzo
1883).

479.   ---.   "La Regenta, mirada y vista."   Insula,
XXXIX, 451 (Junio, 1984): 4.

480.   ---.   "Las dos cajas de Clarín y otras dos de Marsillach: Una fuente literaria desconocida."
HR, LII, 4 (Autumn, 1984): 459-75.

Joaquín Marsillach's short story, "El entierro de un violín" (the text of which is reproduced on pp. 471-75), published in La Ilustración Artística de Barcelona, II, 53 (1 Enero
1883), was probably the source of Clarín's "Las
dos cajas" (June, 1883).   Little is known about
Marsillach, whose book on Richard Wagner was

favorably reviewed by C in <u>El Solfeo</u>, 20 Abril 1878.

481. ---. "Conexiones temáticas y estilísticas entre el libro <u>Pipá</u> y <u>La Regenta</u> de Clarín." <u>Clarín y su obra</u>. Ed. Antonio Vilanova. Barcelona: U de Barcelona, 1985. 229-50.

482. Rico-Avello, Carlos. "Aspectos psicosexuales en <u>La Regenta</u>." <u>BIEA</u>, XXXIX, 116 (Sept.-dic., 1985): 841-72.

Dr. Rico, president of the Spanish Society of Medical Writers, psychoanalyzes Ana Ozores, Fermín de Pas, Alvaro Mesía, and Víctor Quintanar on the basis of the novel itself. Considers Matamoro's conclusions in his <u>CHA</u> article "confusing and unacceptable."

483. Riopérez y Milá, Santiago. <u>Azorín íntegro</u>. Madrid: Editorial Biblioteca Nueva, 1979. 755 pp.

Azorín recalls (pp. 155-60) how he met Clarín in Nov. 1897, at the offices of <u>El Progreso</u>. Asked about "La millonaria," C replied that he had tried very hard to change any similarity with the plot of Echegaray's <u>O locura o santidad</u>. Quotes text of 8 Nov. 1897 letter from Alas enclosing the photo which Azorín had requested.

484. Ríos, Laura de los. "Introducción" a <u>Cuentos de Clarín</u>. Boston: Houghton Mifflin, 1954. xxv + 193 pp.

485. Rivkin, Laura Medelaine. "Extranatural Art in Clarín's <u>Su único hijo</u>." <u>MLN</u>, XCVII, 2 (March, 1982): 311-28.

"Clarín's recurrent use of two literary terms, <u>prosa</u> and <u>poesía</u>, indicates that if <u>Su único hijo</u> is about the creation of life, it is also about the creation of art. We may take these terms to signify the poles of reality and illusion in literary representation, the poles which demarcate the mimesis of a novel . . . although Clarín, like his hero, is a <u>melómano</u> and an addict of melodramatic art, the author of <u>Su único hijo</u> never advocates a labyrinthine story for a high-minded novel. <u>Su único hijo</u> is evidence that what Clarín preaches as good for the novel, is not always what he practices."

486. ---. "Introducción" a <u>Cuesta abajo</u>. Barcelona, 1985. 311 pp.

487.   ---.   Melodramatic Plotting in Clarín's La Regen-
       ta." RQ, XXXIII, 2 (May, 1986): 191-200.

488.   Roberts, Gemma.   "Notas sobre el realismo psicoló-
       gico de La Regenta." Archivum, XVIII (1968):
       189-202.

       An analysis of LR with references to Pérez
       Minik's Novelistas españoles (1957) and Georg
       Lukác's Teorie des Romans (Berlin: Herman Luchter-
       hand Verlag, 1965).   Reprinted in MC's anthology,
       LAC, pp. 194-203.

489.   Rocamora, José.   "Un pensador menos: Leopoldo Alas
       (Clarín)." NT, I, 7 (Julio, 1901): 48-56.

       Denies that Alas plagiarized Flaubert or Fer-
       nanflor.   Zurita is one of the most beautiful,
       original, and profound stories in the Spanish lan-
       guage.   An eye-witness report on C's 1897 lectures
       at the Ateneo.   The first lecture was well attend-
       ed, out of curiosity, but the other four were not,
       because C was not as eloquent as López Muñoz, and
       his audience had never heard of Bergson, Renou-
       vier, Spir, etc.   Later, Clarín explained: "He
       tenido que convertir mis conferencias, por instin-
       to de conversación, en filosofías para literatos y
       señoras, casi casi para niños y soldados."

490.   Rodó, José Enrique.   "La crítica de Clarín." Re-
       vista Nacional de Montevideo, 20 Abril y 5
       Mayo 1895.

       Classifies C's method as "Crítica directa-
       mente literaria . . . impersonal y afirmativa por
       partir de cierta base teórica de criterio y no de
       la veleidad de la impresión" in line with Flau-
       bert's ideas rather than Sainte-Beuve or Taine.
       Since Mezclilla, C's criticism has become broader
       and less "cacería de vocablos." After ER, Rodó
       detects a mystical tone.   Highest praise for C's
       essays on La Terre and La desheredada, "A muchos
       y a ninguno," and the last Folleto literario. Re-
       printed in Rodó's book, El que vendrá (Barcelona:
       Editorial Cervantes, 1920), pp. 30-45 and in his
       OC (1967), pp. 772-78.

491.   ---.   "Correspondencia con Leopoldo Alas." Obras
       completas de J. E. Rodó.   Madrid: Aguilar,
       1957.   1260-63.

       Reproduces text of Alas' letter to Rodó (29
       Dec. 1895) thanking him for the second part of "La
       crítica de Clarín" and requesting a copy of the
       first part.   Also Rodó's reply of 20 Feb. 1896
       enclosing other writings.   In La Saeta (B), 25

Feb. 1897, C wrote a "palique" in which he called Rodó "un crítico de cuerpo entero."

492. Rodríguez, Alfred and Darcy Donahue. "The Exceptional Function of Some Names in Su único hijo." LOS, XI (1984): 197-207.

493. Rodríguez, Alfred and Barbara Jean Kailing. "¿Hay ya intención irónico-burlesca en el título mismo de Su único hijo?" Rom N, XXIV, 3 (Spring, 1984): 226-28.

The title of the novel may have derived from the Creed ("I believe in Jesus Christ, His only Son") but also from the slang expression used in home lottery (bingo) games, as described by A. Ros de Olano in Episodios militares (Madrid: Imprenta de Miguel Ginesta, 1884), pp. 28-29.

493a. Rodríguez-Moñino, Antonio. "Clarín y Lázaro: Un pleito entre escritor y editor." Bibliofilia, V (Valencia: Castalia, 1951): 47-70.

A scholarly study of the literary relations between C and the editor of La España Moderna. Lázaro could not tolerate any disloyalty or injustice; he insisted that Clarín "se portó muy mal conmigo." The appendix contains full text of 19 letters from Lázaro to Clarín, dated between 19 Feb. 1889 and 20 Feb. 1896.

494. Rogers, Douglass. "Don Juan, Donjuanismo, and Death in Clarín." Symposium, XXX, 4 (1976): 325-42.

Don Alvaro Mesía of LR and Don Mamerto Anchoriz, the Don Juan-type of "El caballero de la mesa redonda" (1886). While Don Mamerto may or may not constitute the "reappearance" of the same character, he may be C's "deliberate bringing to justice of his Don Juan figure, not so much for the deeds he did as for the spiritual life he lacked."

495. Rogers, Edith. "Surrogates, Parallels, and Paraphrasing in La Regenta." REH, XVIII, 1 (Jan., 1984): 87-101.

496. Romera Castillo, José. "Espacio y tiempo: Elementos connotadores en El dúo de la tos de Clarín." LdD, XV, 32 (Mayo-agosto, 1985): 199-206.

497. Romero Tobar, Leonardo. "Introducción" a Teresa, Avecilla, El hombre de los estrenos. Madrid: Castalia, 1975.

The introduction (pp. 7-57) discusses C as a theater critic, the elaboration and premiere of _Teresa_, _Teresa_ and the Spanish theater in 1895, and the theater in the narrative works of C. The bibliography (pp. 58-65) includes notes on the first editions of these three works, and studies on _Teresa_ and the Spanish theater of the late 1800's. In the appendix (pp. 173-88) Romero reproduces six critiques of _Teresa_ by Carlos Fernández Shaw, Kasabal, Miquel y Badía, Carlos Díaz Dufóo, etc.

498.   ---. "Clarín, catedrático de la Universidad de Zaragoza (El naturalismo y la mano negra)." _Cinco estudios humanísticos para la Universidad de Zaragoza en su IV centenario_.   Zaragoza, 1983. 528 pp.

499.   Rossini, Flaviarosa.   "Introducción" a _La Presidentessa_. Turin: Unione Tipográfico-Editrice Torinese, 1960. 2 vols.

An italian translation of _LR_. Reviewed by Goytisolo (q.v.)

500.   Round, Nicholas G.   "The Fictional Integrity of Leopoldo Alas' _Superchería_."   _BHS_, XLVII (1970): 97-116.

"The theme of the story is Serrano's recovery of personal wholeness. This theme of integrity subsumes the philosophical question of appearance and reality, deepens the seriousness of the love-story and transcends Clarín's personal preoccupations with childhood and with maternal feeling."■

501.   Rubio Cremades, Enrique.   "Azorín, crítico literario de Leopoldo Alas." _LdD_, XV, 32 (Mayo-agosto, 1985): 185-98.

After a few early attacks, Azorín became C's strongest defender during the first half of the 20th century.

502.   Rubio Jiménez, Jesús.   _Ideología y teatro en España: 1890-1900_. Universidad de Zaragoza: Pórtico, 1982. 244 pp.

Teresa, pp. 158-61. "Clarín . . . opta por una solución (a la cuestión social) evasiva y conformista, acorde con su giro espiritualista de aquellos años." Rubio quotes from Clarín's defense of his play in "La crítica de teatros," _El Imparcial_, I (1 Abril 1895). Present at the performance were Galdós, MMP, Altamira, and PV.

503. Rueda, Salvador. "Los maestros: Leopoldo Alas (Clarín)." La Gran Vía (M), III, 81 (13 Enero 1895).

C's influence on modern Spanish literature has been great. He has taught logic to writers, raised their artistic standards, familiarized them with French literature, and taught them to laugh at the mediocre. Alas is like a conscience in front of us; when a bad poet writes, say in Cádiz, Clarín can hear the poet's pen scratch all the way to Oviedo.

504. Ruiz Contreras, Luis. Memorias de un desmemoria- do. Madrid, 1902.

In "La crítica y los críticos" (pp. 187-90) he accuses C of wasting his time making fun of insignificant writers instead of guiding and ed- ucating the younger generation. In "Los funerales de Clarín" (pp. 191-97) he examines the 190 lines of C's "Crónica literaria" in Los Lunes de El Im- parcial and concludes that it is little more than a list of new books. "Nadie como él (Clarín) metaliza sus pasiones y sus odios, la digestión, la bilis, y la prosa diaria de la vida . . . ni un solo juicio suyo sintetiza ni pone de relieve la obra de un autor famoso." Clarín will witness his own funeral "porque su crítica, fácil y grosera, no ha creado nada y ha pervertido al público, en- señándole a juzgar y no a sentir." These articles are dated Oct. 1902 and 28 Feb. 1899, respec- tively. The book was reprinted in 1946 and 1961. See also his nom de plume, Palmerín de Oliva.

505. Ruiz de la Peña, Alvaro. "Una broma literaria de Clarín: Las vírgenes locas." Argumentos, VIII, 63-64 (Enero-feb., 1984): 56-59.

Overview of this novel. In 1962 MC had as- sumed that "Flügel" was Sinesio Delgado, but in 1984 he learned that it was Clarín.

506. Ruiz Silva, J. C. "Clarín y el amor como imposi- bilidad (en torno a Superchería)." Insula, XXXII, 365 (Abril, 1977): 1 y 12.

Published in 1890, between LR and SUH, Superchería may be "el punto crucial para comprender la evolución del pensamiento clariniano sobre el amor." Ruiz Silva points out some similarities between Superchería and Thomas Mann's "La muerte en Venecia."

507.   Rutherford,   John.   "Introduction"   to   English
         trans. of <u>La Regenta</u>.   Athens: U of Georgia
         P, 1984.   734 pp.

         See pp. 7-17.   <u>LR</u> was well ahead of its time
         in psychological insights (hysteria, sublimation,
         sexual aberrations) and in modern narrative de-
         vices (use of dreams, flashback within a flash-
         back, free indirect style, multiple perspectives,
         dislocated chronology, etc.).   Rutherford's trans-
         lation, the first one in English, is based on So-
         bejano's 1976 ed.   Like Sobejano, Rutherford felt
         a need to furnish some 350 notes (pp. 717-34)
         identifying names, titles, quotations, cultural
         and historical references, etc.   Reviewed by A.
         Gullón, Klein, Seymour-Smith (q.v.)

508.   ---.   Fortunato y Frígilis en <u>La Regenta</u>."   <u>Clarín</u>
         <u>y su obra</u>.   Ed. Antonio Vilanova.   Barcelona:
         U de Barcelona, 1985.   292-316.

509.   Saillard, Simone.   "Documents pour une biographie.
         Le dossier universitaire de Clarín à Sara-
         gosse."   <u>LLNL</u>, LVII, 164 (March, 1963): 37-
         61.

         Publishes C's personnel file as "Catedrático
         de Economía Política y Estadística" at Zaragoza
         from July 1882 to July 1883, at which time he
         transferred to Oviedo as "Catedrático de Historia
         y Elementos de Derecho Romano."

509a. Sáinz Rodríguez, Pedro.   "Clarín y su obra."   <u>Re-</u>
         <u>vista de las Españas</u>, II, 9-10 (Mayo-junio,
         1927): 305-11; No. 11 (Julio, 1927): 441-44;
         No. 12 (Agosto, 1927): 536-38; Nos. 13-14
         (Sept.-oct., 1927): 604-13.

         A selection from his "Discurso" of 1921; see
         the book section of this bibliography.

510.   ---.   <u>Evolución de las ideas sobre la decadencia</u>
         <u>española y otros estudios de crítica litera-</u>
         <u>ria</u>.   Madrid: Ediciones Rialp, 1962.   578 pp.

         Chap. IV, "La obra de Clarín," pp. 334-422,
         discusses Alas' philosophical thought from anti-
         positivism, Krausism, naturalism, to idealism; his
         role as professor, critic, novelist; dates of his
         teaching services; and bibliography.   High praise
         for "Zurita," <u>Apolo en Pafos</u>, and "Un discurso."
         Recalls reading article, "La palmeta de Clarín,"
         published six or eight years after C's death, but
         does not mention author or journal.   States that
         no one has yet studied the parallel between <u>LR</u> and

Eça de Queiroz's _O crime do P. Amaro_.

511. ———. "Nostalgia de Oviedo y de Clarín." _CN_, II, 7 (Mayo-junio, 1981): 94-97.

Recalls how he obtained a position at the University of Oviedo and prepared himself for his 1921 lecture on C, which was highly praised by Pérez de Ayala.

512. Salcedo, Emilio. "Clarín, Menéndez Pelayo, y Unamuno." _Insula_, VII, 76 (Abril, 1952): 5.

Comments on, and excerpts from, the letters published in Adolfo Alas' two-volume _Epistolario_.

513. Sánchez, Elizabeth. "La dinámica del espacio en _La Regenta_ de Clarín." _CN_, II, 7 (Mayo-junio, 1981): 28-35.

A close reading and interpretation of the "living space" ("visión animada del espacio") in C's descriptions, particularly Chap. 1 and 8. Sánchez's objective is to "examinar brevemente algunas de las formas asumidas por la fundamental intuición del espacio que informa _La Regenta_. En el trabajo, trataré de demonstrar cuán eficazmente se prefiguran en las primeras escenas el sujeto esencial y los temas principales de la novela."

513a. Sánchez, Roberto G. "Clarín y el romanticismo teatral: Examen de una afición." _HR_, XXXI (1963): 216-28.

Attempts to explain C's enthusiasm for Echegaray, Sellés, etc. and defense of Rafael Calvo. Like EPB and other intellectuals, C saw the need for a new, realistic theater (such as Galdós' _Realidad_) but at the same time longed for the "national tradition" of Zorrilla, Echegaray, etc. for sentimental reasons. See also book section of this bibliography for Sánchez's book on the theater.

513b. ———. "The Presence of the Theater and 'The Consciousness of Theater' in Clarín's _La Regenta_." _HR_, XXXVII, 4 (Oct., 1969): 491-509.

C uses the theater "to characterize the people of his novel and in one key chapter (strategically located almost at the center of the work) in describing a performance of _Don Juan Tenorio_ he dramatizes the principal conflict through the varying reactions of the main characters of the novel . . . Clarín often views the situations and predicaments of his characters with special ironic detachment: as if they were amateur actors awkwardly rehearsing a scene."

513c.   ---.   "Teatro e intimidad en Su único hijo: Un aspecto de la modernidad de Clarín." Insula, XXVII, 311 (Oct., 1972): 3 y 12.

The role of the theater in the "juego teatrovida" and characterization of SUH, with many references also to LR.

514.   Sánchez Calvo, Estanislao.   "A propósito del libro de D. Leopoldo Alas Solos de Clarín." Revista de Asturias (O), IV (1881): 316-18 y 324-26.

A review of C's first collection of articles. C wrote an obituary of Sánchez Calvo for Revista de Sociología y Derecho (Primer trimestre, 1895).

515.   Sánchez Pérez, Antonio.   "Nueva campaña, por Clarín." La Opinión (M), II, 398 (13 Junio 1887): 1.

516.   ---.   "Su único hijo." MC, XI, 444 (22 Agosto 1891): 6-7.

C called Sánchez Pérez "Pangloss" because SP spent all his time praising him. Determined to find fault with SUH, SP read it twice and did not succeed in finding any faults. He was among the first to predict that young Alas would become a first-class writer. SUH seems to be a fragment of a longer novel. This article is dated 1 Agosto 1891; it was reprinted as "Leopoldo Alas (Clarín), novelista" in the 221-page ed. of Adiós, Cordera y otros cuentos (Buenos Aires: Editorial Tor, 1939), pp. 11-15.

517.   Sanguily, Manuel.   "Críticos y gramáticos." Hojas Literarias (Habana), Año II, Vol. V, 3 (30 Nov. 1894): 365-410.

A lengthy and detailed commentary on Dr. Gener's El caso Clarín, provoked by C's negative review of Literaturas malsanas in Los Lunes de El Imparcial, 30 April 1894. Sanguily refutes Gener, particularly since Dr. Gener did not examine Clarín before pronouncing him a pathological case. Gener's language against Clarín is as abusive as that of the book review by Clarín.

518.   San Miguel, Luis G.   De la sociedad aristocrática a la sociedad industrial en la España del si-

glo XIX. Madrid: Edicusa, 1973.

Pages 131-49 examine Clarín's ideas on aristocracy and "indianos" in LR (Marqués de Vegallana, don Frutos Redondo); conservatives and liberals (pp. 195-97) based on the story "El candidato"; and political ideas (pp. 217-59) based on "Un jornalero," LR, SUH, DB, and the articles on Andalucía which C published in El Día.

519. Sanroma Aldea, José. "Introducción" a Adiós, Cordera y otros cuentos. Madrid: Emiliano Escolar Editor, 1983. 253 pp.

See pp. 9-25. This anthology contains AC and the 12 stories from SDC.

520. Sans, Jaume. "El personaje del intelectual en los cuentos de L. Alas Clarín." Archivum, XXVII-XXVIII (1977-1978): 71-100.

Of the 83 stories analyzed, 36 are devoted to the intellectual. Disillusionment and pessimism are constant characteristics. Sans offers a catalog of the intellectual as main or secondary character, his relations with other characters, and the anti-intellectual.

521. Santullano, Luis. "En el centenario de Clarín. Alabanzas y vejámenes ultramarinos." Insula, VII, 76 (Abril, 1952): 4.

In a 1906 conversation in Paris, Bonafoux attenuated his ascerbic attitude toward Clarín. In the second part of this article, Santullano disagrees with certain ideas expressed by Brent in his book, Leopoldo Alas and La Regenta, and by Bull in his article, "Clarín's Literary Internationalism."

522. ---. "En el centenario de Clarín. La Regenta y su autor en la picota." Asomante, VIII, 3 (Julio-sept., 1952): 5-13.

Disagrees with some aspects of Brent's Leopoldo Alas, which Santullano enumerates. Santullano knew Clarín, Bonafoux, Martínez Vigil, and José Quevedo personally. According to Santullano, C did not attach much importance to the failure of Teresa. "En lo religioso Alas vivió siempre en cierta angustiosa vacilación que, en los últimos años, hubo de acogerse a un espiritualismo deísta, no del todo satisfecho."

523. ---. "Leopoldo Alas, Clarín, cincuenta años des-

pués." <u>CA</u>, LIX, 5 (Sept.-oct., 1951): 267-80.

Personal reminiscences by a contemporary who knew C. Agrees with Azorín that Alas was, above all, a philosopher and moralist, but disagrees that C never found fault with major writers. <u>LR</u> is purely fictitious even though some characters may have been based on actual persons. Brief comparison between C's "La mosca sabia" and Juan Ochoa's "La última mosca."

524.   Sanz Villanueva, Santos. "Ediciones desconocidas de <u>La Regenta</u>." <u>CHA</u>, 370 (Abril, 1981): 173-77.

Why were there no new editions of this great and controversial novel between 1885 and 1900? Sanz has examined several copies of the first ed. and found numerous textual variants. The first scholarly ed. was that by Sobejano, 1976. MC's ed. merely reproduces the first ed., frequently deleting entire paragraphs.

525.   Savaiano, Eugene. "An Historical Justification of the Anticlericalism of Galdós and Alas." <u>Bulletin of the Municipal University</u> (Wichita, KS), XXVII, 1 (Feb., 1952): 3-14.

History justifies Alas' and Galdós' portrayal of vocationless, poorly educated priests, the participation of clergymen in politics, lustfulness among members of the clergy, and a fanatical and bigoted attitude which caused its members to oppose all forms of material and intellectual advancement. In addition to history texts, Savaiano has studied C's two long novels and 12 by Galdós, from <u>La fontana de oro</u> to <u>Halma</u>.

526.   Schraibman, José and Leda Garazzola. "Hacia una interpretación de la ironía en <u>La Regenta</u> de Clarín." <u>Studies in Honor of José Rubia Barcia</u>. Ed. Roberta Johnson and Paul C. Smith. Lincoln, NE: Society of Spanish and Spanish-American Studies, 1982. 175-86.

Types of irony: classical, romantic, aesthetic, tragic, linguistic, etc. and the involvement of narrator, characters, and reader to reflect Alas' moral portrayal of contemporary religious practices, ignorance, and corruption.

527.   Schyfter, Sara E. "La loca, la tonta, la literata: Woman's Destiny in <u>La Regenta</u>." <u>Theory and Practice of Feminist Literary Criticism</u>.

Ed. Gabriela Mora and Karen S. Van Hooft. Ypsilanti, MI: Bilingual P, 1982. 291 pp.

See pp. 229-41. Ana's story is "that of a woman's struggle with sexuality and creativity in a world where woman is offered only three possible ways of life: Virgin, Wife or Whore." A detailed commentary on Ana Ozores since childhood. The title comes from Ana's own words during the Holy Week procession.

528.   Serrano, Eugenia. "Ideales estéticos de uno del sesenta y ocho." RIE, X, 39 (Julio-sept., 1952): 303-12.

Unamuno first placed Clarín in this generation. C's Catholicism in relation to his artistic credo.

529.   Serrano Menéndez, Javier. "La presencia de Clarín en los periódicos gijoneses a finales del siglo XIX y principios del XX." El Comercio (Gijón, Asturias), 25, 28 y 30 Nov. y 2 Dic. 1984.

530.   Serrano Poncela, Segundo. "Un estudio de La Regenta." PSA, XLIV, 130 (Enero, 1967): 19-50.

C's possible objectives in writing LR, and his complexes. Spain as Vetusta, a collective character. Irony as technique. Eros in Ana and other women; as a character, Ana is "la menos satisfactoria," possibly because C did not know too many women. Adultery was common in the European novel, but it is not the central theme in LR. Analysis of Fermín and Alvaro. Also published in CA, 152 (1967): 223-41; reprinted in Beser's C y LR, pp. 139-61.

531.   Sieburth, Stephanie. "James Joyce and Leopoldo Alas: Patterns of Influence." RCEH, VII, 3 (Spring, 1983): 401-06.

"There are many parallels between SUH and Ulysses, which are not explained by the fact that both works are based on the Odyssey, and which suggest to me that Joyce had read SUH."

532.   Silva, J. C. "Clarín y el amor como imposibilidad." Insula, XXXII, 365 (Abril, 1977): 1.

533.   Sobejano, Gonzalo. "Clarín y la crisis de la crítica satírica." RHM, XXXI (1965): 399-417.

A lucid, well-written explanation of criticism and satire, and description of Alas' satiri-

cal criticism. Personal, social, and historical
reasons account for it. Spain has a long tradition of satirical writers, from the two Arcipres-
tes to Larra, some of whom, like Clarín, engaged
in satirizing the misuse of grammar or vocabulary.
The 1880's had many "escritores jocosos" (Bobadilla, Valbuena, Taboada, etc.); this type of literature was attacked by Pompeyo Gener in <u>Literatu-
ras malsanas</u> (1894) and parodied in Antonio Zozaya's <u>Ripios clásicos</u> (1899). Clarín's "crítica
enjuiciativa" gave way to the passive and polite
criticism of Gómez de Baquero (Andrenio). Reprinted in <u>Homenaje a Angel del Río</u> (1966), pp. 399-
417, and in Sobejano's <u>Forma literaria y sensibilidad social</u> (1967), pp. 139-77.

534.   ---. <u>Nietzsche en España</u>. Madrid: Editorial Gre-
        dos, 1967. 287 pp.

        C was not extensively familiar with Nie-
tzsche, and eventually rejected his ideas, but his
influence is evident in "Nietzsche y las mujeres"
(<u>El Español</u>, 6 y 7 Sept. 1899), "Cartas a Hamlet"
(in his book <u>Siglo pasado</u>), his "palique" of 6
July 1899 in <u>MC</u>, his preface to <u>Ariel</u>, etc.

535.   ---. "La inadaptada (Leopoldo Alas: <u>La Regenta</u>,
        capítulo XVI)." <u>El comentario de textos</u>. Ed.
        Emilio Alarcos Llorach et al. Madrid: Cas-
        talia, 1973. 126-66.

        A detailed analysis of Chap. 16, in which Ana
expresses sadness and boredom at the weather and
the stupidity around her. "Del aburrimiento el
sujeto saldrá, en otros momentos de la novela, hacia un entusiasmo, ya místico, ya erótico, tan en-
gañoso como fugaz. Imposible la adaptación. Vetusta logra derrotar a la Regenta, arrastrada por
su lodo: no puede asimilar a Ana, no puede someter
su alma."

536.   ---. "Leopoldo Alas, la novela naturalista y la
        imaginación moral de <u>La Regenta</u>." Prólogo a
        <u>La Regenta</u>. Barcelona: Clásicos Hispánicos
        Noguer, 1976. 932 pp.

        See pp. 11-58. The first scholarly ed. of
this novel. Revised by Sobejano in 1981, 1982,
1983. For comparison with other editions, see
articles by Martínez Torrón and Sanz Villanueva.
Reviewed by Rutherford (q.v.)

536a.   ---. "Introducción" a <u>La Regenta</u>. Madrid: Edito-
        rial Castalia, 1981. 2 vols.

Sobejano's ed. is based on the 1900 ed. with Galdós' preface, which is reprod. here. His 52-page introd. offers a brief biography of C and develops four interpretative aspects of LR: Soledad y corrupción, perversión, condenación." Notable attention to detail, proofreading, and useful footnotes on vocabulary and geographical references. Reviewed by Klein, Round (q.v.) Second ed., revised, 1982. Third ed., 1983. Unquestionably the finest ed. of this novel available today.

537.   ---. "De Flaubert a Clarín." Quimera (B), V (Marzo, 1981): 25-29.

Considers the influence not only of Madame Bovary but also of L'éducation sentimentale.

538.   ---. "Madame Bovary en La Regenta." CN, II, 7 (Mayo-junio, 1981): 22-27.

Adds well-documented details to the broad comparisons already made by Clavería, Laffitte, Melón, Eoff, Agudiez, and López-Rey. Does not accept Ana's bovarysmo altogether, as Clavería did. Symbolism in LR. Attitude of Flaubert and C toward the main character.

539.   ---. "Semblantes de la servidumbre en La Regenta. " Serta Philológica Fernando Lázaro Carreter, II (1983). 519-29.

The role of servants, especially doña Camila, doña Paula, and Petra. Sobejano also discovers a remote but probable parallel between the Quintanar-Ana-Alvaro triangle in LR and Anselmo-Camila-Lotario in Cervantes' El curioso impertinente.

540.   ---. "Clarín y el sentimiento de la Virgen." Aufstieg und Krise der Vernunft (Wien, Köln, Graz), 1984. 157-72.

The Virgin Mary as seen in a sonnet by Antero de Quental (Oporto, 1881), reviewed by Clarín in NC; in Zola's La faute de l'abbé Mouret (1875); and in LR.

541.   ---. "Sentimientos sin nombre en La Regenta." Insula, XXXIX, 451 (Junio, 1984): 1 y 6.

"Lo que buscan esas conciencias supravetustenses (Ana y Fermín) es la elevación del ser a un sentimiento amoroso que era demasiado plenario para ser nombrado." The ending of LR could not have been otherwise; it is a triumph for Ana, Fermín, and the author, because "ellos tres son los únicos que no podrían adaptarse nunca a ese mundo: han eregido contra él lo infinito de su deseo, explorando por los caminos de la tentación (de la tentativa) la verdad de unos sentimientos cuya definición no está en el diccionario."

542. ---. Poesía y prosa en _La Regenta_." _Clarín y su obra_. Ed. Antonio Vilanova. Barcelona: U de Barcelona, 1985. 292-316.

543. Sotelo, Adolfo. "Clarín, crítico de Valera." _CHA_, CXXXIX, 415 (Enero, 1985): 37-51.

C admired Valera's intelligence and discerned three factors in his novels: humor, idealism, and his presence in all of them. Hegel's influence. Clarín's reaction to Valera's _Apuntes_.

544. Sotillo, Antonio. "Semblanza literaria." _La crítica popular_. Valencia: Vives Mora, 1896. v-xvi.

Today C is the writer with the most enemies, among whom Sotillo cites Bonafoux, Ferrari, Grilo, Arimón, and Bobadilla. His lesson is always "la lección de la sátira, tan cruel como la _Lección poética_ de Moratín, pero también beneficiosa y útil." However, C becomes serious when he thinks about Renan, Zorrilla, Moreno Nieto, or Fray Ceferino González. C strikes Sotillo as being "un gladiador literario de otros tiempos, extraviado en una sociedad de polichinelas y perdido entre las frases hechas de nuestra baja y vulgar politiquilla literaria." C is always sincere, but not impartial. In his novels one can always see "el propósito hondamente moral, docente, el empeño de corregir."

545. Suárez, Constantino. "Leopoldo Alas." _Escritores y artistas asturianos. Indice biobibliográfico_, I (Madrid, 1936). 108-33.

An overview of the life and works of C, with long quotations from Azorín, Buylla, Altamira, Sáinz Rodríguez, etc. Suárez: "Está muy lejos Clarín de haber alcanzado en la novela grande las perfecciones conseguidas en la corta y en el cuento . . . Fue un moralista, un profundo creyente, un místico laico." Good bibliography of works by and about Clarín, pp. 129-33.

546. Suárez-Piñera, Rosario. "Algunos recursos e ideas que se desprenden de una lectura crítica de _Su único hijo_, de Clarín." _Archivum_, 29-30 (1979-1980): 59-67.

547. Taylor, Alan Carey. <u>Carlyle et la pensée latine</u>.
     Paris: Boivin, 1937. 317-24, 366-67.

     The first Spanish translation of <u>Heroes</u> was
     actually a commercial venture to launch a new Bi-
     blioteca Selecta Anglo-Alemana. Analysis of Cla-
     rín's introduction, "assez fouillée et remarquable
     surtout pour sa défense enthousiaste des idées de
     Carlyle, ses critiques intéressantes de l'étude de
     Taine et son interprétation plutôt démocratique de
     la doctrine des héros: interprétation d'ailleurs
     parfaitement admissible, mais que l'on n'avait pas
     encore donnée dans les pays latins." Despite the
     excellent introd. and other good qualities of the
     book, it went almost unnoticed because the public
     was unfamiliar with Carlyle, and the two volumes
     appeared three months apart. Reviews were few and
     brief, and the next ed. was not published until
     1930.

548. Thompson, Clifford R., Jr. "Egoism and Alienation
     in the Works of Leopoldo Alas." <u>RF</u>, 81
     (1969): 193-203.

     Alas' most specific indictment of egoism is
     "El pecado original" (from <u>GS</u>). Other examples of
     egoism and social alienation discussed are <u>Cuervo</u>,
     "El caballero de la mesa redonda," "El dúo de la
     tos," "La conversión de Chiripa," and <u>LR</u>. Ana de-
     spises the society of Vetusta and feels that she
     is superior to all the others; egoism is primarily
     responsible for Ana's downfall.

549. ---. "Poetic Response in the Short Stories of Le-
     opoldo Alas." <u>Rom N</u>, XIII, 2 (1971): 272-75.

     The poetry of some stories ("El sustituto,"
     <u>DB</u>, etc.) is revealed principally in the poetic-
     ally idealistic attitudes of the protagonists, not
     in the form or subject matter.

550. ---. "Cervantine Motifs in the Short Stories of
     Leopoldo Alas." <u>REH</u>, X, 3 (Oct., 1976): 391-
     403.

     Cervantes' formula of confronting the real
     and ideal levels of human experience, and the use
     of literature within literature, is reflected in
     "Doctor Sutilis," "Un documento," "La imperfecta
     casada," and <u>DB</u>. If chivalric literature brings
     don Quixote into conflict with the reality of the
     picaresque, it is romantic literature which often
     brings Alas' characters into conflict with the
     reality of naturalism. As in <u>Don Quixote</u>, the
     ideal is reaffirmed rather than negated by the
     triumph of reality.

551.   ---.   "'Un documento' de Clarín: Un paso hacia La
       Regenta." Archivum, 27-28 (1977-1978): 65-
       69.

       In addition to "El diablo en Semana Santa,"
       "Un documento" can be considered as an antecedent
       of LR, from the point of view of plot and charac-
       ter development.

552.   ---.   "Evolution in the Short Stories of Clarín."
       REH, XVIII, 3 (Oct., 1984): 381-98.

       After a survey of earlier opinions on this
       subject, Thompson makes a systematic attempt to
       follow C's progression from satire to sympathy.
       Taking stories involving intellectual activity and
       love (because of their constant recurrence),
       Thompson finds a discernible evolutionary process
       as C moves gradually, if never completely, away
       from the dehumanizing caricature and burlesque sa-
       tire of the early stories toward a more compas-
       sionate attitude.

553.   Tolivar Alas, María Cristina.   "La música en La
       Regenta."   CN, V, 23 (Enero-feb., 1984): 70-
       76.

       The role of popular music, religious music,
       opera, and zarzuela in this novel.   Apparently C
       had no formal training in music.   Around 1890 Fa-
       cundo de la Viña, a musician from Asturias, dedi-
       cated a musical piece for piano, "Palique," to
       Clarín.

554.   Torre, Guillermo de.   "Presencia de Clarín."
       Archivum, II, 1 (Enero-abril, 1952): 221-31.

       "El poderoso novelista de LR nos importa hoy
       más que el satírico de los paliques.   El narrador
       de los CM guarda una vitalidad, una frescura, una
       atracción que el articulista de Solos de Clarín ha
       perdido casi totalmente."

554a. ---.   Del 98 al barroco.   Madrid: Gredos, 1969.
       451 pp.

       See "Clarín, crítico y novelista" (pp. 265-
       81) for an expanded version of his 1952 article in
       Archivum.   Considers comparisons with Madame Bo-
       vary unnecessary because Ana's "frustración de
       mujer malmaridada tiene cierta dimensión univer-
       sal."   C's short stories are "esencialmente senti-
       mentales, quizá en exceso, estremecidos por una
       propensión a lo dramático, o más bien hacia lo
       tragicómico agridulce."

555. Torres, David. "Noticia de otro juicio sobre la
Teresa de Clarín." BIEA, XXXVII, 109-110
(1983): 589-93.

Comments on Luis Alberto's article on this
play, reprod. here.

556. ---. "Juan Ochoa escribe sobre Teresa, de Clarín." BIEA, XXXVIII, 113 (Sept.-dic., 1984):
951-55.

Ochoa published a review of Teresa in RCHL,
I, 2 (Abril, 1895): 61-62, the text of which is
reprod. here.

557. ---. "Clarín y Las vírgenes locas: Doce autores
en busca de una novela." CHA, CXXXIX, 415
(Enero, 1985): 53-63.

Alas contributed two chapters to this 1886
tour de force written by 12 different authors, and
described here in detail.

558. ---. "Tres poesías desconocidas de Leopoldo
Alas." BIEA, XL, 117 (Enero-abril, 1986):
201-06.

559. Torres Nebrera, Gregorio. "Texto de Clarín."
Comentario lingüístico y literario de textos
españoles. Ed. Ariza Viguera, Garrido Medina, y Torres Nebrera. Madrid: Editorial Alhambra, 1981. 211-29.

A formal analysis of the short story, "El
frío del Papa," which originally appeared in Los
Lunes de El Imparcial in 1894 and was later included in CM.

560. Tuñón de Lara, Manuel. Medio siglo de cultura española (1885-1936). Madrid: Editorial Tec-
nos, 1970. 293 pp. (2d ed., 1971, 298 pp.)

See "La España de Galdós y de Clarín," pp.
19-36. In 1885, the year of La Regenta and Lo
prohibido, Spain had 71% illiteracy. LR is the
most profound criticism of Spanish society at the
provincial level. C was anticlerical but not
antireligious; he refused to attend the Congreso
de Librepensadores and was opposed to El Motín and
similar periodicals.

561. Turner, Harriet S. "Vigencia de Clarín: Vistas
retrospectivas en torno a La Regenta."
Arbor, CXVI, 456 (Dic., 1983): 379-402.

562.   ---.   "Vetusta: espacio-fuerza en _La Regenta_."
        Clarín y su obra.   Ed. Antonio Vilanova.
        Barcelona: U de Barcelona, 1985.   31-41.

563.   Ullman, Pierre L.   "The Antifeminist Premises of
        Clarín's _Su único hijo_."   _Estudos Ibero-
        americanos_, I, 1 (July, 1975): 57-91.

        "An attempt to discover the structure of _SUH_
        . . . by positing as its ideological foundation
        the author's antifeminism.   This antifeminism, far
        from being a manifestation of misogyny, is based
        on the premise that there exist two types of al-
        truism, masculine and feminine (which is a distor-
        tion of positivist principles).   Whereas the high-
        est type of male altruism is a universal humani-
        tarian idealism, female altruism expresses itself
        best as woman's total devotion to her children
        . . . Since egoism is but selfish enjoyment, it
        need not be sexually differentiated, and thus
        pseudo-altruism can be treated as a regression to-
        ward mental androgyny.   This is what Clarín ap-
        pears to do in _SUH_, where the exchange of racist
        and romantic attitudes between a shrewish wife and
        milksop husband constitutes the novel's main
        structural element.   Other themes are evident: the
        influence of Aeschylus, etc."

564.   ---.   "Clarín's Androcratic Ethic and the Anti-
        apocalyptic Structure of ';Adiós, Cordera!'"
        _The Analysis of Hispanic Texts: Current
        Trends in Methodology_.   Ed. Lisa E. Davis and
        Isabel C. Tara.   Second York College Collo-
        quium.   Jamaica: York College Bilingual
        Press, 1976.   11-31.

565.   ---.   "Clarín: Ensayos, solos, paliques: A Ques-
        tion of Genre?"   _Los Ensayistas_, 14-15
        (Marzo, 1983): 113-19.

        These and other denominations (preludios, sá-
        turas, revistas, etc.) given by Alas to his non-
        fiction prose do not appear to have any signifi-
        cance for us nowadays if we seek to classify its
        genre and sub-genres.

566.   Unamuno, Miguel de.   _Obras selectas_.   Prólogo de
        Julián Marías.   Madrid: Editorial Plenitud,
        1965.   949-58.

        Reprints text of Unamuno's letter (Salamanca,
        9 Mayo 1900) to Clarín, reacting to C's review of
        Tres ensayos in _El Imparcial_, 7 Mayo 1900.   Una-
        muno regrets that C paid so little attention to
        Ganivet, Campión, or Blasco Ibáñez.   "_La barraca_
        . . . superior para mi gusto a cualquier novela de

Galdós o de Pereda." This letter was originally published in Vol. 1 of Adolfo Alas' Epistolario.

567.   Urmeneta, Fermín de. "Sobre estética clariniana." RIE, XXVII, 107 (Julio-sept., 1969): 255-61.

An analysis of AC.

568.   Urrecha, Federico. "A Clarín, en Oviedo." El Imparcial, 24 Sept. 1894.

569.   ---. "Clarín (A propósito de Cuentos morales)." HM, 27 Enero 1896.

570.   Valbuena, Antonio de. "¡Cómo se escribe!" HM, 2 Julio 1892.

A favorable review of ER.

571.   Valdés, Juan Alfonso. "Prólogo" a Siglo pasado. Madrid: Antonio R. López, 1901. 195 pp.

C had planned to write this preface himself, according to a letter in Valdés' possession. Valdés, whose preface occupies pp. 5-10, considers C "sabio . . . bueno . . . sincero," a man who always told the truth.

572.   Valdivia, Aniceto. "El señorito Octavio, de Armando Palacio Valdés." MC, II, 66 (27 Marzo 1881): 6-7 y No. 67 (3 Abril 1881): 7.

This negative review of PV's novel makes numerous references to Clarín, who had praised it. At the end of the first article, Valdivia mockingly states that the novel sells for 12 reales, a peseta more than Marianela. In the second article, he promises to reply to C's "palique" in El Mundo Moderno, No. 30, in the next issue of MC.

572a. ---. "Al Sr. D. Leopoldo Alas, renombrado Clarín." MC, II, 68 (10 Abril 1881): 7.

The negative review of El señorito Octavio continues. States that Clarín writes for El Mundo Moderno, a daily read by only 200 people. The polemic appears to end with Valdivia's "Punto final" in the April 17th issue, but the April 24th issue of MC carries a "comunicado" in which PV, through his friends Félix González Llana and Tomás Tuero, demands a retraction. Valdivia publishes his reply on the same page.

573.   Valentí Camp, Santiago. Ideólogos, teorizantes y videntes. Barcelona: Editorial Minerva, 1922.

This hard-to-find book, written by one of Alas' former students, contains a chapter entitled "Leopoldo Alas (Clarín)," pp. 113-25. Discerns two stages in C's literary production: "la de iniciación" from 1870-1885, characterized by "radicalismo ingenioso, sátira mordaz, tendencia iconoclasta," and "la de plenitud" from 1885-1901, which "le llevó a ampliar su concepción metafísica, dirigiendo la mirada hacia la restauración de un neocristianismo . . . a pesar de ser Clarín un hombre superior . . . no consiguió substraerse por completo a la influencia que los krausistas ejercieron en su espíritu, y debido a esto, quizá, cuando teorizaba resultaba un tanto obscuro y alambicado."

574.   Valentí Fiol, Eduard.   El primer modernismo literario catalán y sus fundamentos ideológicos. Barcelona: Editorial Ariel, 1973.   357 pp.

"Clarín, modernista" (pp. 69-78) discusses Alas' ideas of a "modernismo católico . . . progresista, humanitario y de veras universal" as described in his review of Víctor Díaz Ordóñez's book, La Unión Católica, and other pages of ER.

575.   Valis, Noël Maureen.   "Leopoldo Alas y los Goncourt: el alma neurótica."   Archivum, 27-28 (1977-1978): 51-63.

Points out stylistic and thematic similarities and differences between Alas and the Goncourt brothers concerning "los temas de la sensación, la frustración sexual y los impulsos latentes de autodestrucción, expresados en personajes inestables y neuróticos," in order to demonstrate "que el universo ficticio de Clarín podría muy bien haber encontrado por lo menos una inspiración parcial en las obras de los hermanos Goncourt." Most of the examples are from Soeur Philomène (1861) and Germinie Lacerteux (1865).

576.   ---.   "Fermín de Pas: Una 'flor del mal' clariniana."   ExTL, VII, 1 (1978): 31-36.

Fermín's pale face and green eyes seem to reflect the "decadent" symbol of the neurotic, corrupt, and cruel character.

577.   ---.   "Romantic Reverberation in La Regenta: Hugo and the Clarinian Decay of Romanticism." Comparatist, III (May, 1979): 40-52.

Similarities and differences between Notre-Dame de Paris (1831-32) and LR, particularly in Chap. 1 of LR.

578.   ---.   "A Spanish Decadent Hero: Clarín's Antonio
        Reyes of 'Una Medianía'." _MLS_, IX, 2 (1979):
        53-60.

579.   ---.   "Leopoldo Alas y Zola: Paralelismos y diver-
        gencias temáticos." _Anuario de Letras_ (Mé-
        xico), XVII (1979): 327-35.

        The themes of fertility, motherhood, sterili-
        ty, and decadence in these two novelists, as re-
        flected in _LR_, _SUH_, _La Terre_, _Nana_, and _L'Assom-
        moir_.

580.   ---.   "The Landscape of the Soul in Clarín and
        Baudelaire." _RLC_, LIV, 1 (Jan-March, 1980):
        17-31.

        Stressing the themes of ennui, death, no-
        thingness, imprisonment, and decay, and their
        metaphorical treatment as expressed in _Les Fleurs
        du Mal_, Valis tries "to demonstrate through af-
        finities in themes and images that the state of
        mind poeticized by Baudelaire is reflected in
        Ana's inner turmoil and in her view of the
        universe."

581.   ---.   "'Tambor y gaita': Clarín's Last Project?"
        _RF_, XCIII, 3-4 (1981): 397-402.

        Includes text of the fragment, posthumously
        published in _Renacimiento Latino_ (M), I, 1 (Abril,
        1905): 26-27, which according to C's son, Leopol-
        do, are the last pages that his father wrote.

582.   ---.   "El 'Pipá ' de Clarín y 'El incendio' de Ana
        María Matute: Una infancia traicionada." _CN_,
        II, 7 (Mayo-junio, 1981): 72-77.

        A comparison between C's "Pipá" (published in
        La Unión in 1879) and "El incendio" from Matute's
        Historias de la Artámila (Barcelona: Destino,
        1961), pp. 7-14.

583.   ---.   "Order and Meaning: Clarín's _La Regenta_."
        Novel: A Forum on Fiction (Brown University),
        XVI, 3 (Spring, 1983): 246-58.

        _LR_ is a complex and disturbing work, so dark
        a novel that at times it seems obsidian. Using
        the "animal trap" incident described in Chap. 10,
        Valis attempts to demonstrate the various levels
        of meaning. The symbolic use of traps, spider
        webs, and brambles to indicate entrapment; thus
        freedom is an illusion for Ana, and Quintanar is
        later entrapped in his code of honor and public
        opinion as he had been entangled in spider webs on

Vegallana's summer estate.

584. ---. "The presence of Nana in Clarín's 'La mosca
      sabia.'" La Chispa. New Orleans: Tulane U,
      1983. 287-96.

585. ---. "Dos artículos olvidados sobre La Regenta de
      Clarín." BIEA, XXXVII, 190-110 (Mayo-dic.,
      1983): 625-52.

      Reproduces reviews by Orlando (Antonio Lara y
      Pedraja) in Revista de España, 106 (10 Sept.
      1885): 124-43, and by J. O. Picón in El Correo (15
      Marzo 1885). Picón's article had been reprinted
      by Amorós in Los Cuadernos del Norte in 1981.

586. ---. "La función del arte y la historia en Doña
      Berta de Clarín." BHS, LXIII 1 (Jan., 1986):
      67-78.

587. Valverde, José María. Azorín. Barcelona: Edito-
      rial Planeta, 1971.

      Briefly reviews, on pp. 34-36 and 41-54, the
      literary relations between C and Azorín, how they
      met, and C's influence on Azorín's style.

588. Varela Jácome, Benito. Estructuras novelísticas
      del siglo XIX. Barcelona: Aubí, 1974. 215
      pp.

      See "Estructuración de Su único hijo," pp.
      185-213. Varela considers it an intellectual no-
      vel, "por la profusión de referencias literarias,
      científicas, educacionales y jurídicas, por su
      alarde de cultura musical. Significa, además, una
      renovación técnica y es la mejor novela de inte-
      rioridad de su tiempo."

589. Vázquez de Prada y Grande, Rodrigo. "La Regenta
      cumple cien años." Argumentos, VIII, 63-64
      (Enero-feb., 1984): 4-7.

      The director of Argumentos presents an over-
      view of Clarín's life and recent interpretations
      of LR.

590. Vázquez Maldonado, F. Pareceres. Almería: Diario
      de Almería, 1930. 311 pp.

      In "Un juicio de Clarín" (pp. 31-36) the
      author disagrees with Alas' comment that one of
      the regrettable defects of La loca de la casa was
      to have Victoria and Pepet engage in a picayune
      struggle in the last two acts of Galdós' play.
      Vázquez feels that C should have interpreted the
      play in a symbolic vein.

591. Vega, Ricardo de la. "Al poeta Velarde en su poema _Fray Juan_." _MC_, 5 (1 Feb. 1880): 3 y 6.

Ridicules Clarín's poem, "El mártir de la duda" (_La Revista Europea_, 3 Marzo 1878) and defends Velarde against C's "palique" in _La Unión_, 25 Enero 1880. C replied in _La Unión_, 3 Feb. 1880. For the continuation of this "polemic" (probably C's first), see next entry.

591a. ---. Al crítico señor de Clarín." _MC_, I, 6 (8 Feb. 1880): 7 y 8.

A colorful squabble between C and the author of _La verbena de la Paloma_, concerning the definition and origin of the word "melena." The ironically respectful title was chosen because C had objected to being addressed as "tú." The argument continues on Feb. 15 with "A mi querido discípulo en peluquería, Clarín," signed Vega, peluquero, because C had called him a barber, a reference to Vega's zarzuela, _Vega, peluquero_ (1877). C suspects that "se conspira contra mi humilde personalidad por todos los malos autores," to which Vega offers the names of Blasco, Ramos Carrión, Vital Aza, Echegaray, Pina Domínguez, and Estremera as the "autorcillos chanflones." In the Feb. 22 issue, "A mi discípulo Clarinito," Vega calls C "gloria mía" and sends regards from Blasco, Catalina, and Campo Arana. In the March 28 issue, "A mi Clarinito," Vega replies to his "lucero de la mañana," expressing surprise that Clarín, who knows it all, has never heard of "sáficos adónicos."

592. Velázquez Cueto, Gerardo. _Galdós y Clarín_. Madrid: Cincel, 1981. 86 pp.

The last third of this book (pp. 77-84) contains an analysis of _AC_.

593. Vida, Jerónimo. "Ultimas Novelas III. _La Regenta_ de D. Leopoldo Alas." _Boletín de la Institución Libre de Enseñanza_, IX, 205 (1885): 246-48.

C's mastery of literary criticism has helped him to write _LR_, which after _La desheredada_ is "la novela de más miga, más seria . . . de cuantas han visto la luz en lengua castellana." Clarín knew exactly what he was doing. Fermín is the best character, Alvaro the weakest. Defects: detailed descriptions, slow action, author's tendency to "talk too much." Reprinted in Beser's _C y LR_, pp. 297-302.

594.   Vigara Tauste, Ana María.   "Clarín ante un actor
       del siglo XIX: Rafael Calvo."   Teatro en
       España (M), 11 (1982): 15-23.

595.   Vilanova, Antonio.   "La Regenta de Clarín y la
       teoría hegeliana de los caracteres indeci-
       sos."   Insula, XXXIX, 451 (Junio, 1984): 1,
       12 y 13.

       Galdós'and MMP's misinterpretation of Ana
       Ozores.   Clarín's change of attitude toward novel-
       istic characters, from the "personaje heroico rec-
       tilíneo" such as Julia in El nudo gordiano, to
       "figuras medianas" such as Doña Perfecta, to more
       complex "caracteres débiles, vacilantes e indeci-
       sos" such as Isidora Rufete in La desheredada or
       Amparo in Tormento, probably derives from Hegel's
       Estética.

596.   ---.   "El adulterio de Anita Ozores como problema
       fisiológico y moral."   Clarín y su obra.   Ed.
       Antonio Vilanova.   Barcelona: U de Barcelona,
       1985.   43-82.

597.   Villa Pastor, Jesús.   "La novela de la generación
       del 68 y el P. Blanco García."   Archivum, II,
       2 (Mayo-agosto, 1952): 303-11.

       Recalls that Father Blanco relegated C to the
       "Etc." section, considering him inferior to Picón,
       and LR a "disforme relato de dos mortales tomos
       . . . rebosa porquerías, vulgaridades y cinismo
       . . . en la forma una premiosidad violenta y can-
       sada, digna de cualquier principiante cerril."

598.   Villar Dégano, Juan F.   "Algunas claves para la
       lectura de Su único hijo de Leopoldo Alas."
       LdD, XV, 32 (Marzo-agosto, 1985): 133-56.

       Parody, irony, morality, and the inversion of
       roles in this novel.

599.   Villavicencio, Laura Núñez de.   "Reiteración y ex-
       tremismo en el estilo creativo de Clarín."
       Hispania, LIV (1971): 459-69.

       Through the insistent interplay of reitera-
       tion and extremism, C creates powerful images that
       bring to life the psychological dimensions of his
       characters and their individual worlds.   Antithe-
       tical tension is the basis of C's artistry in con-
       cept and in form.   Reprinted in Beser's C y LR,
       pp. 273-92.

600.   Weber, Frances Wyers.   "Ideology and Religious
       Parody in the Novels of Leopoldo Alas."   BHS,

XLIII, 3 (July, 1966): 197-208.

"The use of parodic religious symbols that
level all values and demonstrate the unbreakable
continuity of the physical and the spiritual. Religious patterns represent both the drama of love
and the pursuit of sex . . . As in LR, the vision
that underlies Alas' second novel is the baseness
of the material world and the futility of all attempts to escape from it into a purely spiritual
realm." Reprinted in Beser's C y LR, pp. 119-36.

601.   ---. "The Dynamics of Motif in Leopoldo Alas' La
       Regenta." RR, LVII, 3 (Oct., 1966): 188-99.

       Examines some aspects of the "interweaving of
inner and outer realities of sentimental conflict
and social satire in terms of the thematic duali-
ties or tensions that give the work its form."
According to Weber, "love, religion, and the demands of the body are the three motifs (or mo-
tives, for they are both theme and psychological
explanation) that generate the novel's action."

602.   Weiner, Hadassah Ruth. "La Regenta y Su único
       hijo: Revisión del estilo personal de Cla-
       rín." LT, XXIV, 93-94 (Julio-dic., 1976):
       67-83.

       There are more similarities in style, struc-
ture, characterization, and narrative techniques
in these two novels than one might think at first
sight.

603.   ---. "Su único hijo: Desequilibrio y exaltación."
       BIEA, XXX (1976): 431-47.

604.   ---. "Madame Bovary et La Regenta: Etude compara-
       tive." SPFA (1976-1977): 65-79.

605.   ---. "Integralismo de Clarín: Los 'interiores
       ahumados.'" CN, II, 7 (Mayo-junio, 1981):
       84-93.

       C's ideas on the novel, a genre which he con-
sidered very important but never defined: psychology of characters, description, social role of
novel, structure or composition, observation, dis-
like of art for art's sake, etc. Says Weiner: "El
conjunto inseparable de forma y fondo que es la
novela tiene un propósito tanto estético como ético y moral." Weiner detects in the criticism of
Tormento (Sermón perdido) an important change
since Solos de Clarín.

606.   ---. "Cinco breves apuntaciones sobre La Regen-
       ta." CN, V, 23 (Enero-feb., 1984): 30-33.

The five notes are: Sobre el título de la novela, Sobre los personajes secundarios, Sobre la
omnisciencia del narrador, Sobre el paisaje natural, and Sobre los temperamentos indecisos en la
novela.

607.   Wesseling, Pieter. "Structure and its Implica-
        tions in Leopoldo Alas' La Regenta." HR, LI,
        4 (Autumn, 1983): 393-408.

        "The present essay is concerned with overall
structure and its significance with respect to the
novel's themes. It begins with an examination of
the time sequences and the cycles of the plot
. . . then proceeds to an estimate of the relative
placement of the major scenes on the plot's tra-
jectory and of the characteristic method of their
composition . . . The essay ends with some sugges-
tions as to how the structure bears on aspects
such as style and characterization."

608.   Wiltrout, Ann. "El cosmos de La Regenta y el mun-
        do de su autor." Archivum, XXI (1971): 47-
        64.

        Divided into: El concepto clariniano de la
novela; C y Galdós; C y Flaubert; LR. "Igual que
la de Larra, la crítica clariniana es aparentemen-
te ligera, pero con un fondo serio debajo de la
ironía y del humor . . . La Regenta emplea la literatura como espejo de la vida, la ironía siendo
que la literatura en que los personajes se basan
no tiene sus raíces en la realidad vivida."

Wyers, Frances. See Weber, Frances W.

609.   Zeda. "Su único hijo, por Leopoldo Alas (Cla-
        rín)." RE, CXXXV, 4 (Julio-agosto, 1891):
        490-510.

        According to Zeda, Clarín has decided to be-
come a critic and a novelist, even though he has
no aptitude for either genre; he is merely a satirical writer. SUH belongs to a type created by
Zola, now out of fashion. All the characters are
either insane or infamous, every scene is like a
brothel. Clarín obviously did not have a plan or
clear idea before he sat down to write these 436
pages. The style is tedious and the language "en-
cierra también buen número de gazapos." The only
good features are the baptism scene and the cari-
catures. (Zeda's real name was Francisco Fernández Villegas.)

610.   Zuleta, Emilia de. Historia de la crítica espa-
        ñola contemporánea. Madrid: Gredos, 1966.

480 pp.

C was primarily a critic of contemporary authors, especially novelists; the best C is the
critic of Galdós, PV, and Pereda.   C's ideas on
literary criticism.   C ignored Bécquer and Rosalía
de Castro, and exaggerated the importance of Núñez
de Arce and Campoamor, but wrote excellent essays
on Verlaine and Baudelaire.   A second edition,
"notablemente aumentada," appeared in 1974; in the
second ed., see pp. 69-81.

611.   Zulueta, Carmen de.   <u>Navarro Ledesma: El hombre y
su tiempo</u>.   Madrid-Barcelona: Alfaguara,
1968.   389 pp.

See pp. 128-31 for brief description of Navarro's polemic with Clarín.   Reproduces entire
text of Navarro's article from <u>Gedeón</u> (23 Abril
1897) in which he calls C "un ser de tan baja ra-
lea . . . embustero . . . autorcillo silbado."   On
p. 131 she quotes a paragraph from a letter by Ganivet (Helsinfors, 16 Mayo 1897) in which he calls
Alas "el venenoso bichejo" and advises Navarro not
to become involved in duels in the future "porque
eso de lances de honor es cosa inconcebible en es-
tos tiempos en que el honor no vale nada."

C. MASTER'S AND DOCTORAL THESES

612. Bacas, Evan George. "Estudio del estilo y lenguaje en las narraciones de Leopoldo Alas, Clarín." Diss. Universidad de Madrid, 1961.

"El propósito de este trabajo es examinar las formas clarinianas sin hacer un análisis del contenido." Among the topics studied: el uso del adjectivo, estilo indirecto libre, letra cursiva, lenguage figurado, humorismo. Supervised by Rafael Lapesa, but length of study not indicated. See brief abstract in Revista de la U de Madrid, X, 40 (1961): 836-37.

613. Baker, Clayton. "Echegaray and His Critics." Diss. Indiana U, 1969. 254 pp.

To Clarín, Echegaray was "a member of a literary aristocracy in whose works he professed to find the collective thought of that era. C believed he was performing a patriotic and a beneficial function for his country by defending Echegaray's works from adverse criticism. His articles of criticism dealing with Echegaray showed much of the 'benevolence' he so detested in the works of other critics." Baker studies the criticism of Revilla, Clarín, and Azorín.

614. Barrio, Ana. "Las colaboraciones de Clarín a La Ilustración Ibérica. Master's thesis. Université de Toulouse, 1975.

615. ---. "La querelle naturaliste dans la presse madrilène avant la Cuestión palpitante, 1881-1882." Diss. Université de Toulouse, 1979. 254 pp.

616. Bauer, Beth Wietelmann. "Finales de novela en España, 1881-1892." Diss. U of Pennsylvania, 1984. 381 pp.

"The second part of this study concentrates on major realistic or naturalistic novels, beginning with La desheredada and concluding with SUH . . . This approach highlights both the enormous variety of ending strategies used by novelists of Restauration Spain and the specific techniques employed by those who broke with tradition and challenged readers by limiting, altering or withholding what Frank Kermode calls the 'sense of an ending.'"

617.   Bouma, Frederick J.   "The Structure of the Short
        Stories of Leopoldo Alas, Clarín."   Diss.   U
        of Illinois at Urbana-Champaign, 1969.   176
        pp.

        Contents: Introduction; Beginnings (Character
        presentation, setting, in medias res beginnings,
        etc.); Expositions and Entanglements; Climaxes,
        Denouements, and Endings.

618.   Brent, William Albert.   "Leopoldo Alas and the
        Novel from 1875 to 1885 (A Critical Analysis
        of La Regenta)."   Diss.   Princeton U, 1949.

        Published at the U of Missouri in 1951.   See
        book section of this bibliography.

619.   Brown, G. G.   "The Novels and Cuentos of Leopoldo
        Alas."   Diss.   Oxford U, 1962.

620.   Bull, William Emerson.   "Clarín: An Analytical
        Study of a Literary Critic."   Diss.   U of
        Wisconsin, 1940.

621.   Caviglia, John Lawrence.   "Flaubert and Leopoldo
        Alas: An Essay in Comparative Anatomy."
        Diss.   Indiana U, 1970.   232 pp.

        "This essay begins with the analogies in the
        works of the authors under consideration and pro-
        ceeds to their differencies (the specific), as in
        the classification of species . . . Part I: La
        Tentation de saint Antoine and La Regenta; Part
        II: Salammbô and La Regenta; Part III: Madame Bo-
        vary and La Regenta."

622.   Charnon-Deutsch, Mary Louise.   "The Short Fiction
        of Leopoldo Alas, Clarín."   Diss.   U of Chi-
        cago, 1978.

        "A comprehensive survey of Clarín's story-
        telling techniques reveals that the author gave
        every consideration to questions of form and
        style.   Although he thought literature should be
        placed at the service of social reform, it was
        never at the expense of style."

623.   Davies, G. J.   "Leopoldo Alas (Clarín), His Work
        and His Contemporaries."   Diss.   Leeds U
        (England), 1938.

624.   Davies, Martha Leveritt.   "Clarín's Novelistic
        Criticism and La Regenta."   Diss.   Indiana U,
        1972.   167 pp.

"The first objective is to provide an under-
standing of the critical principles adopted by
Clarín in regard to the novel . . . The second
objective is to examine Clarín's own novel, La
Regenta, in relation to his novelistic
principles."

625.   Davis, Dwight M.   "The Attitude of Leopoldo Alas
        (Clarín) Toward Spanish Letters."   Master's
        thesis.   U of Oklahoma, 1934.   111 pp.

626.   Díaz, Luis Felipe.   "Irony and Ideology in La
        Regenta of Leopoldo Alas."   Diss.   U of
        Minnesota, 1984.   298 pp.

627.   Dorwick, Thalia.   "El amor y el matrimonio en la
        obra creacional de Clarín."   Diss.   Case
        Western Reserve U, 1973.   302 pp.

        "Alas vio el amor desde una doble perspec-
tiva: el amor sensual y el sentimental, los dos
presentados como instintos del ser humano.   El
primero, cuando está desprovisto de sentimiento
que lo eleve del nivel animal, constituye un móvil
rebajador, caracterizado por el egoísmo, la desho-
nestidad y el cálculo, capaz de rendir solamente
una satisfacción pasajera.   En cambio, el amor
sentimental se presenta como fuerza sublime y per-
durable . . . El matrimonio se define como una
institución que determina la falta de amor entre
los cónyuges.   Es resultado de preocupaciones fi-
nancieras y sociales por parte de los esposos y
sus padres . . . El fracaso del matrimonio se
cifra en la incomunicación de los esposos y en el
adulterio."

628.   Durand, Frank.   "A Critical Analysis of Leopoldo
        Alas' La Regenta."   Diss.   U of Michigan,
        1962.   192 pp.

        "La Regenta may be considered an extension of
his critical works in its ironic and 'negative'
outlook . . . The actual analysis has been organized around the headings Themes, Narrative Techniques and Form, and Style, with appropriate sub-
divisions."

629.   Echeverría Esponda, María Dolores.   "Análisis
        literario de la obra narrativa de Clarín."
        Diss.   Universidad Complutense de Madrid,
        1975.

        Limits itself to LR and SUH.   "Se aborda la
semiótica del hecho artístico y literario y de los
hechos sociales . . . En La Regenta se estudia el
elemento temporal y espacial . . . la posición del

narrador ante el universo novelesco; tras un censo
de personajes se estudia la función ambiental y
caracteriológica de todos ellos y se traza un sis-
tema de relaciones, reflejado en esquemas gráficas, siguiendo a Todorov y Greimas."

630. García Lorca, Laura de.   "Los cuentos de Clarín.
      Proyección de una vida." Diss. Columbia U,
      1958.

      Published in 1965.   See book section of this
      bibliography under Ríos, Laura de los.

631. García Pavón, Francisco.   "Leopoldo Alas Clarín
      como narrador."   Diss.   Universidad de
      Madrid, 1952.

      "El autor saca la conclusión de que real-
      mente no existen esos dos momentos--uno revolu-
      cionario e iconoclasta seguido de otro espiritua-
      lista y condescendiente--sino que en toda la obra
      de Clarín estas dos posiciones extremas aparecen
      conjunta e irregularmente a lo largo de todo su
      proceso creador." See brief abstract in _Revista
      de la U de Madrid_, I, 3 (1952): 448-49.

632. García Sarriá, Francisco.   "_Su único hijo_: Análi-
      sis de esta novela y de su importancia en la
      obra de Leopoldo Alas, Clarín." Diss. U of
      Edinburgh (Scotland), 1973.

633. Gerrard, Lisa.   "The Romantic Woman in Nineteenth-
      Century Fiction: A Comparative Study of
      Madame Bovary,   _La Regenta_,   _The Mill on the
      Floss_, and _The Awakening_." Diss. U of Cal-
      ifornia at Berkeley, 1979.   157 pp.

      These four novels have a common concern: "the
      problems faced by the romantic individual in an
      unromantic world.   Each novel centers on a char-
      acter whose imaginative apprehension of reality
      conflicts with the workings and values of society
      . . . It is the contention of this study that
      Flaubert, Alas, Eliot, and Chopin all found a fe-
      male protagonist to be a particularly appropriate
      agent for this dilemma . . . because they found
      that the limited role of contemporary middle-class
      women created psychological problems akin to those
      of the dislocated romantic."

634. Gramberg, Eduard Johannes.   "El humorismo de Leo-
      poldo Alas Clarín." Diss. U of California,
      1957.

      Published in Oviedo in 1958.   See book sec-
      tion of this bibliography.

635.   Hamblin, Ellen N.   "Adulterous Heroines in Nine-
       teenth Century Literature: A Comparative Lit-
       erature Study."   Diss.   Florida State U,
       1977.   198 pp.

       "In a comparison and contrast (Clarín, Flau-
       bert, Tolstoy, Hawthorne) carried out by analogy,
       the salient themes of seduction, alienation, and
       motherhood reveal that Spanish Ana Ozores of La
       Regenta emerges a quasi-divine but passive heroine
       who is more a victim of a conquest than a willing
       transgressor."

636.   Hortas Moragón, Carlos Rafael.   "The Moral Vision
       of Leopoldo Alas."   Diss.   Yale U, 1970.   307
       pp.

       Attempts to examine "the central role of
       ethics and morality in the works of . . . Clarín
       . . . to demonstrate that Alas' moral sensibility
       constitutes the dominant feature of his writings."

637.   Ibarra, Fernando.   "Las categorías estéticas en la
       crítica literaria de Leopoldo Alas, Clarín."
       Diss.   U of California at Los Angeles, 1968.
       421 pp.

       "To present a new evaluation of the meaning
       of LAC in the field of aesthetic ideas, and of his
       criticism of the Spanish literature in the last
       quarter of the nineteenth century . . . The dis-
       sertation especially stresses the personal and
       emotional character of Clarin's criticism."

638.   Jones, Julie.   "His Only Son: A Translation of
       Leopoldo Alas' Su único hijo."   Diss.   U of
       Virginia, 1971.   338 pp.

       Published by LSU Press in 1981.   Reviewed by
       Bravo, Johnson (q.v.)

639.   Kronik, John William.   "The Short Stories of Leo-
       poldo Alas (Clarín): An Analysis and Census
       of the Characters."   Diss.   U of Wisconsin,
       1960.   396 pp.

       "An attempt to shed further light on the
       short stories of Alas by means of an analysis and
       evaluation of the narrative element that is shown
       to be of primary significance in them, the char-
       acters.   This is the first and lengthy investiga-
       tion of a specific phase of the stories, and the
       criteria applied to it are entirely esthetic, not
       historical or biographical . . . The census lists
       all the characters that appear in Alas' ninety-
       five collected stories."

640. Küpper, Werner L. "Leopoldo Alas Clarín und der
      französische Naturalismus in Spanien." Diss.
      U of Köln, 1958. 187 pp.

      Reviewed by Gramberg (q.v.)

641. Lebredo, Gerardo Gregorio. "Fermín de Pas y Ana
      Ozores en La Regenta." Diss. Florida State
      University, 1970. 169 pp.

      Contains six chapters: Biography of Clarín,
      general panorama of Spain, a study of La Regenta,
      Fermín de Pas, Ana Ozores, and conclusions.

642. Le Count, Virginia G. "Leopoldo Alas, Clarín: A
      Study of the Nineteenth Century in Spain as
      Depicted in His Novels and Short Stories."
      Master's thesis. Columbia U, 1940.

643. Little, William T. "Don Juanism in Modern Euro-
      pean Literature." Diss. Washington U, 1973.
      440 pp.

      "Using Nietzsche's Zarathustra as a meta-
      phorical prism, Chapter IV analyzes the Don
      Juanesque aspects of Clarín's two novels--La
      Regenta and Su único hijo. In Clarín's post-
      romantic-naturalist fictional world, the seducer
      has degenerated into the figure of an aging dandy
      (Alvaro Mesía), a frustrated priest (Fermín de
      Pas), and an effete husband (Bonifacio Reyes)."

644. Martínez, Renée Corty. "La mujer en la obra de
      Leopoldo Alas." Diss. U of Virginia, 1971.
      212 pp.

      "The purpose of this dissertation has been to
      study the role that women play in Alas' major
      works of fiction, which include La Regenta, Su
      único hijo, his short novel Doña Berta, and his
      only drama Teresa . . . Alas' own literary, social
      and moral preoccupations are, in many instances,
      mirrored in these characters."

645. Matlack, Charles William. "Leopoldo Alas and
      Naturalism in the Spanish Novel, 1881-1892."
      Diss. U of New Mexico, 1954. 177 pp.

      "To define Spanish naturalism in four es-
      sential ways: the influence of Zola, the natural-
      istic rating of the individual authors, the dif-
      ference between naturalism and realism, and the
      significance of Spanish naturalism as a literary
      movement." Chap. IV is devoted to Alas' short
      stories and novels.

646.   McBride, Charles Alfred.   "Narrative Modes in
       Three Works of Leopoldo Alas Clarín."   Diss.
       U of Texas at Austin, 1968.   218 pp.

       The study focuses on the narrative modes
       found in three short novels: <u>Doña Berta</u>, <u>Cuervo</u>,
       and <u>Superchería</u>, published by Alas in a single
       volume, which he declared to be his favorite.

647.   Miller, Michael Barry.   "A Study of Male Charac-
       terization in the Spanish Naturalistic Nov-
       el."   Diss.   George Washington U 1974.   217
       pp.

       Discerns in three novels (<u>LR</u>, <u>Los pazos de
       Ulloa</u>, <u>La barraca</u>) a new type of male character, a
       male who has become an anti-hero, the negation of
       the Romantic hero, and the personification of the
       defects of the Spanish moral, social, and reli-
       gious codes.

648.   Ochart, Luz Ivonne.   "La Restauración española a
       través de las lecturas de los personajes en
       <u>La Regenta</u>."   Diss.   State U of New York at
       Stony Brook, 1981.   221 pp.

       "The aim of this study is to show the links
       between . . . <u>La Regenta</u> and Spanish Restoration
       society . . . through the analysis of the charac-
       ters' literary background."

649.   O'Connor, Dolores Jeanne.   "Leopoldo Alas and the
       Spanish Realist Novel, 1876-1890."   Diss.   U
       of California at Berkeley, 1982.   314 pp.

       "The focus of this study is on Alas' role as
       a critic of culture and as a novelist at the
       turning-point in the development of Spanish liter-
       ary realism."

650.   Proaño-Naveda, Franklin.   "Posibilidades pluralís-
       ticas del 'yo' en los personajes literarios
       de Leopoldo Alas, Clarín."   Diss.   Ohio State
       U, 1971.   318 pp.

       "This dissertation analyzes the pluralistic
       possibilities of the self in the literary charac-
       ters of Clarín's narrative works.   It is the pur-
       pose of this study to investigate Clarín's concept
       of the self and to demonstrate that Leopoldo Alas
       stands out as a synthesizer of the philosophical
       and literary movements of the nineteenth century."

651.   Ramos-Gascón, Antonio.   "Clarín y la gente nueva."
       Diss.   U of California at San Diego, 1970.
       242 pp.

"In spite of Clarín having been one of the critical discoverers of French symbolism in Spain and an active Republican since his youth, the relation between Alas and the gente nueva (Martínez Ruiz, Valle Inclán, Unamuno, Maeztu, and others) is fundamentally polemical. The controversies raised in his polemic, although they manifest themselves on an ideological and aesthetic plane, often originate in contradictions of a political nature."

652.   Richmond, Carolyn.   "Clarín's Su único hijo: A Novel of Ambiguity and Crisis." Diss. U of Wisconsin at Madison, 1975. 386 pp.

"After a brief survey of criticism to date, this study analyzes major aspects of the novel, examines technical devices used by the narrator to create a sense of confusion and ambiguity, and finally considers the work in relationship to Clarín's life and the historical period in which it was written . . . Su único hijo can also be seen as a reflection of an emotional or spiritual crisis from which Clarín appears to have been suffering while writing it."

Ríos, Laura de los. See García Lorca, Laura de.

653.   Rivkin, Laura Madelaine.   "Eclectic Naturalism in the Novels of Leopoldo Alas Clarín." Diss. U of California at Berkeley, 1980. 450 pp.

"By taking up a comparative, intertextual approach, relating Alas' creed and criticism, readings of novels and literary practices, we capture the non-generic quality, the shifting of stances and voices that characterize his eclectic art. The works we examine include Alas' literary criticism, his dissertation, El derecho y la moralidad, his letters, and his novels."

654.   Sánchez, Elizabeth Doremus.   "Madame Bovary and La Regenta: A Comparative Study." Diss. Purdue U, 1980. 290 pp.

"A comprehensive comparison of Flaubert's Madame Bovary and Leopoldo Alas' La Regenta, combining a close reading of the texts with a general presentation of the authors and their works within their respective cultural and historical contexts."

655.   Sieburth, Stephanie Anne.   "Ambivalence in La Regenta: Narratorial Discourse vs. Textual Structure." Diss. Princeton U, 1984. 219 pp.

This novel "generates ambiguity on all levels of its structure. It is a multi-discursive text, containing many different versions of a few events . . . Ambivalence is produced in three ways . . . La Regenta is a quixotic novel, in which characters imitate literary texts, and thus bring them into dialogue with one another."

656.   Thomas, Richard Loyce.   "Sensation and Feeling in Clarín's La Regenta."   Diss.   U of Iowa, 1975.   329 pp.

"This study approaches Alas' novel . . . through its dominant motifs of sense-qualities, emotive elements, and perceptual modes, and through the imagery and symbolic expression of Alas as they are related to these motifs."

657.   Thompson, Clifford Ray.   "A Thematic Study of the Short Stories of Leopoldo Alas."   Diss.   Harvard U, 1965.   224 pp.

A 35-page introduction on the major themes, problems of classification and chronology, naturalistic doctrine, etc. is followed by five chapters on the most frequently treated situations: the lover, the man in search of faith, the intellectual, the creative artist, the family man. Love is often a frustrating and disillusioning experience.   Insisting that faith is a matter of the heart, Clarín portrays "the lonely battle which each individual must wage against reason." The intellectual is most frequently portrayed as a ludicrous figure whose interest in esoteric problems estranges him from his fellow man.   Alas satirizes the versifiers who, concerned only with the success of their works, are entirely lacking in poetic spirit.   As for the family man, only rarely is family life a source of contentment.

658.   Tintoré Espuny, María José.   "La crítica de La Regenta en la prensa del siglo XIX."   Master's thesis, Universidad de Barcelona, 1984.

659.   Tungeln, Annie Laurie von.   "Pessimistic Tendencies of Leopoldo Alas."   Master's thesis.   U of Oklahoma, 1932.   62 pp.

660.   Valis, Noël Maureen.   "The Idea of Decadence in the Novels of Leopoldo Alas (Clarín)."   Diss. Bryn Mawr C, 1975.   402 pp.

"Alas, whose criticism demonstrates his persistent interest in the Spanish decay of morals, politics, religion, and literature, shares the fin

<u>de siècle</u> obsession with decay and degeneration
. . . Alas' attitude toward the French decadents
and their Spanish imitators (mainly the <u>modernis-</u>
<u>tas</u>) was far from favorable . . . Chapters IV and
V attempt to illustrate the complex and rich
depths which the idea of decadence reaches in <u>LR</u>
and <u>SUH</u>."

661. Villavicencio, Laura Núñez de. "La creatividad en
       el estilo de Leopoldo Alas, Clarín."   Diss.
       U of Maryland, 1972.   278 pp.

       The purpose of this study is to analyze Alas'
language, in its affective and imaginative significance, by describing the mechanics of its artistic expression." Published in Oviedo in 1974; see
the book section of this bibliography.

662. Wagner, Miriam.   "<u>La Regenta</u>: Metaphor and Mean-
       ing." Diss. Cornell U, 1972.   183 pp.

       "Clarín's attitude toward the real world in
which he lives is revealed through the fictitious
world of <u>LR</u> by means of the metaphoric technique
. . . Our problem is to discover the metaphorical
structure of <u>LR</u>, with a view toward arriving at
the book's meaning."

663. Weiner, Hadassah Ruth.   "Crítica y creación: Dos
       dimensiones de la novelística de Clarín."
       Diss. Indiana U, 1973.   184 pp.

       "Clarín sees the novel as a vehicle for so-
cial commentary and reform, while recognizing the
importance of its aesthetic aspects as well.   He
therefore demands a balance of form and content,
meaningful and authentic dialogue, and a careful
plan of composition . . . <u>LR</u> is an hermetic novel
which ends on a note of despair, while <u>SUH</u> is an
ascendent, open-ended work, perhaps because it was
intended as the first part of a tetralogy."

664. Wesley, Howard David.   "Clarín and Pérez de Aya-
       la." Master's thesis. U of Texas at Austin,
       1937.   175 pp.

665. Alarcos Llorach, Emilio. "Cuentos de Clarín."
     <u>BIEA</u>, VIII, 21 (Abril, 1954): 137-38.

     A review of MC's 1953 ed. of 19 short stories
     by C, with an introd. by BG.

666. Alvarez, Carlos Luis. Rev. of <u>Fondo y forma del
     humorismo de LAC</u>, by Eduard Gramberg. <u>Punta
     Europa</u>, 55-56 (1960): 100-01.

667. Amorós, Andrés. "Clarín, caso aparte." <u>CHA</u>,
     LXIV, 191 (Nov., 1965): 381-84.

     A review of Laura de los Ríos' <u>Los cuentos de
     Clarín</u>, generally favorable except for the fact
     that it is "más descriptivo que interpretativo,
     más acumulativo que sintético . . . Niega L. de
     los R. el naturalismo de Clarín . . . Sabe ver que
     el amor, la religión y el humor son tres claves
     para comprender a Clarín."

668. Anonymous. "The Toads of Vetusta." <u>The Times
     Literary Supplement</u> (London), 66th Year, No.
     3385 (12 Jan. 1967): 26.

     A review of the new 678-page ed. of <u>LR</u> by
     Alianza Editorial, which the writer predicts will
     outsell all other editions because it is more eco-
     nomical. "Clarín . . . a second-rate literary
     critic . . . a man of confused and vacillating
     political convictions, a writer of short stories
     of uneven and often poor quality, and the author
     of one monumentally fine novel . . . Alas's famous
     anticlericalism turns out to be of a characteris-
     tically Spanish kind--indignation at the harm that
     unworthy ministers are doing to the Church . . .
     <u>LR</u> is the story of a superior, sensitive being,
     inexorably defiled and ultimately destroyed by a
     way of thought which Alas believed to be charac-
     teristic of a whole epoch, and with which he felt
     himself to be violently in conflict. . . . Alas is
     one of those romantic idealists who cannot recon-
     cile true love with physical sexuality . . . There
     is no further escape (for Ana), no further excuse
     for hoping that life is anything but the disgust-
     ing existence of the toad-like inhabitants of
     Vetusta."

669. Araujo-Costa, Luis. "Clarín." <u>ABC</u>, 13 Mayo 1947.

     A review of Adolfo Posada's biography of C.

670. Avrett, Robert.   Rev. of <u>Leopoldo Alas and La Re-</u>
      <u>genta</u>, by Albert Brent.   <u>MLJ</u>, XXXIX, 6 (Oct.,
      1955): 330.

671. Bacarisse, Salvador.   Rev. of <u>La mujer insatisfe-</u>
      <u>cha</u>, by Biruté Ciplijauskaité.   <u>BHS</u>, LXIII, 1
      (Jan., 1986): 94.

672. Bandera, Cesáreo.   Rev. of <u>Clarín o la herejía</u>
      <u>amorosa</u>, by F. García Sarriá.   <u>HR</u>, XLV
      (1977): 462-64.

673. Baquero Goyanes, Mariano.   Rev. of <u>Obras selectas</u>
      <u>de Clarín</u>, ed. by Juan A. Cabezas.   <u>RUO</u>
      (Sept.-dic., 1947): 113-17.

674. Belot, Albert.   Rev. of <u>Clarín político, II</u>, by
      Yvan Lissorgues.   <u>Caravelle</u> (Toulouse), 40
      (1983): 205-07.

675. Beser, Sergio.   Rev. of <u>Los cuentos de Clarín</u>, by
      Laura de los Ríos.   <u>Indice Histórico Español</u>
      (B), XI (1965): 282.

676. ---.   Rev. of <u>La Regenta</u>, ed. by J. M. Martínez
      Cachero.   <u>BHS</u>, XLIII, 4 (Oct., 1966): 303-04.

      Beser recognizes MC's vast knowledge of C's
      personality but would have preferred a more pro-
      found study of the literary aspects of <u>LR</u>.

677. ---.   Rev. of <u>Leopoldo Alas: La Regenta</u>, by John
      Rutherford.   <u>BHS</u>, LIV, 1 (Jan., 1977): 70-71.

678. Bly, Peter.   Rev. of <u>La Regenta</u>, ed. by Gonzalo
      Sobejano.   <u>RCEH</u>, VIII, 2 (Winter, 1984): 304.

679. Bonet, Laureano.   "Clarín y la función de la crí-
      tica."   <u>Insula</u>, XXX, 342 (Mayo, 1975): 12-13.

      Remarks on C's literary criticism as reflec-
      ted in two recent books: Ramos-Gascón's <u>Obra ol-</u>
      <u>vidada</u> (1973) and Martínez Cachero's ed. of <u>Pali-</u>
      <u>que</u> (1973).

680. ---.   "<u>Clarín</u> en imágenes múltiples: Una antología
      de José María Martínez Cachero."   <u>Insula</u>,
      XXXIV, 392-93 (Julio-agosto, 1979): 10.

      The anthology in question is <u>Leopoldo Alas</u>
      <u>Clarín</u>, published by Taurus in 1978.

681. ---.   "Clarín entre el romanticismo y el modernis-
      mo: Una nueva edición de <u>Su único hijo</u>."   <u>In-</u>
      <u>sula</u>, XXXV, 406 (Sept., 1980): 1 y 11-12.

A review of Carolyn Richmond's ed.

682.   ---. "Clarín periodista: Un estudio y antología
        de Yvan Lissorgues." Insula, XXXVI, 418
        (Sept., 1981): 1 y 14.

        A review of Lissorgues' Clarín político, I
        (1980).

683.   ---. "Clarín y el espíritu de la modernidad: Una
        antología de Carolyn Richmond." Insula,
        XXXIX, 446 (Enero, 1984): 1 y 15.

        A review of Richmond's Leopoldo Alas Clarín:
        Treinta relatos, published by Espasa-Calpe in
        1983.

684.   Botrel, Jean-François. Rev. of Clarín político,
        I, by Yvan Lissorgues. BH, LXXXIII, 3-4
        (July-Dec., 1981): 474-76.

685.   Bravo, María Elena. Rev. of Su único hijo, trans.
        into English by Julie Jones. REH, XVII
        (1983): 147-48.

686.   Brown, G. G. Rev. of Leopoldo Alas, crítico lite-
        rario, by Sergio Beser. BHS, XLVII, 4 (Oct.,
        1970): 362-63.

687.   ---. Rev. of Leopoldo Alas: Teoría y crítica, by
        Sergio Beser. BHS, LIII, 4 (Oct., 1976):
        353-54.

688.   ---. Rev. of La creatividad en el estilo de Leo-
        poldo Alas, by Laura N. de Villavicencio.
        BHS, LIV, 1 (Jan., 1977): 69-70.

689.   Cabal, Constantino. Rev. of Leopoldo Alas Clarín,
        by Marino Gómez-Santos. BIEA, VII, 18
        (Enero, 1953): 148-50.

        Considers it fragmentary and deficient ("the
        list of paliques is useless") but approves of the
        wealth of data supplied.

690.   Cano, José Luis. "Clarín y sus cuentos." Insula,
        XX, 227 (Oct., 1965): 8-9.

        A review of Laura de los Ríos' Los cuentos de
        Clarín.

691.   Caso González, José. "Los cuentos de Leopoldo
        Alas." Archivum, III, 2 (Mayo-agosto, 1953):
        297-300.

A review of J. M. Martínez-Cachero's ed. with introd. by BG, published in Oviedo in 1953.

692. Cheyne, G. J. Rev. of <u>Cuentos escogidos de Clarín</u>, ed. by G. G. Brown. <u>BHS</u>, XLIV (1967): 134-35.

693. D'Auria, Riccardo. Rev. of <u>Obra olvidada de Clarín</u>, by Antonio Ramos-Gascón. <u>LT</u>, XXIII, 87-88 (Enero-junio, 1975): 223-26.

694. Davis, Gifford. Rev. of <u>Leopoldo Alas, crítico literario</u>, by Sergio Beser. <u>RR</u>, LXII, 2 (April, 1971): 153-54.

   Points out contradictions in Beser (pp.68-69, 137) regarding C's treatment of great and mediocre writers. Disagrees with Beser's opinion of Bull's and Chamberlin's hard-hitting study.

695. Dial, John E. Rev. of <u>The Decadent Vision in Leopoldo Alas</u>, by Noël M. Valis. <u>REH</u>, XVII, 3 (Oct., 1983): 468-69.

696. Díaz, Janet. Rev. of <u>La creatividad en el estilo de Leopoldo Alas</u>, by Laura N. de Villavicencio. <u>Hispano</u>, LXV (Enero, 1979): 116-19.

697. ---. Rev. of <u>Clarín o la herejía amorosa</u>, by F. García Sarriá. <u>Hispano</u>, LXVI (Marzo, 1979): 126-29.

698. Díez Borque, José María. "Recuperación de un crítico literario: Leopoldo Alas." <u>CHA</u>, 43 (1973): 629-34.

   A review of Sergio Beser's <u>Leopoldo Alas: Teoría y crítica</u>. A similar review appeared in <u>EstLit</u>, 527 (1973): 1512.

699. ---. Rev. of <u>Palique</u>, ed. by J. M. Martínez Cachero. <u>EstLit</u>, 540 (1974): 1722-23.

700. ---. Rev. of <u>Clarín o la herejía amorosa</u>, by F. García Sarriá. <u>EstLit</u>, 580 (1976): 2338-39.

701. D'Ors, Eugenio. "Clarín" y "Más sobre Clarín." <u>Arriba</u> (M), 16 y 17 Marzo 1947.

   A review of Adolfo Posada's biography of Clarín, which D'Ors finds inadequate. Unfavorable comments on <u>LR</u> because it is tedious. More on the Zola-Clarín parallel.

702. Dowling, John. Rev. of <u>Leopoldo Alas, crítico literario</u>, by Sergio Beser. <u>Hispania</u>, LIII (1970): 149-50.

"Even though the period was weak in poetry and C was least sure of himself in this genre, Beser's treatment is exceptionally able." With regard to C's "sincere but by no means unbridled" admiration for Echegaray, Dowling calls attention to Clayton Baker's recent thesis at Indiana, "Echegaray and His Critics."

703.   Entrambasaguas, Joaquín de.   "Notas bibliográficas." RFE, XXV, 3 (Julio-sept., 1941): 405-18.

A review of Adolfo Alas' Epistolario a Clarín (1941), especially Unamuno's "poisonous and resentful" letters trying very hard to obtain a favorable review of Paz en la guerra.

704.   ---.   "Clarín, redivivo." RL, IV, 7 (Julio-sept., 1953): 256-57.

Brief comments on Marino Gómez Santos' Leopoldo Alas Clarín.

705.   Fernández Almagro, Melchor.   "Leopoldo Alas, Clarín." ABC, 8 Sept. 1946.

A review of Adolfo's Posada's biography of C.

706.   ---.   Rev. of Obras selectas de Clarín, ed. by Juan Antonio Cabezas. ABC, 14 Oct. 1947.

"Lo que no se ha dicho todavía es que en LR apuntan asombrosos señales de moderno psicologismo y que en algunas páginas se presiente a Proust."

707.   Fernández de la Vega, Oscar.   Rev. of Inspiración y estética en La Regenta, by Juan V. Agudiez. RIB, XXIII (1973): 99-100.

708.   Fraga, Eduardo de.   "Acuse de lectura." La Nueva España (O), 7 Enero 1953.

A review of Marino Gómez Santos' Leopoldo Alas Clarín.

709.   García Domínguez, Elías.   Rev. of Inspiración y estética en La Regenta, by Juan V. Agudiez. BIEA, XXIV, 71 (Sept-dic., 1970): 561-64.

"Las partes desarrolladas de una manera más orgánica y original parecen ser los capítulos V y VII, por lo que respecta al análisis temático, siendo los capítulos III, IV, VI, y VIII más bien complementarios, pues en ellos la parte analítica es mucho menor."

710. García Sarriá, Francisco. Rev. of <u>The Decadent Vision in Leopoldo Alas</u>, by Noël M. Valis. <u>BHS</u>, LIX, 2 (April, 1982): 155-57.

711. ---. Rev. of <u>Clarín y sus editores</u>, by Josette Blanquat and Jean-F. Botrel. <u>BHS</u>, LXII, 2 (April, 1985): 207-09.

      "Por fascinantes que sean los aspectos humanos y literarios que se revelan en estas cartas, no obstante, su mayor valor reside en los datos que contienen sobre la génesis de <u>SUH</u> y sobre el lugar que C asignaba a <u>Sinfonía de dos novelas</u> entre otras obras suyas."

712. ---. Rev. of <u>Teoría general de la novela. Semiología de La Regenta</u>, by María del Carmen Bobes Naves. <u>BHS</u>, LXIII, 1 (Jan., 1986): 104-06.

713. ---. Rev. of <u>Clarín: Treinta relatos</u>, ed. by Carolyn Richmond. <u>BHS</u>, LXIII, 1 (Jan., 1986): 106-07.

714. Garmendia, Vincent. Rev. of <u>Preludios de Clarín</u>, by Jean-F. Botrel. <u>BH</u>, LXXVIII, 3-4 (July-Dec., 1976): 416.

715. Gich, Juan. "Aportación al estudio de Clarín." <u>Correo Literario</u> (M), No. 67 (1 Marzo 1953).

      A review of Marino Gómez-Santos' <u>Leopoldo Alas Clarín</u>.

716. Goldman, Peter B. Rev. of <u>La novela como acto imaginativo</u>, by Germán Gullón. <u>BHS</u>, LXIII, 1 (Jan., 1986): 93.

717. Gómez Galán, A. "Clarín." <u>Arbor</u>, LXVI, 253 (Enero, 1967): 95-96.

      A bibliographical note on recent books by or about Clarín: Alianza's ed. of <u>LR</u> and <u>SUH</u>, Oxford's ed. of <u>Cuentos</u>, etc. According to Galán, "El Señor" is "una prosa meditativa, seria, con resonancias de interior combate."

718. Goytisolo, José Agustín. "Clarín en Italia." <u>Insula</u>, XVI, 173 (Abril, 1961): 12.

      A review of <u>La Presidentessa</u>, Flaviarosa Rossini's translation of <u>LR</u>, which Goytisolo agrees with José María Castellet may well be the best Spanish novel since <u>Don Quixote</u>.

719.   Gracia, José Ignacio.   Rev. of <u>Los cuentos de</u>
        <u>Clarín</u>, by Laura de los Ríos.   <u>BIEA</u>, XXII,
        64-65 (Mayo-dic., 1968): 457-61.

        According to Gracia, the chapter on humor is
        "esquemático" and establishes artificial differ-
        ences.

720.   Gramberg, Eduard J.   Rev. of <u>Leopoldo Alas Clarín</u>
        <u>und der französische Naturalismus in Spanien</u>,
        by Werner Küpper.   <u>Archivum</u>, XI, 1-2 (1961):
        447-52.

        A precise review of this German doctoral the-
        sis.   Disagrees with Küpper's statement that C
        never wrote anything negative about his favorites
        (Galdós, Echegaray, Valera, PV).   Agrees with Küp-
        per's comparison of <u>LR</u> and <u>Madame Bovary</u>.   Dis-
        agrees that Alas was Spain's only authentic natu-
        ralistic writer, since Alas rejected many of
        Zola's theories.

721.   Gullón, Agnes M.   Rev. of <u>La Regenta</u>, trans. by
        John Rutherford.   <u>HR</u>, LIII, 2 (Spring, 1985):
        250-52.

722.   Gullón, Germán.   Rev. of <u>El teatro en la novela:</u>
        <u>Galdós y Clarín</u>, by Roberto G. Sánchez.   <u>HR</u>,
        XLV (1977): 460-61.

723.   Gullón, Ricardo.   Rev. of <u>Leopoldo Alas Clarín</u>, by
        Adolfo Posada.   <u>BBMP</u>, XXII, 2 (Abril-junio,
        1946): 190-91.

        Likes the sincere tone and simple style, and
        the wealth of data, but regrets that Posada did
        not publish the letters in their entirety.

724.   ---.   "Una interpretación de <u>La Regenta</u>."   <u>CHA</u>,
        XIV, 38 (1953): 219-20.

        A review of Albert Brent's <u>Leopoldo Alas and</u>
        <u>La Regenta</u>.

725.   ---.   Rev. of <u>El teatro en la novela: Galdós y</u>
        <u>Clarín</u>, by Roberto G. Sánchez.   <u>Insula</u>, XXX,
        341 (Abril, 1975): 10.

726.   Hall, H. B.   Rev. of <u>Leopoldo Alas and La Regenta</u>,
        by Albert Brent.   <u>BHS</u>, XXIX, 114 (April-June,
        1952): 122-23.

        "The scope of the book is . . . disappoint-
        ingly limited . . . The book thus shows a certain
        lack of balance and a marked preponderance of the
        expository over the critical."

727.   ---. Rev. of <u>Cuentos escogidos de Clarín</u>, ed. by
       G. G. Brown. <u>MLR</u>, LXIII (1968): 734-35.

728.   Helman, Edith F.   Rev. of <u>Leopoldo Alas and La
       Regenta</u>, by Albert Brent. <u>HR</u>, XX, 3 (July,
       1952): 347-50.

       Praise for Brent's "thorough, and often pene-
       trating" analysis of the novel, but disagrees that
       C wrote it to compensate for his own disappoint-
       ments.

729.   ---. Rev. of <u>Una novela de Clarín: Su único hijo</u>,
       by Mariano Baquero Goyanes.   <u>HR</u>, XXII, 1
       (Jan., 1954): 81-84.

       "We do not concur with Goyanes' opinion that
       the novel is coldly impersonal, the work of a de-
       tached pure intellectual.   It seems to us, rather,
       a spiritual autobiography, agonizingly felt and
       recounted with intense feeling, even if in bit-
       terly humorous caricature."

730.   Jackson, Robert M.   Rev. of <u>Leopoldo Alas, crítico
       literario</u>, by Sergio Beser.   <u>MLN</u>, LXXXVI, 2
       (March, 1971): 306-09.

       Beser's most important achievement is the
       clear presentation of the concept of <u>oportunidad</u>
       as the basis for the evolution of Alas' literary
       theories . . . Beser has given C's writings on
       poetry and drama more attention than those sub-
       jects deserve; yet, Beser omits the area of C's
       enthusiastic appreciation for Zorrilla's theater.

731.   ---. Rev. of <u>Su único hijo</u>, ed. by Carolyn Rich-
       mond. <u>Hispania</u>, LXVI, 2 (May, 1983): 296.

       Despite the sketchy "Datos biográficos,"
       Richmond is especially helpful in suggesting the
       relationship with the concerns and techniques of
       the writers of 1898.   She aids the reader with
       thorough explanations of literary and musical
       references.

732.   Johnson, Harvey L.   Rev. of <u>Su único hijo</u>, trans.
       by Julie Jones.   <u>South Central Bulletin</u>
       (Houston, TX), XLII, 1-2 (1982): 22.

733.   Klein, Richard B.   Rev. of <u>La Regenta</u>, ed. by
       Gonzalo Sobejano. <u>Hispania</u>, LXVI, 3 (Sept.,
       1983): 434-35.

       Sobejano's ed. is based on the 1900 edition,
       with Galdós' preface, which Sobejano considers the

definitive one. The 52-page introd. shows a complete and sensitive grasp of both Alas and LR. Good bibliography which, however, deletes Jeremy Medina's 1979 book on realism. Extremely useful footnotes.

734.   ---. Rev. of La Regenta, trans. by John Rutherford. REH, XIX, 1 (Jan., 1985): 139-40.

735.   Kronik, John W. Rev. of Clarín: The Critic in Action, by William Emerson Bull and Vernon A. Chamberlin. Hispano, 25 (1965): 57-62.

736.   ---. Rev. of Cuentos escogidos de Clarín, ed. by G. G. Brown. HR, XXXV (1967): 202-03.

737.   ---. Rev. of Leopoldo Alas, crítico literario, by Sergio Beser. HR, XXXIX (1971): 329-34.

738.   ---. Rev. of Palique, ed. by J. M. Martínez Cachero. HR, XLIV (1976): 299-301.

739.   ---. Rev. of The Decadent Vision in Leopoldo Alas, by Noël M. Valis. Hispania, LXV, 3 (Sept., 1982): 463-64.

740.   Le Bouill, J. Rev. of Leopoldo Alas, crítico literario, by Sergio Beser. BH, LXXI, 3-4 (July-Dec., 1969): 697-99.

741.   Ledesma Miranda, Ramón. "Clarín en edición de lujo." Arriba (M), 9 Oct. 1947.

A review of the Obras selectas ed. by Juan A. Cabezas.

742.   López-Morillas, Juan. Rev. of Clarín, crítico literario, by Sergio Beser. Comparative Literature Studies, IX, 2 (June, 1972): 234-37.

C did not think it was possible to criticize solely on aesthetic values. He was not sure how to approach poetry. The theater was his true passion, even though he was more recognized as a critic of novels. Beser's study is of cardinal importance.

743.   Marañón, Gregorio. "Menéndez Pelayo y Clarín: Reflexiones sobre un epistolario." LN, 21 Nov. 1943.

Concerning Adolfo Alas' Epistolario de Clarín y Menéndez Pelayo.

744.   Maravall, José Antonio. "La mascarilla de Clarín." Arriba (M), 27 Dic. 1941.

A review of Adolfo Alas' <u>Epistolario a Cla-</u>
<u>rín</u>. The "mascarilla" refers to the fact that the
volume does not contain Clarín's replies to letters from MMP, Unamuno, and PV.

745.   Martínez Cachero, José María.   "Bibliografía re-
       ciente sobre Clarín." <u>BIEA</u>, XIII, 38 (Dic.,
       1959): 469-72.

       A brief and highly favorable review of
Blanquat's "Clarín et Baudelaire" and Gramberg's
<u>Fondo y forma del humorismo de Leopoldo Alas</u>
<u>Clarín</u>.

746.   ---. Rev. of <u>Fondo y forma del humorismo de Leo-</u>
       <u>poldo Alas Clarín</u>, by Eduard J. Gramberg.
       <u>RL</u>, XXI (1962): 208-09.

       Speaks highly of the "lucid analysis" made in
the last chapter.

747.   Martínez San Martín, Angel. Rev. of <u>Teoría gene-</u>
       <u>ral de la novela</u>, by María del Carmen Bobes
       Naves.   <u>RL</u>, XLVII, 94 (Julio-dic., 1985):
       300-04.

748.   Mathías, Julio.   Rev. of <u>Leopoldo Alas, crítico</u>
       <u>literario</u>, by Sergio Beser.   <u>EstLit</u>, 463
       (1971): 486.

749.   Mayoral, Marina.   Rev. of <u>Leopoldo Alas, crítico</u>
       <u>literario</u>, by Sergio Beser. <u>CHA</u>, LXXVII, 230
       (Feb., 1969): 458-63.

       Mayoral is surprised that Clarín did not
write on Rosalía de Castro and that Beser did not
justify this silence.

750.   Méndez Riestra, Eduardo.   Rev. of <u>La Regenta</u>, ed.
       by Gonzalo Sobejano. <u>CN</u>, 12 (1982): 88-89.

751.   Menéndez Onrubia, Carmen. Rev. of <u>El teatro en la</u>
       <u>novela: Galdós y Clarín</u>, by Roberto G. Sán-
       chez. <u>Segismundo</u> (M), XV, 33-34 (1981): 294-
       97.

       However, the reviewer concentrates on Galdós.

752.   Moreno Baez, E.   Rev. of <u>Cuentos de Clarín</u>, ed. by
       José María Martínez Cachero.   <u>Arbor</u>, 27
       (1954): 480-81.

753.   Muñiz, Angelita.   Rev. of <u>Fondo y forma del humo-</u>
       <u>rismo de Leopoldo Alas Clarín</u>, by Eduard J.
       Gramberg. <u>NRFH</u>, XVII (1963-64): 407-08.

754.   Muñoz Cortés, M. Rev. of <u>Una novela de Clarín: Su</u>
        <u>único hijo</u>, by Mariano Baquero Goyanes.
        <u>ASNS</u>, CLXXXIX (1953): 399.

755.   Ortega, R. G. de. Rev. of <u>La obra de Clarín</u>, by
        Pedro Sáinz Rodríguez. <u>RFE</u>, VIII, 4 (Oct-
        dic., 1921): 417-18.

        According to Ortega, Chap. 4 of <u>LR</u>, which
        Sáinz Rodríguez cites as diffuse, is the best one
        in which to note the difference between Zola's
        naturalism and Clarín's.

756.   Pattison, Walter T. Rev. of <u>Clarín: The Critic in</u>
        <u>Action</u>, by William E. Bull and Vernon A.
        Chamberlin. <u>HR</u>, 34 (1966): 192-93.

757.   Pazos, Manuel R. Rev. of <u>El gallo de Sócrates y</u>
        <u>otros cuentos</u>, by Leopoldo Alas. <u>AIA</u>, XXXIV,
        136 (1974): 696.

758.   Pino, Juan del. Rev. of <u>La Regenta de Clarín y la</u>
        <u>Restauración</u>, by Jean Bécarud. <u>Archivo His-</u>
        <u>palense</u> (Sevilla), 123 (1964): 91-92.

759.   Quiroga Clérigo, Manuel. "Casi crítica a un crí-
        tico: <u>Clarín, La creatividad en el estilo de</u>
        <u>Leopoldo Alas</u>." <u>CHA</u>, CVIII, 324 (Junio,
        1977): 573-75.

        A review of Laura N. de Villavicencio's book,
        which Quiroga considers "obra profunda donde la
        figura literaria de C es analizada con vigor y
        donde se estudia con detenimiento los varios as-
        pectos (literarios, gramaticales y temperamenta-
        les) de la ingente obra comentada."

760.   Richmond, Carolyn. "Una espléndida edición de <u>La</u>
        <u>Regenta</u>." <u>Insula</u>, XXXIV, 392-393 (Julio-
        agosto, 1979): 10.

        A review of Gonzalo Sobejano's ed.

761.   ---. "Clarín periodista. Una nueva aportación de
        Ivan Lissorgues." <u>Insula</u>, XXXVII, 433 (Dic.,
        1982): 5.

        A review of Yvan Lissorgues' <u>Clarín político,</u>
        <u>II</u>.

762.   Rivkin, Laura. Rev. of <u>Los prólogos de Leopoldo</u>
        <u>Alas</u>, by David Torres. <u>Hispania</u>, LXVIII, 3
        (Sept., 1985): 518-19.

763. Rogers, Douglass M. Rev. of <u>The Decadent Vision in Leopoldo Alas</u>, by Noël M. Valis. <u>SAR</u>, XLII, 2 (May, 1982): 110.

764. Rossi, Guiseppe Carlo. "Clarín." <u>Idea</u> (Rome), 5 April 1953.

A review of the 1952 issue of <u>Archivum</u> devoted to C.

765. Round, Nicholas C. Rev. of <u>La Regenta</u>, ed. by Gonzalo Sobejano, and <u>The Decadent Vision in Leopoldo Alas</u>, by Noël M. Valis. <u>MLR</u>, LXXIX (1984): 217-19.

766. Rutherford, John. Rev. of <u>La creatividad en el estilo de Leopoldo Alas</u>, by Laura N. de Villavicencio. <u>MLR</u>, LXXI (1976) 940-41.

767 ---. Rev. of <u>Clarín o la herejía amorosa</u>, by F. García Sarriá. <u>BHS</u>, LIV, 3 (July, 1977): 254-56.

768. ---. Rev. of <u>La Regenta</u>, ed. by Gonzalo Sobejano. <u>BHS</u>, LV, 2 (April, 1978): 165-66.

769. Sánchez Arnosi, Milagros. Rev. of <u>Clarín y La Regenta</u>, ed. by Sergio Beser. <u>Insula</u>, XXXVIII, 434 (Enero, 1983): 9.

770. Seymour-Smith Martin. "Fiction: Spanish Passion." <u>Financial Times</u> (London), 11 Feb. 1984.

A review of John Rutherford's English translation of <u>LR</u>.

771. Sobejano, Gonzalo. Rev. of <u>Su único hijo</u>, ed. by Carolyn Richmond. <u>HR</u>, L (1982): 496-99.

772. Southworth, E. A. Rev. of <u>La Regenta</u>, ed. by Mariano Baquero Goyanes. <u>BHS</u>, LXIII, 1 (Jan., 1986): 104.

773. S. R., I. Rev. of <u>Leopoldo Alas Clarín</u>, by Marino Gómez-Santos. <u>BEP</u>, XVII (1953): 273-74.

774. Tejedor, Matilde. Rev. of <u>Los cuentos de Clarín</u>, by Laura de los Ríos. <u>RLMM</u>, VI (1967): 139-40.

775. Thompson, Clifford R. Rev. of <u>Los cuentos de Clarín</u>, by Laura de los Ríos. <u>RF</u>, LXXIX (1967): 251-56.

A well-informed and favorable review of Dr. de los Ríos' 1965 book.

776. ---. Rev. of <u>Leopoldo Alas Clarín: Treinta rela-</u>
      <u>tos</u>, ed. by Carolyn Richmond. <u>Hispania</u>,
      LXVII, 3 (Sept., 1984): 474.

777. Ullman, Pierre L. Rev. of <u>La creatividad en el</u>
      <u>estilo de Leopoldo Alas</u>, by Laura N. de
      Villavicencio. <u>Hispania</u>, LIX, 2 (May, 1976):
      375.

778. Valdeavellano, Luis G. de. "Clarín visto por
      Adolfo Posada." <u>Insula</u>, I, 12 (15 Dic.
      1946): 2.

      A review of Posada's biography of C.

779. Valis, Noël M. Rev. of <u>Clarín, político, I</u>, by
      Yvan Lissorgues. <u>HR</u>, LI, 3 (Summer, 1983):
      336-38.

      In addition to the editing of thousands of
      newspaper articles by C, the reviewer admires
      Lissorgues' well-documented introduction and
      thematic presentation of the material. The major
      defect is the large number and length of the
      footnotes.

780. ---. Rev. of <u>La Regenta</u>, trans. by John Ruther-
      ford. <u>BHS</u>, LXIII, 1 (Jan., 1976): 102-03.

781. ---. Rev. of <u>La Regenta</u>, ed. by Juan Oleza. <u>BHS</u>,
      LXIII, 1 (Jan., 1986): 103-04.

782. ---. Rev. of <u>Clarín en su obra ejemplar</u>, by Gon-
      zalo Sobejano. <u>Hispania</u>, LXI, 3 (Sept.,
      1986): 544-45.

783. Villa Pastor, Jesús. "Homenaje a Clarín." <u>La Voz</u>
      <u>de Asturias</u> (O), 20 Dic. 1952.

      A review of the 1952 issue of <u>Archivum</u> de-
      voted to C.

E. MISCELLANEOUS

784. Acebal, Francisco. "Los paisajes de Clarín." RP
     (1 Julio 1901): 12-13.

785. Aggeler, William F. Baudelaire Judged by Spanish
     Critics, 1857-1957. Athens: U of Georgia P,
     1971. 115 pp.

     Critical extracts (pp. 9-15, 22) of Clarín's
     articles on Baudelaire from La Ilustración Ibérica
     and elsewhere. Unlike Valera, C was more toler-
     ant, flexible, and objective toward the French
     poet. Reviewed by R. A. Cardwell in BHS, LI
     (1974): 304-05.

786. Agramonte Cortijo, Francisco, ed. "Clarín, Leo-
     poldo Alas." Diccionario cronológico biográ-
     fico universal. Madrid: Aguilar, 1961. 291.

     Refers to a so-called Novela incoherente
     (1900), written by C in collaboration with another
     author, whom Agramonte does not identify. Appar-
     ently he considers it a different work from Las
     vírgenes locas, which he also lists. Contains
     several errors of classification and dates.

787. Aguas Alfaro, J. J. "Clarín, creador de tipos
     clásicos." El Universal (Caracas), 28 Agosto
     1952.

788. "Alas, Leopoldo." Enciclopedia universal ilus-
     trada. Madrid: Espasa-Calpe, 1958. 4: 41-
     42.

789. ---. The New Encyclopedia Britannica. Chicago,
     1980. 1: 186-87.

790. Albornoz, Alvaro de. "La Universidad de Oviedo."
     EM, 21 (1908): 153-65.

     Devotes three laudatory pages to Clarín, even
     though editor Lázaro had promised to remove his
     name from this journal. See Rodríguez-Moñino's
     article on this "pleito."

791. Alonso Cortés, Narciso. Jornadas. Valladolid,
     1920.

     Describes the polemic between C and the poet
     Manuel del Palacio, pp. 68-73.

792.   ---.   "Armonía y emoción en Salvador Rueda."   CLC,
       VII (1943): 36-48.

       Literary relations between C and the young
       poet.   Excerpts from Alas' "Cartas a Salvador
       Rueda" (Los Madriles, 27 Julio 1889).

793.   ---.   "Zorrilla y Clarín."   Amigos de Zorrilla
       . . . Colección de artículos dedicados al
       poeta.   Valladolid: Imprenta Castellana,
       1933.   134 pp.

       On pp. 47-49 reproduces two unpublished let-
       ters from C to Zorrilla (2 April 1885 and 3 March
       1892) concerning the poet's government pension and
       his poem "Cádiz" in El Liberal.   Alas claims to
       have been an admirer of Zorrilla since the age of
       five, and to know El zapatero y el rey by heart.

794.   ---.   Crítica belicosa."   El Norte de Castilla
       (Valladolid), 14 Nov. 1952.

       Laments that C wasted so much time and energy
       in intemperate disputes with Bonafoux and Bobadi-
       lla.   Makes one of the earliest references to Mar-
       tinete's Autopsia de Clarín, studied by MC in
       1959.

795.   Alonso Iglesia, Leontina y Asunción García-
       Paredes.   "La Extensión Universitaria de
       Oviedo, 1898-1901."   BIEA, 81 (Enero-abril,
       1974): 119-69.

796.   Alonso y Orera, E.   "Correspondencia española:
       Revista literaria."   Revista Ilustrada de
       Nueva York, XII, 12 (Dic., 1893): 616-20.

       Comments on SDC, p. 618.

797.   ---.   "Revista teatral: La Dolores - Teresa."   Il
       Ib, XIII, 661 (31 Agosto 1895): 554-55.

       C is a playwright, despite defects of Teresa.
       Alas should not have replied to attacks against
       his play.   Alonso announces that he plans to write
       a study entitled Clarín.

798.   Altamira, Rafael.   "Paliques."   RP (1 Julio 1901):
       12.

799.   ---.   "Leopoldo Alas."   Anales de la Universidad
       de Oviedo, 1902.

       Some "apuntaciones necrológicas" by one of
       Alas' faculty colleagues.

800. ---. <u>Tierras y hombres de Asturias</u>.   México: Re-
      vista Norte, 1949.   284 pp.

      The Clarín Theater was inaugurated in Soto in
      1921.   Perhaps <u>Teresa</u> may some day be performed
      here.   In 1895 the play was "tan injustamente
      rechazada por un público prevenido, que iba dis-
      puesto a no escuchar ni la primera escena."

801. Alvarez, Blanca.   "Ana."   <u>CN</u>, V, 23 (1984): 58-59.

      Alvarez Buylla, A.   See Buylla, Adolfo A.

802. Anonymous.   "<u>Sermón perdido</u>."   <u>RE</u>, CVII, 426 (Nov.-
      dic., 1885): 309-11.

      "Y como posee (Clarín) un talento perspicaz,
      buen gusto e instrucción variada y profunda, hace
      con gran facilidad la anatomía completa de cual-
      quier libro."

803. ---.   "<u>Pipá</u>."   <u>RE</u>, CIX, 434 (Marzo-abril, 1886):
        318-19.

      "En todas (las narraciones) se deja ver la
      pluma penetrante, intencionada y sangrienta de
      Clarín y en algunas, como en <u>Pipá</u>, un talento de
      primer orden."

804. ---.   "Critica de <u>Su único hijo</u>."   <u>HM</u>, 4 Julio
        1891.

805. ---.   "Los funerales de Clarín."   <u>RN</u>, I, 2 (25
      Feb. 1899): 69-75.

      The analysis of a weak "crónica literaria"
      published by Clarín in <u>Los Lunes de El Imparcial</u>
      leads the writer to announce Clarín's "death."
      The entire <u>Revista Nueva</u> has been reprinted in
      facsimile.

806. ---.   "Clarín industrial."   <u>RN</u>, II, 26 (25 Oct.
      1899): 120-21.

      An attack on C and <u>MC</u>.   Accuses C of lack of
      integrity and "caza de gazapos" for economic
      reasons.

807. ---.   "Una necrología."   <u>El Carbayón</u> (O), 14 Junio
      1901.

808. ---.   "Honrando la memoria de un ilustre profe-
      sor."   <u>El Carbayón</u> (O), 5 Mayo 1931.

809. ---.   "Las cosas en su punto."   <u>Región</u> (O), 26
      Abril 1952.

> Objects, on religious and moral grounds, to the tributes being paid to Clarín on the centenary of his birth.

810.   ---. "Ya estuvo bien." _Región_ (O),   27   Abril 1952.

> Again objects to the centenary.

811.   ---. "Nuestro artículo en el centenario de Clarín." _El Pregonero de San Juan_ (Mieres, Asturias), Junio, 1952: 6.

> Wishes to go on record on the centennial of "nuestro escritor más representativo."

812.   ---. "Encuesta sobre _La Regenta_." _Insula_, XXXIX, 451 (Junio, 1984): 1,8-9.

> The editors of _Insula_ asked 10 top Spanish writers (Rosa Chacel, Cela, Torrente Ballester, Delibes, Benet, Hortelano, Lourdes Ortiz, Carmen Martín Gaite, J. Fernández Santos, García Pavón) to answer these two questions: When did you first read _LR_, and what interested you most about it? From a current perspective, how do you perceive _LR_ today, its meaning and importance within the panorama of our novel?

813.   Antón del Olmet, Luis y José de Torres Bernal. _Los grandes españoles: Palacio Valdés_.   Madrid: Imprenta de Juan Pueyo, 1919.   55-57.

> Alas, PV, and Tomás Tuero were inseparable friends.   PV recalls the titles of two early plays by young Alas: "Tras los muros de Zamora," a historical drama in verse, and "Por un real," a comedy.

814.   Aramburu, Félix.   "Eternos discípulos."   _RP_ (1 Julio 1901): 7.

815.   Araujo Costa, Luis.   "Zorrilla, Arriaza, y Clarín. Un autógrafo, una autocrítica y un corazón sincero."   _El Español_ (M),   225   (15 Feb. 1944): 4.

> Reproduces a letter from Zorrilla to C, dated Berne, 25 Mayo 1885.   C criticized Calderón y Herce and others who were opposed to the government granting Zorrilla a pension.

816.   Arcadio.   "Yo fui el monaguillo en la boda de Clarín." _Voluntad_ (Gijón), 18 Junio 1952.

An interview with Rafael Loredo, who was 12 years old on 29 August 1882, when C married Onofre García Argüelles.

817. Arciniega, R. "Un gran novelista silenciado." El Universal (Caracas), 13 Nov. 1958.

818. Arias, Pedro G.   "A Clarín, en su centenario." Asturias (M), XIII (1952): 12-13.

819. Arimón, Joaquín F.   "Teresa."   El Liberal (M), 21 Marzo 1895.

"No hay actor posible donde no hay caracteres que representar."

820. Artigas Ferrando, Miguel and Pedro Sáinz y Rodríguez, ed.   Epistolario de Valera y Menéndez Pelayo. Madrid: Compañía Ibero-Americana de Publicaciones, 1930. 253 pp.

In letters dated between 1882-85, Valera and MMP criticize C for "dando y quitando reputaciones" (p. 127), his excessive praise for Sellés and Galdós (pp. 142, 145), his "tonterías" (p. 161), and LR (pp. 225,230). See also pp. 147, 148, 191, 242.

821. Asterisco, Apunte.   "Clarín, maestro de maestros." Proa (Leon), 24 Nov. 1949.

822. Astur Fernández, Néstor.   "Clarín."   Asturias (Buenos Aires), 339 (1952): 9.

A sonnet in honor of the centenary of C's birth.

823. ---. "El asturianismo de Clarín." El Progreso de Asturias (La Habana), Oct., 1952.

824. ---. "Palique de Clarín y de Vetusta." CN, II, 7 (Mayo-junio, 1981): 120-22.

Excerpts from a lecture on C which the Argentine police prevented Astur from delivering at the Ateneo Ibero-Americano of Buenos Aires in 1952. Autobiographical details in Superchería. At the end of the article, Astur includes his sonnet on C mentioned above.

825. Aub, Max. "Discurso de la novela española contemporánea."   Jornadas, 50.   El Colegio de México, 1945: 27-29.

C's fame as a critic probably will not last. Compared to Galdós, C is too satirical. He attacked minor writers but overlooked defects of major writers.

826. Avecilla, Ceferino R. "El centenario de Leopoldo Alas y la sombra de su hijo." España Libre (Brooklyn, NY), 2 Enero 1953.

In mentioning the University of Oviedo's tribute to Clarín, headed by President Jorge Miranda, Avecilla recalls that C's son, Leopoldo, was also President of the University at the time of his death sentence.

827. Avello, Manuel F. "Clarín, otra vez." El Eco de Luarca (Luarca, Asturias), 42 (14 Dic. 1952).

828. ---. "El día que don Saturnino Bermúdez entrevistó a Leopoldo Alas Clarín." CN, II, 7 (Mayo-junio, 1981): 123-30.

An imaginary 1883 interview between Saturnino Bermúdez (from La Regenta) and Clarín, using information known about C. Illustrations include two letters from C to Juan Ochoa. C predicts that Spain will have freedom of the press in 1983.

829. ---. "Clarín, Oviedo, Vetusta." Argumentos, VIII, 63-64 (1984): 28-32.

830. ---. "Clarín y el periódico dominguero Tambor y Gaita." BIEA, XXXIX, 114 (Enero-abril, 1985): 301-11.

Reproduces several quips by an anonymous contemporary of Alas, published in this Oviedo newspaper in 1885.

831. ---. "La Regenta, 1884-1984. Cien años." La Nueva España, 20 Feb. 1983: 29.

832. Ayala, Francisco. "Clarín, en su tiempo y en el nuestro." El País (M), 13 Junio 1981: 11.

"Leopoldo Alas desarrolló su tarea literaria en continua zozobra, en medio de vacilaciones y dudas. Se ha apuntado hacia una crisis suya, pero lo cierto es que vivió en continua crisis, y ello se refleja a lo largo de toda su obra." Reprinted in Ayala's Palabras y letras (Barcelona: Edhasa, 1983), pp. 275-77.

833. Ayesta, Julián. "Estilo de Clarín. La corriente germánica en la literatura." El Español (M), 121 (17 Feb. 1945).

834.   Azorín. "La crítica literaria en España." OC, I.
        Madrid: Aguilar, 1959. 22-25.

        C's best critical articles are those on "de-
fective" works. He is less rhetorical than EPB or
Picón. From a speech delivered at the Ateneo de
Valencia on 4 Feb. 1893, published as a 22-page
pamphlet signed by "Cándido."

835.   ---. "El misticismo de Ureña (Boceto de un estu-
        dio)." Buscapiés. Madrid, 1894. 212 pp.

        This time Martínez Ruiz signed his name
"Ahrimán." See his OC, I (1959), pp. 141-45.

836.   ---. "Echegaray-Clarín." El Pueblo, 25 Marzo
        1895.

        Apparently not reprinted in his OC or in José
María Valverde's Artículos olvidados de José Martínez Ruiz (1972).

837.   ---. Literatura. Madrid, 1896. 48 pp.

        See "Revista literaria: Leopoldo Alas, Cla-
rín." Remarks on Teresa and its stoic philosophy.
Reprinted in OC, I (1959), pp. 229-33.

838.   ---. "Charivari: Crítica discordante." OC, I
        (1959). 256, 272-73, 277.

        Originally published in 1897 as a 55-page
pamphlet. Reproduces brief letter from C encour-
aging Martínez Ruiz to continue writing. Does not
believe C's praise for Balart's Horizontes. Considers it strange that Gedeón should call C insignificant.

839.   ---. "Un recuerdo: Clarín." España (M), 24 A-
        gosto 1904.

        Concerning DB. Reprinted in his Tiempos y
cosas (1948) and later in his OC, VII (1959), pp.
187-91.

840.   ---. "Clarín." ABC, 13 Junio 1906.

        Sees three periods or "momentos" in the life
of C: LR, SUH, and "Cambio de luz." Reprod. in
his book Escritores (1956), pp. 25-28.

841.   ---. España: Hombres y paisajes. Madrid, 1909.
        166 pp.

        Contains "Nicolás Serrano," a "recreation" of
the character who appears in Alas' Superchería.
Reprinted in OC, II (1959), pp. 482-84.

842.   ---.   <u>El paisaje de España visto por los españo-</u>
       <u>les</u>. Madrid: Renacimiento, 1917.

　　　　In Chap. 4 ("Asturias") recalls that he and C
went to the Teatro Lara to see Benavente's <u>La fa-</u>
<u>rándula</u> in the winter of 1897.   According to Azo-
rín, C was too kind toward established authors
such as MMP, Echegaray, and Núñez de Arce.   Describes a visit to C's home four years after C's
death.   Long quotations from <u>DB</u>.   Reprod. in <u>OC</u>,
III (1959), pp. 1180-86.

843.   ---.   "El homenaje a Clarín."   <u>ABC</u>, 8 Sept. 1925.

　　　　The Tirso de Molina locomotive reminds Azorín
of C's story of the same title.   Recalls C's article on an imaginary tribute to Campoamor (<u>MC</u>, 17
Feb. 1894) and also that C did not help Rubén Darío.   Reprinted in <u>Escritores</u> (1956), pp. 29-34.

844.   ---.   "Página histórica: Una opinión autorizada."
       <u>La Libertad</u> (M), 6 Marzo 1934.

　　　　Quotes from two speeches given by Clarín at
the Ateneo de Madrid in 1886.

845.   ---.   <u>La farándula</u>.   Madrid, 1945.

　　　　In "La <u>Teresa</u> de Clarín," Azorín gives the
plot of the play and reasons why it failed.   Reprinted in his <u>OC</u>, VII (1962), pp. 1163-68.

846.   ---.   "Corresponsales en París."   <u>ABC</u>, 25 Feb.
       1946.

　　　　Believes that Bonafoux's accusation of plagiarism was unjustified.   During the first part of
his literary career, C was inspired by Emma
Bovary, then by Ernest Renan, but C's Renan was
the sentimental one.   The other correspondents
mentioned here are Eusebio Blasco and Enrique
Gómez Carrillo.   Reprinted in <u>OC</u>, IX (1954), pp.
1120-22.

847.   ---.   "Clarín."   <u>ABC</u>, 11 Oct. 1947.

848.   ---.   "<u>Teresa</u>."   <u>ABC</u>, 17 Enero 1948.

　　　　Teresa, the main character in C's play, is a
model of a Christian wife.   One reason for the
failure of this play was its dialog, which tried
very hard to sound natural.   Reprinted in <u>OC</u>, IX
(1954), pp. 1204-06.

849.   ---.   "Una novela."   <u>ABC</u>, 1 Feb. 1950.

Concerning <u>SUH</u>.

850.   ---.   "La campana de Huesca."   <u>ABC</u>, 25 Enero 1951.

851.   Balart, Federico.   "Correspondencia particular: Al
        Sr. Leopoldo Alas, de Oviedo."   <u>El Imparcial</u>
        (M), 5 Enero 1891.

852.   Baquero Goyanes, Mariano.   "La literatura narra-
        tiva asturiana en el siglo XIX."   <u>RUO</u> (Enero-
        abril, 1948): 81-99.

853.   ---.   "La novela española en la segunda mitad del
        siglo XIX."   <u>Historia general de las litera-
        turas hispánicas</u>.   Ed. Guillermo Díaz Plaja.
        5 vols.   Barcelona: Editorial Barna, 1958.
        V: 53-143.

        See especially "Las novelas de Clarín," pp.
        120-26.

854.   Barja, César.   <u>Libros y autores modernos: Siglos
        XVIII y XIX</u>.   Madrid, 1924.   644 pp.

        High praise for <u>LR</u>, which Barja considers the
        most naturalistic novel of Spain.   In second ed.
        (Los Angeles, 1933), see pp. 367-76.

855.   Barutell, Teresa.   "Retrato de Ana Ozores."
        <u>Argumentos</u>, VIII, 63-64 (1984): 34-37.

856.   Bell, Aubrey F. G.   <u>Contemporary Spanish Litera-
        ture</u>.   New York, 1933.

        <u>LR</u> is "the novel of an intellectual, a phil-
        osopher, a self-critic and a critic of others."

857.   Benet, Juan.   <u>En ciernes</u>.   Madrid: Taurus, 1976.
        35-39.

        Concerning the seating arrangement of the
        guests in <u>LR</u>, Chap. 13, p. 270 of the Alianza
        edition.

858.   Bermejo Marcos, Manuel.   <u>Don Juan Valera, crítico
        literario</u>.   Madrid: Editorial Gredos, 1968.

        Although C and MMP were Valera's greatest ad-
        mirers, Valera seldom approved of C's virulent
        "crítica policiaca."   He praised C's talent and
        wit but disliked his harshness.   Valera considered
        <u>SUH</u> very inferior to <u>LR</u>, about which he never
        wrote.   See especially Chap. IX, "La crítica," pp.
        205-07.

859.   Blanco Asenjo, R. "La literatura en 1885." Il
        Ib, III, 156 (26 Dic. 1885): 819, 822-23.

860.   Blanco García, Francisco. La literatura española
        en el siglo XIX. Madrid: Sáez de Jubera
        Hnos., Editores, 1891. 2 vols.

        Undoubtedly the most negative evaluation of
        Clarín in any history of Spanish literature.
        Father Blanco accuses Alas (Vol. 2, p. 353) of
        writing a "poisonous article" on Ferrari and
        refers to C as "el desdichado autorcillo de La
        Regenta" (p. 531). According to Blanco, C's lit-
        erary campaigns "no han sido nunca de verdadera
        crítica, sino de difamación calumniosa" (p. 610).
        C's reaction may be found in "Palique," MC, XII,
        469 (13 Feb. 1892): 3 and 6.

861.   Blasco, Eusebio. "Leopoldo Alas Clarín."   Re-
        lieves (M), 138 (21 Junio 1901).

        An obituary which describes C as the "tyrant"
        of Spanish letters but remembers his works with
        justice and respect, despite the fact that C and
        Blasco had had some disagreements. It is inter-
        esting to note that Blasco had not mentioned C at
        all in his book, Mis contemporáneos (Madrid: Al-
        varez, 1886).

862.   Bleiberg, Germán y Julián Marías, ed. "Clarín."
        Diccionario de literatura española.   4a ed.
        Madrid: Revista de Occidente, 1972. 194-95.

        This brief article, apparently prepared by
        Marías, states that C wrote five volumes of Solos
        from 1890 to 1898.

863.   Bonafoux y Quintero, Luis. Coba. Madrid: Impren-
        ta Popular, 1889. 191 pp.

        Contains "Más sobre D. Leopoldo," pp. 182-85,
        in which Bonafoux accuses C of demanding payment
        for an article from a literary journal, and sug-
        gests that C take Novo y Colson's place on a sub-
        marine so that he can drown.

864.   ---. "Cuba desguarnecida. A Clarín." HM, 17
        Oct. 1895.

865.   ---. "Explosión de un traductor." El Heraldo de
        París, 33 (22 Junio 1901).

        A hostile obituary on C, later reprinted in
        Bonafoux's book, Bilis (Paris, 1908), pp. 265-70.
        The "traductor" in the title refers to the fact
        that C translated Zola's lengthy novel, Travail,
        shortly before his death.

866.   Bonet, Laureano.   De Galdós a Robbe-Grillet.
         Madrid: Taurus, 1972.   121 pp.

         Pages 79-83 examine C's severe criticism of
the "novela hablada" such as El abuelo and
Realidad.

867.   Bravo-Villasante, Carmen.   Biografía de don Juan
         Valera.   Barcelona: Editorial Aedos, 1959.
         366 pp.

         Agrees with C's statement that Valera is a
"figura desconcertante y contradictoria."   Comments on C's article, "Valera" (La Opinión, 26
Junio 1886) reviewing Valera's poetry.

868.   Bremón, José F.   "Crónica general."   Il EA, XXX, 8
         (28 Feb. 1886).

         An unfavorable review of C's speech on Anto-
nio Alcalá Galiano at the Ateneo de Madrid.   Reprinted in MGS's LAC, pp. 203-04.

869.   ---.   "Crónica general."   Il EA, XLV, 23 (22 Junio
         1901): 370.

         C and Bremón went their separate ways at the
Teatro de la Alhambra at the end of 1882.   Alas
thought that Bremón had played a part in the failure of Teresa and in his severance from El Liberal, but Bremón denies both charges.

870.   Brenan, Gerald.   The Literature of the Spanish
         People from Roman Times to the Present.
         Cambridge: Cambridge UP, 1951.   409-10.

         Devotes one paragraph to Alas: "LR has many
of the marks of a good novel: the characters are
finely analyzed, the plot is adequate and the comment intelligent and spiced with irony.   Yet the
book is dead.   The author lacks the secret of making his scenes come alive and is besides extra-
ordinarily long-winded."   Later editions exist.

871.   Brouta, Julio.   "Respuesta a Clarín."   HM, 8 Mayo
         1895.

872.   Brown, Donald F.   "Successive Variations on the
         Theme of the Priest in Love."   The American
         Hispanist (Clear Creek, IN), IV, 34-35
         (March-April, 1979): 8-10.

         The priest as villain or victim in Azevedo,
Zola, Eça, Valera, and PV; the role of the
priest's mother in Zola and Alas; the priest in

Barrios' <u>El hermano asno</u> and Manuel Gálvez's <u>Miércoles santo</u> and <u>Perdido en su noche</u>. "Clarín's novel is the first to protest outright the rule forcing a man to dress in a long black robe."

873. Bustillo, Eduardo. "Los teatros." <u>Il EA</u>, XXXIX, 12 (30 Marzo 1895): 198-99.

Reprinted by MC in "Noticia del estreno de <u>Teresa</u> . . . y de algunas críticas periodísticas," <u>Archivum</u>, XIX (1969): 270-72 and in his book, <u>Las palabras y los días</u>, pp. 289-90.

874. Buylla, Adolfo A. "Alas, sociólogo." <u>RP</u> (1 Julio 1901): 16-17.

875. ---. "Leopoldo Alas. Sus ideas pedagógicas y su acción educadora." <u>Boletín de la Institución Libre de Enseñanza</u> (M), XXV (1901): 263-64.

"Leopoldo Alas, filósofo . . . dice y repite con laudable insistencia que Dios es el principio de la sabiduría . . . Ha sido, ante todo, un pedagogo."

876. Caba, Pedro. "La crítica literaria como creación, como noticiario y como comadreo." <u>Correo Literario</u> (M), I, 13 (1 Dic. 1950): 1 y 9.

"La verdadera crítica es obra de arte de complemento, es subsidiariamente creadora. Lo fue en Saint Bauve <sic>, en George Brandés y hasta en Clarín, alguna vez."

877. Cabezas, Juan Antonio. "Aniversario: Clarín, un provinciano universal." <u>El Sol</u> (M), Mayo, 1935.

Excerpts from his forthcoming biography of C.

878. ---. "Cosas de Clarín." <u>ABC</u>, Enero, 1946.

879. ---. "Estanislao Sánchez-Calvo. Un filósofo y filólogo olvidado." <u>El Español</u> (M) (21 Sept. 1946): 4.

Clarín had praised Sánchez-Calvo, who died in 1895 and left an unpublished work, "La elección de fe en el mundo moderno," dedicated to Alas.

880. ---. "Centenario de Clarín." <u>Revista Oviedo</u> (San Mateo) (1951): 53.

881. ---. "El centenario de Clarín." <u>España</u> (Tánger), 3 Marzo 1952.

882. Cantelli, Juan. "Anecdotario del autor y sus personajes. Clarín en Oviedo. Hace cuarenta y tres años de su muerte y sesenta que nació La Regenta. El secreto y el pateo histórico de Teresa." El Español (M), 89 (8 Julio 1944): 5.

883. Caramés, Francisco. "Enalteciendo a Clarín." La Libertad (M), 5 Mayo 1931.

884. Carretero, Tomás. "Revista literaria, por Clarín." Las Novedades de Nueva York, 11 Julio 1895.

885. ———. "Don Leopoldo Alas." MC, 3a época, XXI, 25 (22 Junio 1901): 199.

Spain's greatest critic was difficult to understand at the Ateneo because of his digressions and the flow of ideas. Not since the death of Moreno Nieto has the nation felt so much grief. Clarín was buried in Oviedo next to Tomás Tuero and Juan Ochoa.

886. Casielles, Ricardo. "Mi dolor." RP (1 Julio 1901): 17.

A poem in memory of Clarín.

887. Cavia, Mariano. "Crónicas teatrales. Cuatro letras a Clarín." El Imparcial, 5 Abril 1896.

Concerning Teresa. (Cavia used the nom de plume "Sobaquillo." According to the 21 April 1895 issue of La Iberia, Clarín and Cavia began writing for HM on that date.)

888. Cejador y Frauca, Julio. "El modelo del casticismo." Los Lunes de El Imparcial, 13 Agosto 1906.

Recalls a conversation in which Alas had said the following about Catholicism: "Hay que tentarse mucho la ropa, y yo cada vez tiemblo más de hacerlo, en eso de hablar sin ton ni son contra una institución que ha pasado ilesa al través de tantos siglos y de tantas inteligencias superiores, a lo menos tan entendidas como las nuestras."

889. ———. Historia de la lengua y literatura castellana. Madrid, 1918. IX: 263-70.

Excelente novelador realista; por cima de todo, crítico literario, sagaz y ameno . . . un segundo Larra del siglo XIX . . . En el estilo fue igualmente mejorando, desde la intemperancia y el despilfarro desleído de sus comienzos, hasta la condensación, sencillez, armonía y templanza de sus últimos escritos . . . Las críticas de Clarín son amenas . . . y chispeantes, y enseñan más que muchos tratados de preceptiva teórica, porque son una preceptiva práctica y viviente."

890.   Chandler, Richard E. and Kessel Schwartz, ed. <u>A New History of Spanish Literature</u>.   B a t o n Rouge: LSU Press, 1961.   696 pp.

Alas, pp. 220-22 and 547-49.   "<u>LR</u> excoriates the envy, intrigue, false erudition, and mental stultification to be found in Vetusta, Oviedo, and thus, in all Spain . . . He was considered a follower of Zola, and possibly was the real leader of the movement instead of Pardo Bazán."

891.   Cimorra, Clemente.   "Es hora de decir . . ." <u>Asturias</u> (Buenos Aires), 339 (Abril, 1952): 6.

892.   Ciplijauskaité, Biruté.   "El narrador, la ironía, la mujer: perspectivas del XIX y del XX." <u>Homenaje a Juan López-Morillas</u>.   E d .   J o s é Amor Vázquez y A. David Kossoff.   Madrid: Editorial Castalia, 1982.   129-49.

Devotes four pages (pp. 137-41) to the use of irony and ambiguity in <u>LR</u>.

893.   ---.   <u>La mujer insatisfecha: El adulterio en la novela realista</u>.   Barcelona: Edhasa, 1984. 187 pp.

Compares and contrasts this subject in <u>LR</u>, <u>Madame Bovary</u>, <u>Ana Karenina</u>, and Fontane's <u>Effi Briest</u> (1895).   Separate chapters on <u>Fortunata y Jacinta</u>, <u>The Portrait of a Lady</u>, <u>Casa de muñecas</u>, and <u>La Gaviota</u>.

894.   "Clarín."   <u>Diccionario enciclopédico Salvat universal</u>.   20 vols.   Barcelona: Salvat Editores, 1969.   7: 102.

Illustrates the front cover of the first ed. of <u>LR</u>, and one of J. Llimona's drawings for the novel, both in full color.   The front cover of <u>LR</u> was designed by F. Jorba.

895.   Conde Gargollo, Enrique.   "Clarín, universitario." <u>Insula</u>, XV, 167 (Oct., 1960): 12 y 16.

"Percibimos en C dos factores fundamentales para su labor fecunda de escritor: un temperamento

íntegro y sensible de espíritu y una inagotable
pasión por el estudio doctrinal y por la lectura."
In Nov. 1876 C lost his position at Salamanca because the Count of Toreno had not forgotten certain satirical remarks in El Solfeo.

896.   Correa Rodríguez, Pedro.   "Clarín."   Enciclopedia
       Rialp. Madrid, 1971. V: 735-56.

897.   Cuenca, Carlos Luis de.   "Leopoldo Alas Clarín:
       Necrología."   Il EA, XXIII (22 Junio 1901):
       371.

       Cuenca had dedicated his poem "Gramática" in
Alegrías (M, 1900) to Clarín.

898.   Cueto Alas, Juan.   "La cuarta persona del singu-
       lar. El humor literario: dos ejemplos astu-
       rianos."   El Urogallo (M), III, 16 (Julio-
       agosto, 1972): 83-90.

       Irony and humor in LR and Belarmino y Apo-
lonio. Reprinted as "Desde la cuarta persona del
singular" in El País (M), 13 Junio 1981): 31.

899.   Darío, Rubén.   España contemporánea.   París:
       Garnier Hermanos, 1901.

       In "La crítica," pp. 340-46, Darío expresses
his opinion that Spain has few good literary critics. Valera prefers to write novels, Balart has
returned to poetry, MMP does not often write on
contemporary authors, Picón writes about art, and
the public seems to prefer Clarín's "paliques"
rather than his more serious essays.

900.   Davis, Gifford.   "The Critical Reception of Nat-
       uralism in Spain before La cuestión palpi-
       tante."   HR, XXII, 2 (April, 1954): 97-108.

       EPB's book marked the culmination rather than
the inception of the Spanish debate on naturalism.
Davis has found 130 pertinent items in 14 periodicals published from 1876-1882. Clarín's opinion
of De tal palo tal astilla, La desheredada, and
his ideas on pessimism, impersonality, and determinism.

901.   Delgado, Sinesio.   "Súplica (a los señores Alas y
       Palacio)."   MC, IX, 342 (7 Sept. 1889): 6.

       A poem by the editor, asking his two contrib-
utors to put their "navajas" aside. Palacio replied with a sonnet, "A Sinesio Delgado" in MC,
IX, 343 (14 Sept. 1889): 3.

902.   Del Río, Angel.   Historia de la literatura espa-
       ñola.   2 vols.   New York: Holt, Rinehart and
       Winston, 1948.   II: 149-50.

       In revised edition, 1967, see Vol. 2, pp.
       214-17.

903.   Díaz, Edmundo.   "Leopoldo Alas Clarín."   El Nalón
       (Muros de Pravia) 105 (15 Junio 1901): 2.

904.   Díaz Estévanez, Maximino.   "Don Leopoldo en su
       cátedra de Derecho Natural--Final de una
       conferencia."   RP (1 Julio 1901): 5.

905.   ---.   "Non omnis moriar."   RP (1 Julio 1901): 18-
       20.

906.   Díez Borque, José María, ed.   Historia de la lite-
       ratura española.   Madrid: Taurus, 1980.

       Vol. 3, Chap. XXI, pp. 351-438, prepared by
       Juan Ignacio Ferreras, devotes slightly more than
       two pages to Clarín.

907.   Díez-Echarri, Emiliano y José María Roca Fran-
       quesa.   Historia de la literatura española e
       hispanoamericana.   Madrid: Aguilar, 1960.
       1590 pp.

       Clarín as critic of Pereda (pp. 1087-89) and
       PV (pp. 1091-94); as novelist, short story writer,
       and critic (pp. 1111-15).   Structure of LR, a
       great psychological novel.   Two types of literary
       criticism.

908.   Domínguez, Antonio.   "En el Ateneo."   CE, 19 Oct.
       1897.

       Concerning a lecture by C.

909.   ---.   "En el Ateneo."   CE, 12 Nov. 1897.

       This time C spoke on José Moreno Nieto and
       Franciso Giner de los Ríos.

910.   Don Cualquiera.   "Éxitos y fracasos.   Teatro
       Español."   La Justicia, 22 Marzo 1895.

       Before analyzing Teresa and its three main
       characters, the anonymous writer asks: Why did
       María Guerrero consent to play a role in this
       drama?   Why did she (or the company) not foresee
       its failure during rehearsals?   Reprinted in
       Romero's ed. of Teresa, pp. 175-78.

911.   D'Ors, Eugenio. <u>El Valle de Josafat</u>.   Buenos
        Aires: Losada, 1946.

        Agrees with Alas' opinion of Cánovas and his
        style. See pp. 121-22, 124, 126.

912.   ---. <u>Nuevo glosario</u>.   3 vols.   Madrid: Aguilar,
        1947-49.

        Vol. 1 contains brief remarks on C's descrip-
        tion of the cathedral in <u>LR</u>, "vista por un incom-
        petente" (p. 380); C's ridicule of Antonio M.
        Fabié's introd. to Hegel's <u>Lógica</u>; and C's regret
        of such ridicule, according to José de Velarde.
        Vol. 2, comments on the monument to C.   In Vol. 3
        he calls C "inolvidable y olvidado."

913.   E.   "Boletín bibliográfico: <u>Las dos cajas</u>." <u>RC</u>,
        116 (30 Nov. 1899): 447-48.

        Calls Alas "uno de los mejores cuentistas
        españoles" but believes that "la crítica al día y
        el semanario . . . han perjudicado no poco al
        Clarín de los <u>Cuentos morales</u> y otras producciones
        del mismo género."

914.   Echegaray, José de.   "Cuatro palabras a manera de
        prólogo." <u>Solos de Clarín</u>.   4a ed.   Madrid:
        Librería de Fernando Fé, 1891.   5-9.

915.   Echevarría, María de las Nieves.   "Responso a
        Leopoldo Alas." <u>Asturias</u> (Buenos Aires), 339
        (Abril, 1952): 10-12.

        Recalls seeing articles by C in the Buenos
        Aires press, probably <u>LN</u>.   According to Arturo
        Farinelli's memoirs, it is also possible that the
        Italian Hispanist published works by C in Zurich
        and Milan.

916.   Estepa, Francisco de (El Bachiller). <u>Académicos
        en cuadrilla</u>.   Madrid: Fernando Fé, 1897.
        119 pp.

        This criticism of Valera's <u>Cuentos y chasca-
        rrillos andaluces</u> (1896) makes several references
        to C, who had praised the <u>Cuentos</u>.   Alas himself
        mentioned <u>Académicos en cuadrilla </u>in <u>MC</u>, 15 Mayo
        1897: 153.   Estepa's real name was Francisco Teo-
        domiro Moreno y Durán.

917.   Etreros, Mercedes.   "El naturalismo español en la
        década de 1881-1891." <u>Estudios sobre la no-
        vela española del siglo XIX</u>.   Madrid: Consejo
        Superior de Investigaciones Científicas,
        1977.   49-131.

For Clarín, see pp. 102-04. <u>LR</u> is "una obra
naturalista en toda la extensión de la palabra,
aunque adaptada por la exigencia de una mímesis
exacta, a una realidad española en la que faltan
condiciones para un naturalismo como el de Zola, a
la realidad española, carente del desarrollo social y filosófico del país vecino."

918.   Fabbiani Ruiz, J. "Como gorgonas infernales." <u>El</u>
        <u>Universal</u> (Caracas), 15 Enero 1957.

919.   ---. "Pórtico de <u>La Regenta</u>."   <u>El Universal</u>
        (Caracas), 22 Enero 1957.

920.   ---. "Sola y rodeada de silencio."   <u>El Universal</u>
        (Caracas), 5 Feb. 1957.

        Concerning <u>LR</u>.

921.   Fernández Almagro, Melchor.   "Leopoldo Alas
        Clarín." <u>Almanaque Literario 1935</u>. Madrid:
        Editorial Plutarco, 1935. 188-91.

        Among other qualities, C possessed "genio del
        idioma y sentido de la raza." C was satirical in
        his "paliques" but essayist in <u>Rafael Calvo</u>, <u>Un</u>
        <u>discurso</u>, or the introd. to Carlyle's <u>Los Heroes</u>.
        His naturalistic novel, <u>LR</u>, contains some of the
        best pages of the modern Spanish novel.

922.   ---. "Leopoldo Alas y Clarín."   <u>Insula</u>, III, 31
        (Julio, 1948): 1.

        Some people still make a distinction between
        Leopoldo Alas the novelist and Clarín, the writer
        of popular "paliques." Almagro regrets that Cabe-
        zas included only three essays by C in the recent
        ed. of <u>Obras selectas</u> (1947).

923.   ---. <u>Cánovas: Su vida y su política</u>. Madrid:
        Ediciones Ambos Mundos, 1951.

        After a long quotation (pp. 347-50) from
        Alas' <u>CST</u>, Almagro disagrees with C's totally
        negative portrayal of Cánovas. Cánovas was not
        "the worst Spanish poet of the century."

        Fernández Arimón, J. See Arimón, Joaquín F.

        Fernández Bremón, J. See Bremón, José F.

924.   Fernández Juncos, Manuel.   <u>De Puerto Rico a</u>
        <u>Madrid. Estudios de viaje</u>.   Puerto Rico,
        1886. 162-65.

Pereda had asked Juncos to visit Clarín on his behalf. People in Oviedo were still discussing C's polemic with the bishop. C told Juncos that he had decided to write only about good authors, in order to avoid further entanglements with minor figures.

Fernández Rodríguez-Avello, M. See Avello, Manuel F.

925. Fernández Sevilla, J.   Erudición y crítica en los siglos XIX y XX.   Madrid: La Muralla, 1975. 52 pp.

Brief comments (pp. 15-17) on C's two types of literary criticism and his attitude toward Galdós, Pereda, EPB, and Echegaray. The volume contains 60 color slides of personalities and libraries (especially the Biblioteca de Menéndez Pelayo in Santander), of which No. 17 is a portrait of Clarín.

926. Fernández Shaw, Carlos. "Veladas teatrales." La Epoca, 21 Marzo 1895.

María Guerrero, Díaz de Mendoza, and Perrín did their best in Teresa, but the final scenes were difficult to hear because of the audience's disapproval. Was it because the audience did not understand the play, or because Alas had made an unfortunate mistake? Reprinted in Romero's ed. of Teresa, p. 173.

927. Ferrari, Emilio.   "A un enemigo (Epístola en tercetos)."   Los Lunes de El Imparcial, 11 Marzo 1895.

Ferrari's reply (reprinted in his OC, I, 111-14) to Clarín's criticism of his poetry. Although the poem does not mention C by name, the Conde de las Navas believes (in his article "Ferrari," Cultura Española, XVI, Nov. 1909: 890) that the target was Clarín.

928. Fitzmaurice-Kelly, James.   A History of Spanish Literature. New York, 1898.

A staunch defense of Alas, rare at that time. "There is something noble in the intrepidity with which he handles an established reputation, in the infinite malice with which he riddles an enemy. An ample knowledge of other literatures than his own, a catholic taste, as pretty a wit as our days have seen, and a most combative, gallant spirit." Much less space was devoted to C in the Oxford, 1926 ed. The 1898 ed. was reviewed by C himself in MC, XVIII, 812 (10 Sept. 1898): 639.

929.   Flórez, Adriano. "Hay que humanizar a Clarín."
        El Carbayón (O), 7 Mayo 1931.

930.   Fox, Edward Inman. Azorín as a Literary Critic.
        New York: Hispanic Institute, 1960. 176 pp.

        "Although Clarín greatly influenced Azorín's
        personal outlook and although Azorín's critical
        essays on Teresa, Superchería, and Su único hijo
        were most favorable, their conflicting judgments
        on Balart, Echegaray, Núñez de Arce, and Menéndez
        Pelayo were never reconciled. Azorín felt deep
        respect for Alas, but he always doubted his sin-
        cerity as a critic."

931.   Fraga, Eduardo de. "Clarín."   La Nueva España
        (O), 21 Feb. 1952.

932.   Francés, José.   De la condición del escritor.
        Madrid: Editorial Páez-Bolsa, 1930.

        In "Clarín o la poligrafía apasionada," pp.
        153-59, considers C and EPB as the most admired
        short story writers of the 19th century. Finds an
        auto-portrait of C in "El sombrero del señor
        cura." Describes C as a near-sighted little man,
        absent-minded, with reddish beard and mustache,
        with his coat pockets full of books and
        newspapers.

933.   ---. "Tributo a Clarín."   Madre Asturias.   Ma-
        drid, 1945. 37.

934.   Francos Rodríguez, José.   Cuando el Rey era niño
        . . . De las memorias de un gacetillero
        (1890-1892). Madrid: Morales, 1895.

        Briefly describes (pp. 160-62) C's duel with
        Bobadilla in 1892. After the duel, C's friends
        (PV, Taboada, Vico, Morote, Grilo, etc.) offered
        him a banquet at the Hotel Inglés. It is inter-
        esting to note Grilo among the guests, considering
        the vitriolic articles that C had written about
        him.

935.   ---. Contar vejeces (De las memorias de un gace-
        tillero, 1893-1897). Madrid: Compañía Ibero-
        Americana de Publicaciones, 1928. 359 pp.

        In Chap. 14, entitled "Teresa, drama de Cla-
        rín" (pp. 154-56), Francos states that C, replying
        to his critics, proposed that his play be judged
        by a literary panel consisting of EPB, Cánovas,
        Pidal, Tamayo, and Coloma, none of whom had any
        literary ties or obligations with him.

936. ———. "Páginas asturianas: Clarín." <u>Norte</u> (M),
         Feb., 1932.

937. Fuente, Ricardo. <u>De un periodista</u>. Prólogo de
         Joaquín Dicenta. Madrid: Casa Editorial de
         Mariano Núñez Samper, 1897. 221 pp.

         Contains "Los paliques de Arimón" (pp. 79-
         84), in which Fuente defends C against attacks by
         Joaquín Arimón in <u>El Liberal</u>. Clarín may be
         "soberbio" and "vanidoso," but he is not a
         "currinche."

938. García López, José. <u>Historia de la literatura
         española</u>. Barcelona: Editorial Vicens-Vives,
         1977. 575-76.

939. García Rosales, Carlos. "A Clarín." <u>La Voz de
         Asturias</u>, 2506 (3 Mayo 1931).

         A poem in honor of the unveiling of a
         monument to C.

940. García Santos, M. "Cuando Clarín, harto de pre-
         dicar, quiso dar trigo. El violín de Ingres
         de Leopoldo Alas." <u>Proa</u> (León), 17 Sept.
         1946: 3.

         Concerning a conversation between C and
         Salvador Canals on <u>Teresa</u>.

941. García Valero, Eloy. <u>La novela contemporánea</u>.
         Sevilla, 1889. 67 pp.

         Devotes two pages to Zola and Daudet, two to
         Clarín (pp 38-39), two to Galdós, especially <u>Lo
         prohibido</u>, and two to Pereda, whom Father Valero
         considers Spain's finest. He recognizes the tal-
         ent and psychological analysis of <u>LR</u> but believes
         that ordinary readers will find it tedious and
         others may dislike the author's pessimism and
         emphasis on moral misery.

942. Gener, Pompeyo. "Carta máxima a mi amigo Clarín."
         <u>La Publicidad</u> (B), 12 Sept 1893.

943. Gil Cremades, Juan José. <u>El reformismo español:
         Krausismo, escuela histórica, neotomismo</u>.
         Barcelona: Ediciones Ariel, 1969. 410 pp.

         Brief comments (pp. 264-67) on Clarín's <u>El
         derecho y la moralidad</u> and preface to <u>La lucha por
         el derecho</u>. Between pp. 280 and 281 there are
         glossy photos of Clarín and Adolfo Posada, and a
         cartoon of Buylla, Sela, and Posada.

944.   Godínez. "A Bonafoux el desmedrado . . . carta le
        escribo." RP, I, 4 (16 Julio 1901): 9-10.

        Concerning Bonafoux's "Explosión de un
        traductor."

945.   Gómez, Ulpiano. "Recuerdo: Al maestro de maes-
        tros, Leopoldo Alas." RP (1 Julio 1901): 10-
        11.

        Reprod. in MGS's LAC, pp. 200-02.

946.   Gómez de Baquero, Eduardo. El renacimiento de la
        novela española en el siglo XIX. Madrid:
        Editorial Mundo Latino, 1924. 269 pp.

        Places C in Chap. 9 under "Los novelistas
        menores" (pp. 92-93), after Alarcón and Picón, but
        before Coloma. Chap. 6, 7, and 8 had dealt with
        Galdós, Valera, Pereda, EPB, and PV. C's two long
        novels demonstrate that he could have been a great
        novelist if his literary criticism had not taken
        up so much of his time. Sees an affinity between
        LR and Eça de Queiroz.

947.   ---. "Clarín y la crítica." El Sol (M), IX, 2406
        (24 Abril 1925): 1.

        C had the advantage of writing away from Ma-
        drid. His literary criticism caused panic, like
        the rural police, while Valera used chloroform in
        his.

948.   Gómez Carrillo, Enrique, ed. Cuentos escogidos de
        los mejores autores castellanos contemporá-
        neos. París: Casa Editorial Garnier Herma-
        nos, 1880.

        An anthology of 27 short stories by as many
        authors, each preceded by a brief introduction, of
        which C and AC appear first.

949.   Gómez Marín, José Antonio. Aproximaciones al re-
        alismo español. Madrid: Miguel Castellote
        Editor, 1975. 398 pp.

        "Clarín, crítico," pp. 79-85.

950.   Gómez Molleda, María Dolores. Los reformadores de
        la España contemporánea. Prólogo de Vicente
        Palacio Atard. Madrid: Consejo Superior de
        Investigaciones Científicas, Escuela de
        Historia Moderna, 1966. 522 pp.

See especially "Alas y el problema de
España," pp. 350-54.

951. Gómez Santos, Marino. "Después del centenario de
Clarín." Correo Literario (M), IV, 68 (15
Marzo 1953): 11.

952. Gómez Tabanera, José Manuel. "Luis Bonafoux, el
hombre que intentó asesinar literariamente a
Clarín." La Voz de Asturias (O), 1976.

953. González Bardón, Francisco. "Clarín, el naturalismo y los escritores jóvenes." El Español,
(M), 9 Marzo 1946: 7.

954. González Blanco, Andrés. Historia de la novela en
España desde el romanticismo a nuestros días.
Madrid: Sáenz de Jubera, 1909. 1020 pp.

The author, from Asturias, places C and PV in
Chap. VII, entitled "La novela humorística" (pp.
495-511). "LR es quizás la novela más detallista
y en ese sentido la más naturalista que se escri-
bió en España . . . Sólo Clarín es el Zola puro,
el documentado, el recargado . . . Su vida fue un
mariposeo continuo por todos los campos intelec-
tuales." Defends C against Blanco García and
claims to have read C's books at least 12 times.

955. González Blanco, Pedro. "Cómo conocí a Clarín."
Asturias (Buenos Aires), 333 (1951): 7-8.

956. González López, Emilio. Historia de la literatura
española. La edad moderna (Siglos XVIII y
XIX). New York: Las Américas, 1965. 861 pp.

See Chap. XLI, entitled "Entre el naturalismo
y el espiritualismo: Clarín," pp. 501-12. Disagrees with Sáinz Rodríguez, Marías, Hurtado y
Palencia, Valbuena Prat, and others who have classified LR as a naturalistic novel. In fact, of
the three novelists generally included in this
generation (EPB, C, and PV), "es Alas quien se
resistió más a la influencia del naturalismo de
Zola."

957. Granell, Manuel. "Clarín y Oviedo." El Español
(M), 13 Feb. 1943: 5.

958. ---. "Mi Clarín en el recuerdo." El Nacional
(Caracas), 14 Nov. 1951.

959. ---. "Clarín y la filosofía." El Universal (Caracas), 12 Marzo 1952.

960.   ---.   "Un drama de Clarín."   _Elite_ (Caracas), 19
       Abril 1952.

961.   ---.   "Clarín y el ambiente literario de su tiem-
       po."   _Cultura Universitaria_ (Universidad Cen-
       tral de Venezuela), 31 (Mayo-junio, 1952):
       73-88.

       Comments on C's critique of books by Gómez
       Carrillo, Azorín, and Unamuno.

962.   ---.   "La unidad de la cultura hispanoamericana."
       El Universal (Caracas), 13 Junio 1952.

       Remarks on C's article on Rodó's _Ariel_.

963.   Granés, Salvador M.   _Calabazas y cabezas_.   Madrid:
       M. Romero, 1880.

       A collection of short poems by this popular
       humorist, also known as "Moscatel."   Page 153
       contains the following on Clarín:

              Cuando no quiere apuntar
              detalles, generaliza;
              mas si entrevé una paliza,
              se complace en detallar.
              Con sus ribetes y puntas
              de sabio, es algo pedante,
              y hay quien le augura el instante
              de pagarlas todas juntas.

964.   Grau, Jacinto.   _Estampas_.   Buenos Aires: Librería
       Hachette, 1941.   221 pp.

       Un viaje a Madrid, _CST_, and _AP_ deserve to be
       reprinted soon, according to this well-known dram-
       atist.   Alas' short stories show no French or
       Italian influence.   His Christianity was predom-
       inantly emotional.   His son Leopoldo, an innocent
       victim of politics, was shot by a firing squad.

965.   Gregersen, Halfdan.   _Ibsen and Spain.   A Study in
       Comparative Drama_.   Cambridge: Harvard UP,
       1936.   xiv + 209 pp.

       Clarín, pp. 42, 47, 51, 92.   C's observations
       on the theater, as expressed in _Solos_, _Los Lunes
       de El Imparcial_ (July-Aug. 1896 article), _ER_, and
       especially "Ibsen y Echegaray" (_La Correspondencia
       de España_, 23 and 28 Apr. 1892).

966.   Gubernatis, Angelo de, ed.   "Alas, Leopoldo."
       _Dictionnaire international des écrivains du
       jour_.   Florence, 1891.   29.

C merits only one paragraph, which describes him as a professor of literature (sic) at Zaragoza, the author of <u>LR</u>, and a man who is known in Madrid "par sa critique agressive et personnelle qui lui a procuré beaucoup d'ennemis." C's reaction to this last statement can be found in his preface to the fourth ed. of <u>Solos de Clarín</u>.

967. Gullón, Ricardo. <u>Vida de Pereda</u>. Madrid: Editora Nacional, 1944. 281 pp.

After his trip to Portugal with Galdós, Pereda decided to visit Clarín in Oviedo, to thank him personally for his article on <u>Sotileza</u>. C and the university organized a reception in Pereda's honor. See pp. 178-80.

968. ---. "Un centenario actual." <u>CHA</u>, 36 (Dic., 1952): 270-71.

"Hay en ella (la crítica clariniana) demasiada cominería, demasiada atención a lo pequeño circunstancial . . . sacrificó los valores permanentes al chisporroteo del momento." Nevertheless, quoting from C's preface to <u>SP</u>, Gullón believes that C is very timely.

969. Gutiérrez Nájera, Manuel. <u>Obras</u>. México: Tip. de la Oficina Impresora del Timbre, 1910.

Vol. 2, pp. 211-14, contains "El último folletín de Clarín," a heretofore unreported review of <u>Museum</u>. Agrees with C on Campoamor's <u>Poética</u> but disagrees on EPB's style. According to the Mexican poet, EPB's works lack tenderness and love.

970. Hall, H. B. "The Working Man in Late Nineteenth-Century Drama." <u>BHS</u>, XXVIII, 111 (July-Sept., 1951): 173-85.

<u>Teresa</u> is "a painstaking attempt to re-create the atmosphere of working-class life and to penetrate the working-class mind . . . The play has many faults . . . The author did not take sides in the class struggle, but the very admission of the existence of conflict between bourgeoisie and proletariat was repugnant to the well-to-do theatregoer."

971. Haro Tecglen, Eduardo. "La sombra de la provincia." <u>CN</u>, V, 23 (Enero-feb., 1984): 34-36.

When Haro was a young man, Madrid was still provincial in more ways than one. Leopoldo Alas' name disappeared from school textbooks, only to be briefly mentioned later on, in derogatory terms.

972. Hermanz, Norberto. "Leopoldo Alas Clarín, 1852-
      1901." Revista de Pedagogía (B), XVII
      (1938).

973. Huelga González, Vicente. En recordación del
      ilustre crítico, novelista y jurisconsulto D.
      Leopoldo Alas García Clarín. Mieres (Astu-
      rias): Imprenta Francisco Bárcena Sordo,
      1952.

974. Hurtado, Juan y Angel González Palencia. Historia
      de la literatura española. Madrid: Tip. Rev.
      de Archivos, 1921. 1106 pp.

      The 6th ed. was published by Saeta of Madrid
      in 1949.

975. Icaza, Francisco A. de. Examen de críticos. Ma-
      drid. Rivadeneyra, 1894. 141 pp.

      Contains "La crítica en la literatura contem-
      poránea," a speech delivered at the Ateneo de Ma-
      drid in 1893. On Clarín: "Téngolo por muy versado
      en literaturas antiguas y modernas, modernas sobre
      todo, por sagaz en muchas apreciaciones, profundo
      en no pocas e ingenioso en todas . . . gran cono-
      cedor del lenguaje castellano, aunque no por
      estilista."

976. ---. Páginas escogidas. México: Universidad Na-
      cional Autónoma, 1958. 186-87.

      In "La crítica española en la actualidad,"
      Icaza writes: "Considero a Clarín, a pesar de todo
      . . . como uno de los primeros críticos españoles.
      Su estudio de la Poética de Campoamor, sus Ensayos
      y revistas, y sus prólogos a la traducción de Car-
      lyle, al hermoso libro que sobre Goethe escribió
      González Serrano, y a la Primera campaña . . .
      bastarían de sobra para probar lo dicho."

977. Iglesias Eguren, Ricardo. "D. Leopoldo Alas (Cla-
      rín): Los cuatro amores del maestro." La Voz
      de Asturias, 7866 (1 Mayo 1949).

978. Jove y Bravo, Rogelio. "Un siglo de prensa astu-
      riana (1808-1916)." Nota liminar de J. M.
      Martínez Cachero. BIEA, III, 7 (Agosto,
      1949): 45-92.

      States that C wrote for El Anunciador, El Eco
      de Asturias, and Revista de Asturias. C's anger
      at Juan Menéndez Pidal's 1883 article about him in
      El Trasgo. Prof. Jove y Bravo was one of Alas'
      faculty colleagues.

979. L. <Eduardo de Lustonó?>. "Alas, Leopoldo." El
libro del año. Ed. Ricardo Ruiz y Benítez de
Lugo con la colaboración de D. Eduardo de
Lustonó . . . Madrid: Est. Tipolitográfico
Sucesores de Rivadeneyra, 1899. 11-14.

The brief biographical sketch is followed on
pp. 14-19 by C's essay on "Filosofía y letras."

980. Ladrón de Guevara, Pablo. Novelistas malos y
buenos. Bilbao: Edit. El Mensajero del
Corazón de Jesús, 1910.

This priest calls Alas a "crítico presuntuo-
so, de mala ley . . . En el fondo (de La Regenta)
rebosa de porquerías, vulgaridades y cinismo."

981. La Llave Alas, Pedro. "En el centenario de Clarín." Arriba (M), 25 Abril 1952.

Clarín's grandson denies that the author was
an Atheist.

982. Lázaro, José. "Un folleto y una novela de
Clarín." EM, II (Junio, 1889): 181.

Merely announces that C is finishing a folleto in three parts: Rafael Calvo y el teatro español, Horacio en la tertulia de Commelerán, and Las
últimas novelas. Also, C has finished a long novel, "La viuda y el libro," for La España Moderna.

983. Lillo, Juan de. "Clarín, evocado por su hija."
Alerta (Santander), 17 Nov. 1966.

Personal reminiscences by Elisa Alas.

984. López Jiménez, Luis. El naturalismo y España.
Madrid: Editorial Alhambra, 1977. 385 pp.

See especially pp. 296-303 for C's reaction
to Valera's Apuntes sobre el nuevo arte de escribir novelas (1886-87).

985. López Martínez, José. "Se cumplen cien años de la
publicación de La Regenta." R Letras, X
(Abril, 1984): 27-29.

986. López Sanz, Mariano. "Los escritores de la
Restauración y las polémicas literarias del
siglo XIX en España." BH, LXXXI (1979): 51-
74.

Mostly about the debate on realism-
naturalism.

987.   ---. "Los escritores de la Restauración ante la
       España política y religiosa de su tiempo."
       CA, XXXIX, 1 (Enero-feb., 1980): 137-46.

       The period 1868-1898 as viewed by C, Galdós,
       and EPB.

988.   M. "Boletín bibliográfico: Doña Berta . . ." RC,
       85 (29 Feb. 1892): 440-41.

989.   Maeztu, Ramiro de. "Apuntes para un manual sobre
       el vigente Katipunan literario." Las Noti-
       cias (B), 14 Dic. 1900.

       Satirizes Katipunan, an imaginary Madrid so-
       ciety that promotes its authors (Clarín, Blasco
       Ibáñez) and also has branches in the provinces.

990.   Manent, J. R. "Alas y Ureña, Leopoldo." Diccio-
       nario de autores. Ed. González Porto-
       Bompiani. Barcelona: Montaner y Simón, 1973.
       1: 39-40.

       Calls Alas "idealista difuso . . . pensador
       impresionable . . . socialista teórico." Among
       C's works Manent mentions a Novela incoherente.

991.   Marañón, Gregorio. Ensayos liberales. Buenos
       Aires: Espasa-Calpe, 1946. 132-46.

       Brief remarks on MMP's respect for C, EPB's
       disdain for MMP's new books, C's financial need to
       write many newspaper articles; MMP's (and Mara-
       ñón's) defense of Cánovas, MMP's contempt for
       Commelerán and praise for Costa.

992.   Martínez Cachero, José María. "El poeta Ventura
       Ruiz Aguilera y Asturias." RUO (Mayo-agosto,
       1948): 65-89.

       When Ruiz Aguilera visited Oviedo in the
       summer of 1880, C read one of Ruiz Aguilera's
       poems, "El dolor de los dolores," at the uni-
       versity reception. Nothing else on C, but this
       article contains a glossy photo of the poet.

993.   ---. "Un dato para la fortuna de Grün en España."
       Archivum, I (1951): 157-58.

       Reprints C's translation (from Revista de
       Asturias, 25 Abril 1879) of a poem by Antonio
       Alejandro María Auesperg, better known by the
       pseudonym of Athanasius Grün.

994.   ---.   "Clarín, cien años después."   _Ateneo_ (M),
        VII (26 Abril 1952): 3.

995.   ---.   "Más noticias para la bio-bibliografía de
        Ceferino Suárez Bravo."   _BIEA_, XIV, 40
        (Agosto, 1960): 195-216.

        Pages 204-10 discuss Suárez Bravo's novel,
        Guerra sin cuartel (1885) and C's negative review
        in _NC_. The first part of this article appeared in
        BIEA, IX (Abril, 1950): 49-63.

996.   ---.   "Leopoldo Alas Clarín desde hoy."   _ABC Sába-
        do Cultural_, 34 (13 Junio 1981): 1-2.

        Recalls C's greatness but also his "cerrada
        incomprensión y la injusticia" toward Rubén Darío
        and modernismo.   Wonders "si la Restauración ca-
        novista fue solamente eso, si LAC no tuvo o no
        quiso tener ojos para mirar otras distintas
        realidades asimismo existentes en ella."   This
        article became the introd. to MC's _Las palabras y
        los días_, pp. 11-16.

997.   Martínez Espada, M.   _Teatro contemporáneo: Apun-
        tes para un libro de crítica_.   Madrid: Im-
        prenta Ducazcal, 1900.   270 pp.

        Believes that _Teresa_ was not a failure but
        "un _asesinato_ con premeditación y alevosía; algo
        así como un desquite que trataron de tomar deter-
        minadas personalidades, haciendo a la obra blanco
        de añejos odios."   Agrees that Galdós and C were
        right in rebelling against "esta crítica menuda,
        indocta, gacetillesca."

998.   Martínez Olmedilla, Augusto.   "Muertos ilustres
        contemporáneos: Leopoldo Alas, Clarín."   _ABC_,
        Marzo, 1931.

        Believes that the poet José Velarde stopped
        writing because of C's constant attacks.

        Martínez Ruiz, José.   See Azorín.

999.   Mella, R.   "A Clarín."   _El Progreso_ (M), I, 39 (3
        Dic. 1899): 3.

        A commentary on C's reply to an article about
        him in _La Protesta_ of Valladolid, and a reference
        to C's article, "El libre pensador" in _El Progre-
        so_, I, 31 (8 Oct. 1899): 3.

1000.   Mendoza, Carlos.   "Bibliografía: _La Regenta_, por
        Leopoldo Alas (Clarín)."   _Il Ib_, III, 109
        (31 Enero 1885): 71.

A brief (three paragraphs) laudatory review of <u>LR</u>, which the reviewer expects will cause controversy. This novel reminds him of Daudet in its style and of Galdós in its intent. According to Mendoza, the characterization of Paula is admirable.

1001.   ---.   "Bibliografía: <u>Folletos literarios</u> de Clarín: <u>Cánovas y su tiempo</u>."   <u>Il Ib</u>, V, 220 (19 Marzo 1887): 190.

According to Mendoza's one-paragraph review, if anything were needed to crown C's reputation, it would be this pamphlet. It demonstrates that C not only makes insipid writers uneasy but also puts "big wigs" in their place.

1002.   ---.   "Bibliografía: <u>Folletos literarios</u>, III: <u>Apolo en Pafos</u>."   <u>Il Ib</u>, V, 251 (22 Oct. 1887): 686.

Brief, laudatory review. If the satire seems a bit too strident to some readers, Clio's speech is more harmonious. Spanish letters should be proud to have a literary critic like LA.

1003.   ---.   "Bibliografía: <u>Folletos literarios</u>: <u>Mis plagios</u>."   <u>Il Ib</u>, VI, 278 (28 Abril 1888): 270.

Disagrees that Echegaray's <u>Haroldo el Normando</u> resembles any of Oehlenschläger's tragedies.

1004.   ---.   "Bibliografía: <u>Mezclilla</u>."   <u>Il Ib</u>, VII, 321 (23 Feb. 1889): 126.

A brief (two paragraphs) review praising the exuberance of ideas and observations.

1005.   ---.   "Celebridades españolas contemporáneas: <u>Galdós</u>, por Clarín."   <u>Il Ib</u>, VII, 322 (2 Marzo 1889): 142.

1006.   ---.   "Bibliografía: <u>Folletos literarios</u>, VI: <u>Rafael Calvo y el teatro español</u>."   <u>Il Ib</u>, VIII, 370 (1 Feb. 1890): 75 y 78.

The best article on this actor and on contemporary Spanish stage, according to Mendoza. C is not only a first-class critic but also an educator.

1007.   ---. "Bibliografía: <u>Doña Berta</u>." <u>Il Ib</u>, X, 483
        (2 Abril 1892): 215.

        Brief review (three paragraphs) praising the
        three short novels in this volume. According to
        Mendoza, one of them, <u>Superchería</u>, was already
        known to the reviewer's readers because it had
        appeared originally in <u>La Ilustración Ibérica.</u>

1008.   Menéndez Arranz, Juan. "Una tarde con Unamuno."
        <u>IAL</u>, XI, 102 (Julio, 1957): 4.

        When Arranz chatted with him in the summer
        of 1933 or 1934, Unamuno still seemed resentful
        that C had so many reservations about <u>Tres ensa-</u>
        <u>yos</u>. Unamuno had visited Gijón, Asturias, in
        Aug. 1901, just two months after C's death.

1009.   Menéndez y Pelayo, Marcelino. <u>Estudios de crí-</u>
            <u>tica literaria</u>. 5a. serie. Madrid: Tip. de
        la Revista de Archivos, 1908. 286.

        "L. Alas, tan rico de felices intuiciones,
        tan original y agudo en su pensar, tan varia y
        profundamente versado en la cultura de nuestros
        tiempos." MMP never wrote an article on C, but
        his opinion of <u>LR</u> and <u>SUH</u> may be found in his
        letters to C, Valera, and others. See also
        Baquero Goyanes' <u>La novela española vista por</u>
        <u>Menéndez Pelayo</u> (Madrid, 1956), pp. 200-02.

1010.   Mérimée, Ernest. <u>A History of Spanish Litera-</u>
            <u>ture</u>. Trans. and rev. by S. Griswold
        Morley. New York: Holt, 1930. 635 pp.

        "<u>La Regenta</u> . . . the leading example in
        Spain of naturalistic writing after the French
        formula. It is a work rich with philosophic ob-
        servation; the style is like granite, the view of
        life objective, cold, and almost scornful."

1011.   Miguel Traviesas, M. "Leopoldo Alas, profesor."
        <u>España</u> (M), 24 Julio 1919.

1012.   Miranda García, Soledad. <u>Pluma y altar en el</u>
            <u>XIX. De Galdós al cura Sta. Cruz</u>. Madrid:
        Ediciones Pegaso, 1983. 350 pp.

        See "Clarín o la religiosidad de la élite,"
        pp. 310-04.

1013.   Molina Foix, Vicente. "Cinco poetas del 62 (Ma-
            rio Míguez, Luis Cremades, Leopoldo Alas,
            Amadeo Rubio, Alfredo Francesch)." <u>Poesía</u>
        (M), XV (1982): 123-32.

1014.   Monner Sans, Ricardo.   Breves noticias sobre la
        novela contemporánea española.   Buenos Ai-
        res: Félix Lajouane, 1889.   30 pp.

        Clarín, pp. 17-18.

1015.   Morgan, C. Lewis Jr.   "Alas, Leopoldo."   The
        Encyclopedia Americana.   30 vols.   1985 ed.
        1: 456.

1016.   Muñiz, María Elvira.   Historia de la literatura
        asturiana en castellano.   Salinas (Astu-
        rias): Ayalga Ediciones, 1978.   308 pp.

        Clarín, pp. 127-37.

1017.   Muñoz de Diego, Alfonso.   "Actualidad asturiana:
        El discípulo que habló con el maestro."
        Norte (M), Marzo, 1931.

        Concerning a monument in honor of C at the
        Campo de San Francisco.   Apparently this article
        was reprinted in La Aurora Social, 8 Mayo 1931.

1018.   Muruais, Jesús.   "Los plagios de Clarín."   Gali-
        cia Humorística, 30 Abril 1888.

        Supports Bonafoux in his accusations of
        plagiarism.

1019.   Narbona, Rafael.   "Misión de la crítica.   Evoca-
        ción de Clarín."   La Tarde (M), 4 Sept.
        1948.

        "Su concepto de la justicia le lleva a ser
        cáustico y despiadado en sus juicios, porque su
        sensibilidad y buen gusto no admiten la mezquin-
        dad ni la chabacanería."

1020.   Navarro, Calixto y E. Navarro Gonzalvo.   "Carta."
        MC, II, 72 (8 Mayo 1881): 7.

        A letter protesting C's review (in Mundo
        Moderno, No. 60) of their play, Ley de amor.

1021.   Neira Martínez, Jesús.   "Clarín, símbolo de
        Oviedo y de Asturias."   La Nueva España (O),
        25 Abril 1952.

1022.   Northup, George Tyler.   An Introduction to
        Spanish Literature.   Chicago: The U of
        Chicago P, 1925.   473 pp.

        See p. 376.   Alas is considered "a regional
        novelist of Asturias . . . The principal interest
        of LR consists in the pitiless analysis of the

heroine's false mysticism . . . he outrivaled
Larra in trenchancy and abusiveness of style, if
not in brilliance." The second ed. (July, 1936)
repeats the same information, p. 380.

1023.   Nozick, Martin. "Alas y Ureña, Leopoldo." Euro-
pean Authors, 1000-1900. Ed. Stanley J.
Kunitz and Vineta Colby. New York: H. W.
Wilson Co., 1967. 11.

1024.   Obregón, Antonio de. "Cada día: Clarín." Madrid, 12 Mayo 1952.

1025.   Ochoa, Juan. "Mezclilla, de Clarín." El
Atlántico (Santander), 25 Feb. 1889.

1026.   Opisso, Alfredo. "Necrología: Leopoldo Alas Clarín - José Luis Pellicer." Iris (B), 111
(22 Junio 1901).

Two unnumbered pages on C and the artist
Pellicer, who died on 13 and 15 June 1901, re-
spectively. Opisso remembers "una preciosísima
novela, con trazas de autobiografía titulada
Cuesta abajo, que no sabemos si terminaría." He
also recalls C's article on El Niño de la Bola,
which upset Alarcón so much.

1027.   Oria, José A. "Cuesta abajo, obra inédita de
Clarín." LN, 15 Abril 1956.

1028.   ---. "Vislumbres sobre la 'Cuesta abajo' de
Clarín." LN, 27 Mayo 1956.

1029.   Pageard, Robert. Goethe en España. Trad. de
Francisco de A. Caballero. Madrid: Consejo
Superior de Investigaciones Científicas,
1958. 236 pp.

See especially pp. 108-13 for Urbano González Serrano's ideas on Goethe, and pp. 113-16
("El intelectualismo de Clarín") for Alas' admiration for Goethe as poet and intellectual,
particularly Guillermo Meister.

1030.   Palacio, Eduardo de. "Carta a Clarín." MC, XIV,
572 (3 Feb. 1894): 59.

Praises C for honoring Galdós, Balart, Campoamor, Pereda, Tamayo, and Echegaray while they
are still alive. C's initiative was seconded by
Félix Llana, Kasabal, Palacio, etc.

1031.   Palacio, Manuel del. "A Clarín, para su corona
poética." MC, IX, 341 (31 Agosto 1889): 2-
3.

A two-stanza poem calling C "a bowl of soup without substance and a little bit of chicken." Another two-stanza poem appeared in the next issue, No. 342 (7 Sept. 1889): 2-3.

1032. ---. <u>Mi vida en prosa</u>. Madrid: Victoriano Suárez, n.d.

On pp. 253-56, entitled "Sepan cuantos . . ." Palacio still resents C's classification of him as a "half poet" and corrects or denies some of the statements in C's fifth <u>Folleto</u>. Palacio's book is signed 30 Marzo 1904.

1033. Palacio Valdés, Armando. <u>La novela de un novelista</u>. Buenos Aires, 1957.

Reminiscences of friendship with Alas, Tomás Tuero, Pío Rubín, and others; at times they performed plays (including at least two by Clarín) at the home of two Cuban boys on Cimadevilla Street. In his <u>OC</u> (Madrid: Aguilar, 1959), see Vol. 2, pp. 789-92.

1034. ---. "Testamento literario." <u>Obras completas</u>. Madrid: Aguilar, 1959. 2: 1278, 1289.

Quotes part of a letter by C on <u>Maximina</u>. On p. 1289 states: "No fue un humorista en el sentido verdadero de la palabra. Para ello le faltaba la piedad . . . Fue al mismo tiempo un crítico de gran relieve, aunque su influencia sobre las letras patrias no ha sido tan feliz como debiera a causa de su falta de ponderación. Era extremoso y apasionado en sus juicios. Tuvo siempre ídolos, a los cuales no permitía que se tocase."

1035. Palacios, Leopoldo. "El filósofo." <u>RP</u> (Junio, 1901): 21-23.

1036. París, Luis. "Clarín." <u>El Cascabel</u> (M), 1139 (10 Dic. 1891): 9.

1037. ---. "<u>Novelas cortas</u>, de Clarín." <u>CE</u>, 12 Abril 1892.

1038. ---. <u>Gente nueva: Semblanzas</u>. Madrid, n.d. 200 pp.

Briefly describes personality differences between Alas and Bonafoux. The fact that C had to publish a "defense" (against accusations of plagiarism) encouraged other writers to break their silence. París' reference to the Clarín-

Bonafoux affair was reprinted in J. F. Dicenta's
biography of Bonafoux, p. 130.

1039.   Patac y Pérez, Ignacio.   "El ensayo de Clarín."
El Carbayón (O), 5191 (26 Abril 1895).

Concerning Teresa.

1040.   Pattison, Walter T.   El naturalismo español.
Madrid: Editorial Gredos, 1965.   190 pp.

Although Pattison does not devote a separate
chapter to C, as he does to Pereda, there are
numerous references throughout this book to C's
speeches at the Ateneo, ideas on naturalism, Galdós, Champsaur's remarks on SUH, etc.

1041.   Pedro, Valentín de.   "Clarín y Rodó."   Asturias
(Buenos Aires), 339 (Abril, 1952): 8-9.

1042.   Peña, Vidal.   "Crítica ideológica en La Regenta."
Asturias Semanal, 42 (27 Dic. 1969): 52-55.

1043.   Peña y Goñi, Antonio.   "Cuyadas."   MC, IX, 315 (2
Marzo 1889): 3 y 6.

A reply to C's palique of 23 Feb. concerning
the proper use of "cuya."   In the 9 March issue,
C admits that he was wrong but continues the discussion anyway.   Continued in No. 317 (16 March).
Sánchez Pérez ends the grammar discussion in No.
318 (23 March) by informing C and Peña y Goñi
that he, Sánchez Pérez, has found the improper
use of "acaparar" in Valera and the misuse of
"primer" in the Dictionary itself.

1044.   Perés y Perés, Ramón Domingo.   Historia de la
literatura   española   e   hispanoamericana.
Barcelona: Editorial Sopena, 1960.   551-52.

1045.   Pérez de Castro, José Luis.   "Clarín, crítico e
introductor de Rodó."   Juventud Americana
(Montevideo), 24 Julio 1960.

1046.   ---.   "Leopoldo Alas Clarín y José Enrique Rodó."
Cuatro Vientos (México), 189 (1963): 145-47.

1047.   Pérez de la Dehesa, Rafael.   "Zola y la literatura española finisecular."   HR, XXXIX, 1
(Jan., 1971): 49-60.

Of special interest is Dehesa's review of
reviews of Travail (translated by Clarín),
written by Posada, Rovira, Guerra, González
Serrano, and Monegal.

1048.   Picón, Jacinto Octavio.   "Libros."   El Correo
(M), 6 Mayo 1888.

A review of Mis plagios.

1049.   Pons y Umbert, Adolfo.   Vagando.   Madrid: Hernán-
dez, 1903.   299 pp.

In a chapter entitled "Clarín" (pp.
61-65) and dated June, 1901, Pons states that he never
met C but followed his literary career closely
and felt a certain affinity.   Pons felt hurt when
C called Cánovas a "pedante."   According to Pons,
C was fortunate not to live in Madrid.   C was not
"popular" but was highly respected by many, including Eusebio Blasco.

1050.   Posada, Adolfo.   "Alas y la idea divina."   RP (1
Julio 1901): 7-9.

1051.   ---.   Para América desde España.   París: Ollendorff, 1910.   334 pp.

See "De Vetusta a Oviedo," dated 26 Sept.
1907, pp. 217-29.   Oviedo has changed much since
C and Posada walked together and admired the
tower described in LR.   "No pocos de los
personajes que juegan papel en LR han sido a su
hora vecinos de la ciudad astur . . . Es un
placer para mi . . . releer LR y recordar . . .
los vivos, de carne y hueso, en que Alas se
inspiró para sus creaciones maravillosas."   On p.
208 Posada states that he still has the three
pages of "Tambor y gaita," C's unfinished novel
about Oviedo.

1052.   ---.   "Apreciación."   Cuentos de Leopoldo Alas
(Clarín).   Colección Ariel.   San José de
Costa Rica: Imprenta Alsina, 1914.   5-8.

This little 59-page pamphlet contains Bo-
roña, AC, GS, and El dúo de la tos.   Posada remembers Alas' Krausist education and a lecture he
gave on St. Thomas.   Posada's introd. appeared
originally in the August, 1913, issue of Hispania
(London).

1053.   ---.   "Leopoldo Alas Clarín.   Fragmentos biográ-
ficos (De un libro en preparación)."   Verba
(Gijón, Asturias), 2 (Feb., 1926): 23-24.

Apparently no more passages appeared, according to Luciano Castañón's index of this local
periodical in BIEA, XXIX, 86 (Sept.-dic., 1975):
475-87.

1054. ---. "Clarín y Vetusta." LN, 12 Junio 1927.

1055. Quevedo, José F. "Triste recuerdo." El Progreso de Asturias (O), I, 65 (16 Junio 1901).

The text of this article, by one of Alas' closest friends, can be read in Appendix 8 of MGS's LAC, pp. 207-09.

1056. ---. "Leopoldo Alas. El hombre." RP (1 Julio 1901): 13-15.

1057. ---. "Un recuerdo en verso." La Ilustración Asturiana (San Esteban de Pravia), Junio, 1904.

1058. R. "Boletín bibliográfico: Nueva campaña." RC, 66 (30 Junio 1887): 670.

1059. ---. "Boletín bibliográfico: Folletos litera-rios, V." RC, 75 (15 Agosto 1889): 335.

1060. ---. "Boletín bibliográfico: Folletos litera-rios, VII." RC, 79 (15 Agosto 1890): 335-36.

1061. ---. "Boletín bibliográfico: El Señor . . ." RC, 91 (15 Agosto 1893): 335.

1062. Río, Germán del. "Hace un siglo . . . y La Re-genta." Ateneo (M), VII (26 Abril 1952): 3.

1063. Rioja, Eugenio de. "Polémica y manzanilla en torno a Clarín." Ateneo (M), X (7 Junio 1952): 15.

A review of events in Oviedo on 25 April 1952, the centenary of C's birth.

1064. Rivas Santiago, Natalio. Retazos de historia. Madrid: Editora Nacional, 1952.

See pp. 205-08 for "Manuel del Palacio y Leopoldo Alas Clarín."

1065. Robles, Alfredo. "Clarín, el español universal." La Nueva España (O), 7 Feb. 1952.

1066. Ródenas, M. A. de. "El Modernismo." El Nuevo Mercurio (Junio, 1907): 642-54.

A survey of this literary movement, including C's opposition to it.

1067. Rodríguez, José Francisco. "Páginas asturianas: Clarín." Norte (M), Feb., 1932.

1068.   Rodríguez Alonso, Angel.   "Incidencias."   La Cruz
        de la Victoria, 2629 (8 Enero 1895).

        One of several attacks on C by a priest
        known as "Angelón."   C's replies appeared in an
        Oviedo daily newspaper, El Correo de Asturias,
        signed "Diana Cazadora."   This polemic was de-
        scribed in MGS's LAC, pp. 136-39.

1069.   Rodríguez Bravo, Juan L.   "La Regenta y La Con-
        quête de Plassans: Notas sobre una posible
        relación."   RL, XLVII, 94 (Julio-dic.,
        1985): 179-86.

1070.   Rodríguez Díez, Bonifacio.   "Un modelo de análi-
        sis crítico para los cuentos de Clarín."
        Homenaje a Don Emilio Hurtado Llamas:
        Estudios Humanísticos y Jurídicos.   León:
        Colegio Univ. de León, 1977.   337-53.

1071.   Rodríguez y García, Fabián.   Ensayo para una
        galería de asturianos ilustres y distin-
        guidos.   Oviedo: Cebú, 1888.   665 pp.

1072.   Rodríguez Marín, Rafael.   La novela en el siglo
        XIX.   Madrid: Editorial Playor, 1982.   132
        pp.

        Clarín, pp. 30-31.   Brief analysis of Chap.
        9 and 29 of LR, pp. 107-12.

1073.   Romera-Navarro, Miguel.   Historia de la litera-
        tura española.   Boston: D. C. Heath, 1928.
        701 pp.

        "Notable es . . . La Regenta . . . novela
        muy extensa, pero gustosa, donde bulle un mundo
        entero de figuras graves, risueñas, ridículas, y
        la entera vida clerical, social y política de una
        atrasada capital de provincia . . . En la última
        parte de su vida, se inclinó a la mayor senci-
        llez, a la profunda reflexión y al idealismo sim-
        bólico."   A later ed. exists.

1074.   Roque.   "Un recuerdo a Clarín."   La Ilustración
        Asturiana (San Esteban de Pravia), I, 1
        (Enero, 1904): 7.

1075.   Rubín, Antonio ("Tarari").   "Clarín, el crítico y
        Palacio Valdés, el novelista."   Región (O),
        15, 18, 20, 21, 23 Nov. 1951.

        "Tarari" was the son of Pío Rubín, an inti-
        mate friend of C and PV since childhood.

1076.   Rubín, Pío.   "En el tren."   El Correo de Asturias
        (O) (18 Junio 1901): 2

1077.   Ruiz de la Peña, Alvaro.   Introducción a la lite-
        ratura asturiana.   Oviedo: Biblioteca Popu-
        lar Asturiana, 1982.

        Does not devote a chapter to C, but there
        are numerous references to him in the preface and
        in the sections on the 19th and 20th centuries.

1078.   Ruiz González, David.   El movimiento obrero en
        Asturias.   Oviedo, 1968.   280 pp.

        "Hasta el período huelguístico 1916-1917
        persistió (en Oviedo), el tono de vida provin-
        ciana de una sociedad clasista que Clarín extre-
        mando la realidad inmortalizó en La Regenta . . .
        Clarín . . . colaboró junto con Giner de los
        Ríos, Unamuno, y el anarquista Ricardo Mella en
        la Revista Blanca, fundada por Anselmo Lorenzo,
        rompiendo muy pronto y de forma violenta con la
        publicación más importante de la acracia
        española."

1079.   Sáinz de Robles, Federico Carlos.   Cuentistas
        españoles del siglo XIX.   Madrid: Aguilar,
        1954.   548 pp.

1080.   ---.   "Alas y Ureña, Leopoldo."   Ensayo de un
        diccionario de la literatura.   4 v o l s .
        Madrid: Aguilar, 1964.   2: 32-33.

1081.   Salcedo Ruiz, Angel.   La literatura española.   4
        vols.   Madrid: Calleja, 1917.   4: 608-09.

        "La Regenta parece . . . una paráfrasis de
        Doña Perfecta, de Galdós; Vetusta es Orbajosa."

1082.   Sánchez Cantón, F. J.   "Don José Lázaro y su
        legado a España."   Arbor, IX, 26 (Feb.,
        1948): 215-31.

        Mostly about Lázaro Galdiano's art collec-
        tion, but on pp. 216-18 discusses briefly the
        founding of La España Moderna and Clarín's
        resignation, as explained in Museum.   One of the
        books which C was supposed to review was Insola-
        ción, "novela con clave, según las malas len-
        guas."   Not so, states Rodríguez-Moñino (q.v.)

1083.   Sánchez Pérez, Antonio.   "No hay tales borregos."
        MC, XI, 416 (7 Feb. 1891): 6.

        A reply to C's "palique" in the previous
        issue (31 Jan. 1891), in which C had made a bet

with Sánchez Pérez that C would not change his opinion of Dicenta's Los irresponsables in 10 years.

1084. ---. "Bibliografía festiva (Cuentas atrasadas)." MC, XIII, 530 (15 Abril 1893): 3 y 6.

Agrees with C that Spain should be a republic, but not with Castelar as President. Brief comments on Alas' prefaces to Carlyle's Los héroes and Altamira's Mi primera campaña.

1085. ---. "A romper tocan." Il Ib, XI, 554 (12 Agosto 1893): 502.

1086. ---. "¿Subvenciones? (A Clarín)." Il Ib, XIII, 672 (16 Nov. 1895): 730-31.

Considers government subsidies impractical, in fact impossible, even if limited to Madrid theaters. Urrecha had proposed subsidies for the Teatro Español (instead of the Teatro Real), while Clarín had proposed a Teatro Nacional.

1087. ---. "Para rectificar . . . A Leopoldo Alas (Clarín)." Il Ib, XIV, 694 (18 Abril 1896): 246-47.

Denies being "decano de los optimistas" as Clarín had called him in HM, and also denies having stated that the public of the opening nights is infallible. What Sánchez Pérez had said was that the general public does not normally go to the theater to judge a play or a concert, but simply for entertainment.

1088. ---. "Para alusiones." Il Ib, XIV, 716 (19 Sept. 1896): 598-99.

Suspects he may be the journalist whom Clarín accused, in the article "Roma y Rama," of never having read Valmiki's Ramayana, and of having admitted so "sin empacho." Repeats his unfamiliarity with the famous Indian poem and suggests that C probably is equally unfamiliar with "cálculo infinitesimal" or "geometría analítica." (Note: Sánchez Pérez had studied to be a math teacher!)

1089. ---. "Clarín." Il Ib, XV, 750 (15 Mayo 1897): 315-16.

Refuses to join those who believe it is "fashionable" to attack Clarín, whom he considers one of Spain's greatest literary critics. Two circumstances have impaired Clarín: his harsh

criticism, and the fact that he lives so far from
Madrid. According to Sánchez Pérez, C has taken
too seriously "su misión de enderezador de en-
tuertos literarios."

1090. Sandoval, Manuel de. "Palacio y Clarín." Homenaje a Manuel del Palacio.   Madrid, n.d.
110-14.

Originally published in La Epoca, 2 Jan.
1932. The author promises that some day he will
demonstrate that Clarín was not a critic but "un
satírico feroz, un cuentista notabilísimo y un
novelista aceptable."

1091. San Juan, Mario. "Don Leopoldo Alas Clarín." La
Ilustración Gallega y Asturiana (M), 8 Sept.
1881.

Mentions a book by Clarín, El cerebro de
España, allegedly being printed in Barcelona in
1881, but Constantino Suárez (in Escritores y
artistas, p. 129) doubts that such a work was
ever published.

1092. ---. "Nuestros críticos: Don Leopoldo Alas y
Ureña, Clarín." Asturias (M), Nov.-dic.,
1899.

1093. Santullano, Luis. "Recuerdos y nostalgias: Clarín en Cimadevilla." España Peregrina (México), IV (1940): 172-74.

1094. ---. "Una lectura de Clarín en la Universidad de
Oviedo."   Suplemento de El Nacional (Méxi-
co), 9 Mayo 1948.

1095. ---. "Clarín: Sus amigos, sus enemigos." El Nacional (Caracas), 5 Agosto 1950.

1096. Sela, Aniceto. "Alientos." RP (1 Julio 1901):
15.

1097. ---. "Once años de extensión universitaria."
Memorias correspondientes a los años de 1888
a 1899 de la Universidad de Oviedo. Madrid,
1910.

1098. Señas Encinas, F. "La casa del Maestrante y el
caserón de la Regenta." Boletín de la Sociedad Ovetense de Festejos, IV (M a y o ,
1953): 2 y 3.

Suggests that the Ozores mansion described
in LR may have been inspired by this house on the
Plaza del Ayuntamiento.

1099.   Serrano Anguita, Francisco. "Cuando Clarín no
         tenía tiempo para ser reo." Región (O), 24
         Marzo 1949.

         When Sinesio Delgado, director of Madrid
         Cómico, notified Alas that someone had sued his
         newspaper for a "palique agresivo" attributed to
         C, the critic replied that he had already testi-
         fied before the local judge and that he, Clarín,
         was too busy to be a defendant.

1100.   Shaw, Donald L.   Historia de la literatura espa-
         ñola: El siglo XIX.   Barcelona: Editorial
         Ariel, 1973. 212-19.

         Originally published as A Literary History
         of Spain: The Nineteenth Century (London: Ernest
         Benn Ltd., 1972).   Clarín had a clear theory on
         the novel but not on poetry or the theater, hence
         his acceptance of Echegaray, Campoamor, and Núñez
         de Arce.   Plot and structure of LR.   His four
         volumes of short stories place him among Alarcón,
         PV, and EPB as the outstanding figures in this
         genre; surely his AC ranks as the best Spanish
         short story of the century.

1101.   Sousa, Paco. "Clarín en América." Asturias (M),
         XIII (1952): 6.

1102.   S. S. "Vida y obra de Leopoldo Alas (Clarín)."
         Adiós Cordera y otros cuentos de Leopoldo
         Alas Clarín.   Buenos Aires: Editorial Tor,
         1939. 5-9.

1103.   Suárez, Constantino, ed. "Leopoldo Alas Clarín."
         Cuentistas asturianos.   Madrid: Renacimien-
         to, 1930.

         Reprints "Boroña." Suárez was also known as
         "Españolito."

1104.   ---. "Revisiones: Leopoldo Alas, Clarín." Solar
         Norteño (O), 3 (1934).

1105.   Taboada, Luis. "A Clarín." MC, XV, 666 (23 Nov.
         1895): 390.

         Alas' friend admits that he may have exag-
         gerated a bit when he wrote about how little
         writers earn in Spain. Taboada charges at least
         25 pesetas per article; some editors try to pay
         less. He also thanks C for praising his book,
         Cursilones.

1106.   ---.   <u>Intimidades y recuerdos: Páginas de la vida</u>
        <u>de un escritor</u>.   Madrid: Administración de
        El Imparcial, 1900.   301 pp.

        Devotes one chapter (pp. 141-47) to the
Bilis Club and another (pp. 125-32) to the editorial offices of <u>El Solfeo</u>.   In the latter he
tells the anecdote about a playwright who was
always threatening to kill Clarín, but did not
dare to do so when Taboada introduced Clarín to
the playwright.

        Tarari.   See Rubín, Antonio.

1107.   Tarfe.   "<u>Teresa</u>."   <u>El Comercio</u> (Gijón, Asturias),
        Marzo, 1895.

        The author, whose name was Ataulfo Friera,
defended C against attacks on his play by Joaquín
Arimón of <u>El Liberal</u>, and others.

1108.   Tomasso, Vincenzo de.   <u>Il significato dei riferi-</u>
        <u>menti   letterari   ne   La Regenta   di Clarín</u>.
        Roma, 1968.

1109.   Torre, Guillermo de.   <u>Tríptico del sacrificio</u>.
        Buenos Aires: Losada, 1948.

        See "Unamuno y Clarín," pp. 29-30, for a
brief commentary on Unamuno's letters to C, published in Adolfo Alas' <u>Epistolario</u>.

1110.   ---.   "En el cincuentenario de Leopoldo Alas,
        Clarín."   <u>LN</u>, 14 Oct. 1951.

1111.   Torrente Ballester, Gonzalo.   <u>Literatura española</u>
        <u>contemporánea (1898-1936)</u>.   Madrid: Afrodi-
        sio Aguado, 1949.   464 pp.

        See especially pp. 126-41.   "La ejemplaridad
del caso Clarín consiste precisamente en la intención moral de sus críticas.   Cree firmemente
en la necesidad del juicio justo y exacto, sin
componendas ni paliativos, y lo cree necesario
por un cúmulo de razones que van desde la honra-
dez al patriotismo . . . Clarín constituye hoy un
arquetipo de lo que debe ser el crítico literario, considerado como ser moral."

1112.   ---.   <u>Panorama de la literatura española contem-</u>
        <u>poránea</u>.   Madrid: Guadarrama, 1956.   815 pp.

        Repeats entry of 1949 book but adds a note
on "Clarín novelista" (pp. 92-94).   C is neither
regionalist nor naturalist.   <u>LR</u> is the best 19th
century novel after <u>Fortunata y Jacinta</u>, which it

excels "indiscutiblemente en arquitectura y en penetración psicológica." According to Torrente Ballester, Clarín's only descendent is Pérez de Ayala, who wrote better prose.

1113. ---. "La verdad como escándalo." <u>CN</u>, V, 23 (Enero-feb., 1984): 25-28.

When Torrente Ballester was 15 years old, <u>LR</u> was banned, but today it could hardly be considered "scandalous." Also wonders why no Spanish artist ever bothered to paint a portrait of C.

1114. Torrente-Legazpi, Ramón Luis. "Del ideal hispánico de Clarín." <u>EstLit</u>, 343 (7 Mayo 1966): 34.

"La resurrección de España que más tarde preconizaría Angel Ganivet, era la gran constante del pensamiento del escritor asturiano. Patria y Dios eran las grandes preocupaciones de Alas."

1115. Traviesas, M. Miguel. "Leopoldo Alas, profesor." <u>España</u> (M), 24 Julio 1919.

1116. Valbuena Prat, Angel y Agustín del Saz. <u>Historia de la literatura española (Siglos XIX-XX)</u>. Barcelona: Editorial Juventud, 1951. 328 pp.

Classifies Alas under the Generation of 1898. "En la novela y el cuento representa un avance notable . . . lo mejor de su producción es . . . <u>LR</u>."

1117. Valera, Juan. <u>Ecos argentinos: Apuntes para la historia literaria de España, en los últimos años del siglo XIX</u>. Madrid: Fernando Fé, 1901. 14-15.

These two pages were originally published as a letter to <u>El Correo de España</u> (Buenos Aires), 28 August 1896. Praise for Clarín as a novelist; if C's reputation is not as great as it should be, it is probably because of the enemies he has made through his critical essays.

1118. Vargas Llosa, Mario. <u>La orgía perpetua (Flaubert y Madame Bovary)</u>. Madrid: Taurus, 1975. 254.

Calls <u>LR</u> the best novel of 19th-century Spain.

1119. Vázquez Zamora, Rafael. "Clarín, novelista." <u>Destino</u> (B), XI, 534 (11 Oct. 1947): 10-11.

"Ningún otro escritor contemporáneo suyo logró ese ritmo en la narración ni tal naturalidad en los diálogos."

1120.   ---. "El látigo de Clarín." Destino (B), XI, 535 (18 Oct. 1947): 11-12.

1121.   Vega Pico, J. "Personajes de Clarín. Doña Berta en el mapa de Madrid." Asturias (M), XIII (1952): 15.

1122.   Vela, Fernando. "Un día de Clarín en Oviedo." El grano de pimienta. Buenos Aires: Austral, 1950. 30-32.

1123.   Vigil, Manuel. "Clarín, obrero." RP (1 Julio 1901): 20-21.

1124.   Vincent, Ephrem. "Lettres espagnoles: Trabajo, par Emilio Zola, traduction et prologue de Leopoldo Alas (Clarín). Barcelona: Maucci." Mercure de France, XXXIX, 140 (Aug., 1901): 542.

Merely one paragraph, to announce this translation and to praise the late Clarín, "dévoué à ses amis et oublieux de ses ennemis, vivant en pleine culture européene, connaissant mieux que beaucoup d'entre nous la philosophie française. . . ."

1125.   Walton, L. B. Pérez Galdós and the Spanish Novel of the Nineteenth Century. London: J. M. Dent and Sons, 1927. 250 pp.

The first public expression of general admiration for Galdós took the form of a banquet in his honor, organized by Clarín in March, 1883. At this banquet speeches were delivered by Cánovas, Castelar, and Echegaray.

1126.   Ward, Philip, ed. "Alas, Leopoldo." The Oxford Companion to Spanish Literature. Oxford: Clarendon Press, 1978. 9-10.

Repeats the statement that Solos consisted of five volumes published from 1890 to 1898.

1127.   Warren, L. A. Modern Spanish Literature. 2 vols. London: Brentano's Ltd., 1929. 1: 172-79.

1128.   Zozaya, Antonio. Ripios clásicos: Lucubraciones de crítica barata procedentes de un saldo de paliques. Madrid: Librería de Fernando Fé, 1899. 207 pp.

Without mentioning Clarín by name, Zozaya states on p. 16: "Y ¿qué? ¿Creerán vuesas mercedes que es cosa fácil hinchar un palique? Hay que empezar por adquirir renombre de gracioso ¡aquí donde lo es Rodríguez San Pedro! Hay que adular no poco a los dioses mayores de la Literatura, aunque suelten un par de <u>humoradas</u>; hay que reventar muchos Grilos y aun Arechavalas. Pero, en cambio, se llega . . . Se llega al fin con una o dos <u>Teresas</u> a decirle a Pompeyo Gener: ¡Tú no sirves! y a aconsejar a los vates futuros que comulguen y vuelvan . . ." On p. 158 he adds: "Y vivo y con Alas (o con García) está Clarín, lo cual, no me impide decir que después de tener mucho, pero mucho talento, su crítica <u>paliquera</u> es menuda y grotesca, por lo cual quedará pronto muerta y sepultada."

SUBJECT INDEX

Numbers refer to entries, not pages.

Bibliographical Data

11, 16, 29, 36, 40, 47, 58, 75, 125, 220, 259, 332, 340, 344, 359, 368, 462, 476, 524, 529, 585, 614, 658, 745, 830, 978, 993, 1091

Biography

19, 22, 29, 46, 55, 76, 77, 104, 151, 152, 162, 163, 164, 165, 172, 185, 187, 246, 248, 284, 286, 289, 298, 314, 329, 343, 346, 359, 379, 382, 414, 428, 431, 451, 463, 483, 498, 509, 510, 523, 544, 545, 651, 924, 934, 955, 964, 967, 1026, 1033, 1034, 1038, 1055, 1078, 1092, 1093, 1094, 1095, 1099, 1106

Correspondence

2, 3, 13, 74, 80, 85, 92, 93, 94, 95, 117, 119, 154, 171, 174, 183, 186, 213, 219, 221, 222, 223, 237, 244, 249, 251, 268, 329, 333, 334, 342, 352, 366, 385, 419, 491, 512, 566, 793, 815, 820, 1034

Doña Berta, Cuervo, Superchería

87, 100, 107, 108, 149, 355, 358, 374, 376, 420, 436, 500, 506, 586, 644, 646, 824, 839, 841, 988, 1007, 1121

Folletos Literarios

26, 45, 79, 134, 139, 205, 224, 253, 258, 341, 392, 473, 490, 510, 594, 921, 923, 969, 982, 1003, 1006, 1032, 1048, 1059

Literary Criticism

4, 10, 11, 16, 18, 24, 25, 39, 40, 47, 54, 58, 60, 62, 75, 120, 128, 131, 132, 133, 134, 153, 160, 161, 200, 217, 231, 232, 255, 256, 257, 260, 261, 262, 263, 273, 274, 356, 360, 361, 371, 383, 384, 427, 445, 490, 503, 504, 514, 515, 533, 543, 565, 570, 573, 613, 620, 637, 649, 785, 858, 924, 925, 930, 947, 949, 968, 995, 1019, 1089, 1111, 1120

189

Naturalism

158, 218, 319, 367, 377, 411, 421, 423, 536, 615,
640, 645, 653, 900, 917, 953, 956, 984, 986, 1040, 1047

Poetry

7, 42, 238, 250, 336, 558, 591

Polemics

15, 28, 32, 38, 42, 45, 50, 53, 81, 89, 90, 102,
135, 136, 137, 138, 139, 140, 144, 145, 150, 166, 167,
168, 168a, 169, 176, 188, 191, 192, 196, 207, 258, 288,
323, 324, 331, 335, 341, 347, 365, 391, 402, 403, 404,
469, 493a, 572, 572a, 591, 591a, 597, 611, 794, 805,
806, 846, 863, 865, 869, 901, 937, 942, 944, 989, 1018,
1032, 1038, 1043, 1063, 1064, 1068, 1090

Politics

34, 35, 122, 146, 285, 310, 311, 950, 987, 1084

La Regenta

1, 8, 9, 12, 14, 17, 21, 33, 51, 59, 60, 63, 65,
66, 67, 68, 69, 73, 84, 86, 88, 91, 96, 105, 111, 114,
115, 116, 124, 126, 141, 142, 143, 166, 170, 177, 178,
189, 190, 197, 198, 199, 201, 202, 204, 206, 210, 211,
216, 225, 242, 243, 266, 269, 270, 272, 278, 279, 280,
283, 291, 292, 293, 306, 307, 317, 318, 321, 322, 328,
330, 351, 363, 368, 369, 372, 378, 380, 395, 398, 399,
400, 405, 407, 408, 411, 412, 413, 417, 418, 422, 426,
429, 430, 432, 441, 446, 447, 453, 454, 455, 456, 457,
460, 466, 467, 468, 477, 478, 479, 481, 482, 487, 488,
494, 495, 499, 507, 508, 513, 513b, 522, 524, 526, 527,
530, 535, 536, 536a, 537, 538, 539, 541, 542, 554a, 561,
562, 576, 577, 583, 585, 593, 595, 596, 600, 601, 602,
604, 606, 607, 608, 618, 619, 621, 624, 626, 628, 629,
633, 635, 641, 643, 644, 647, 648, 654, 655, 656, 658,
662, 854, 872, 892, 907, 1010, 1042, 1069, 1072, 1073,
1098, 1100, 1108, 1112

Religious Ideas

5, 27, 37, 78, 83, 85, 97, 129, 130, 156, 203, 227,
234, 240, 241, 249, 290, 309, 312, 394, 407, 418, 442,
453, 458, 525, 600, 987, 1012, 1050

Short Stories

43, 48, 64, 83, 109, 110, 112, 113, 121, 157, 182,
228, 229, 239, 245, 247, 267, 275, 297, 299, 301, 308,
317a, 320, 339, 345, 375, 389, 396, 406, 415, 464, 465,
471, 473, 474, 476, 478, 480, 481, 484, 496, 518, 519,
520, 548, 549, 550, 551, 552, 559, 564, 567, 569, 582,
584, 592, 617, 619, 622, 630, 639, 646, 657, 803, 913,
1070, 1079

Style and Techniques

14, 17, 20, 30, 63, 67, 68, 70, 96, 127, 147, 148,
155, 159, 182a, 210, 233, 265, 292, 302, 322, 330, 387,
393, 395, 396, 401, 405, 428, 459, 466, 494, 495, 496,
513, 513c, 526, 528, 548, 553, 567, 575, 579, 580, 599,
605, 606, 607, 612, 616, 617, 626, 627, 631, 636, 637,
643, 644, 646, 647, 650, 655, 656, 657, 660, 661, 663,
833, 872

Su Único Hijo

6, 59, 60, 96, 105, 106, 112a, 139, 175, 184, 209,
235, 264, 266, 271, 294, 313, 315, 316, 381, 397, 410,
433, 470, 471, 472, 475, 485, 492, 493, 513c, 516, 531,
546, 563, 588, 598, 602, 603, 609, 629, 632, 633, 638,
643, 644, 652, 660, 804, 849

Teresa

57, 72, 167, 168, 168a, 169, 180, 181, 194, 208,
252, 268, 296, 354, 357, 390, 409, 416, 434, 450, 497,
502, 522, 555, 556, 797, 800, 819, 845, 848, 887, 910,
926, 935, 940, 960, 970, 997, 1107

Unfinished Works

3, 60, 118, 123, 129, 276, 277, 336, 350, 362, 448,
449, 470, 472, 486, 578, 581, 1027, 1028, 1051